THE MASSIVE™

"[Brian] Wood's post-Crash world is still just as big as it was before, and he continues to find intriguing ways to explore it, while building up enough history and characters within the context of the series to keep it exciting."

—Comic Book Resources

"THE MASSIVE HAS NEVER BEEN MORE EXCITING."
—COMICS BULLETIN

"Comic book fans should jump on immediately."
—Unleash the Fanboy

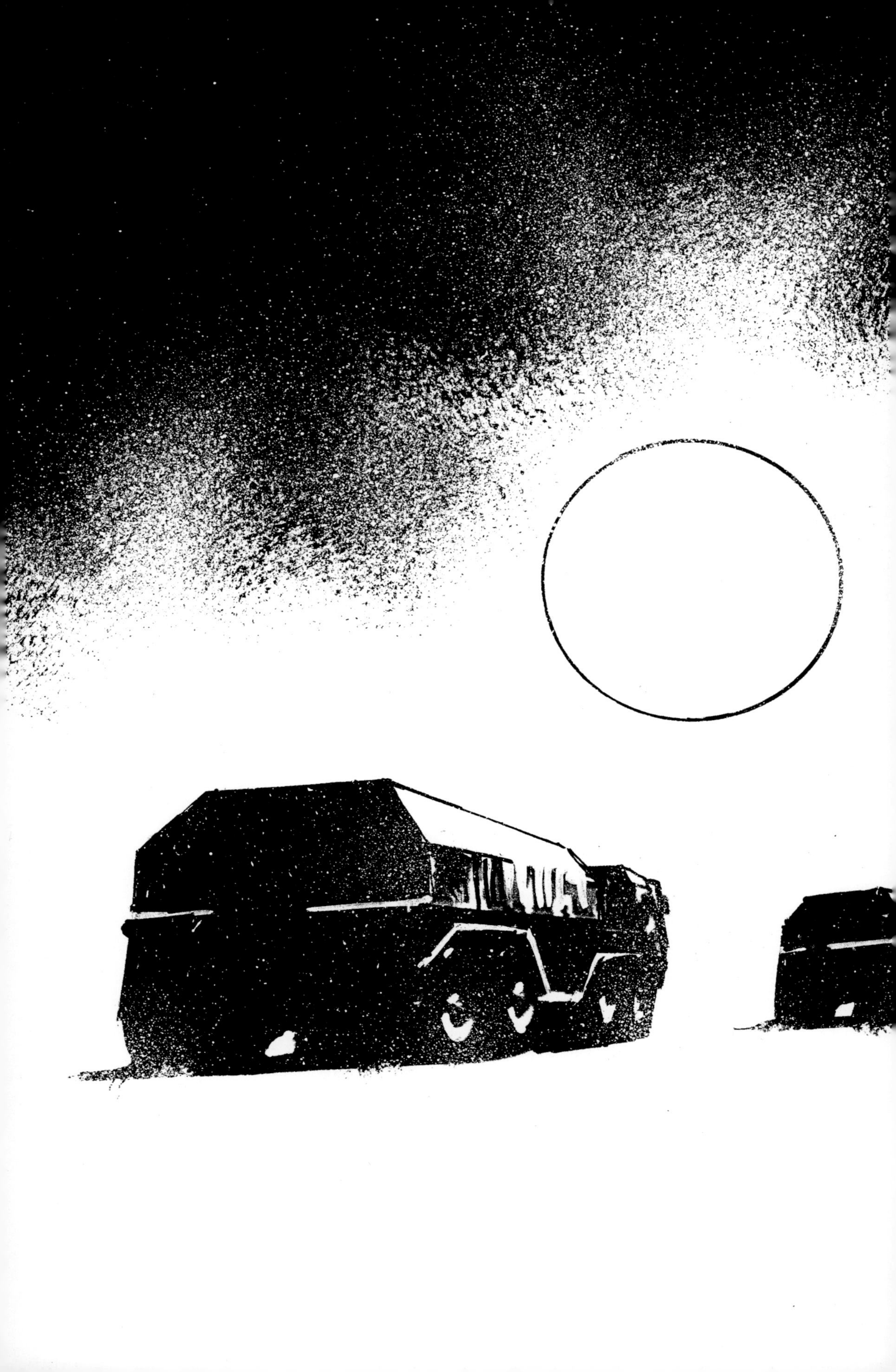

THE MASSIVE

SAHARA

BRIAN WOOD
STORY

Bloc
GARRY BROWN
ART

Sahara
DANIJEL ZEZELJ
ART

JORDIE BELLAIRE
COLORS

JARED K. FLETCHER
LETTERING

J. P. LEON
COVER ART

DARK HORSE BOOKS

MIKE RICHARDSON
PRESIDENT & PUBLISHER

SIERRA HAHN
EDITOR

SPENCER CUSHING
ASSISTANT EDITOR

JUSTIN COUCH
COLLECTION DESIGNER

Published by **DARK HORSE BOOKS**
A division of Dark Horse Comics, Inc.
10956 SE Main Street, Milwaukie, OR 97222

DARKHORSE.COM

First edition: December 2014
ISBN 978-1-61655-508-5

1 3 5 7 9 10 8 6 4 2

To find a comics shop in your area, call the Comic Shop Locator Service toll-free at (888) 266-4226.
International Licensing: (503) 905-2377

Library of Congress Cataloging-in-Publication Data

Wood, Brian, 1972-
The massive. Volume 4, Sahara / story, Brian Wood ; art, Garry Brown, Danijel Zezelj ; colors, Jordie Bellaire ;
lettering, Jared K. Fletcher ; cover art, J. P. Leon. – First edition.
pages cm
Summary: "Captain Callum Israel continues the search for the Massive in Post-Crash Europe. Mary disappears to
the Sahara guarding a secret"– Provided by publisher.
ISBN 978-1-61655-508-5 (paperback)
1. Graphic novels. I. Brown, Garry, 1981- illustrator. II. Žeželj, Danijel, illustrator. III. Bellaire, Jordie, illustrator. IV.
Title. V. Title: Sahara.

PN6727.W59M38 2014
741.5'973–dc23

2014031089

Neil Hankerson Executive Vice President · Tom Weddle Chief Financial Officer · Randy Stradley Vice Presicent of
Publishing · Michael Martens Vice President of Book Trade Sales · Anita Nelson Vice President of Business Affairs
Scott Allie Editor in Chief · Matt Parkinson Vice President of Marketing · David Scroggy Vice President of Product
Development · Dale LaFountain Vice President of Information Technology · Darlene Vogel Senior Director of Print,
Design, and Production · Ken Lizzi General Counsel · Davey Estrada Editorial Director · Chris Warner Senicr Books
Editor · Diana Schutz Executive Editor · Cary Grazzini Director of Print and Development · Lia Ribacchi Art Director
Cara Niece Director of Scheduling · Mark Bernardi Director of Digital Publishing

This volume collects the comic-book series The Massive #19–#24 from Dark Horse Comics.

LIFE GOES ON
BASIL TSIMOYIANIS

August 24, 2012: What the fuck are we doing? The question kept echoing in my ears. It was mixed with a loop of inaudible yelling, breaking waves, roaring engines, and blasts of water cannons.

I was far from home. A foreigner. Suspended from an oil rig in the Pechora Sea. Our ship, the Arctic Sunrise, *waded in the distance.*

Extremely low temps and violent storms are ordinary here. Ice and darkness stick around for much of the year. It's a pretty lonely place if you don't have a fur coat or a base layer of fat. This is the new frontier of oil extraction. Rising global temps and shrinking icecaps have made it profitable to take once-inaccessible resources, and the wolves are circling—with guns. Here sits Gazprom's first "Arctic-class ice-resistant oil rig," the Prirazlomnaya. A syringe capable of destroying the last remaining wilderness and any potential we have to live on this planet. And I've come with some Greenpeace comrades to confront them.

In *The Massive*, Brian Wood presents a world in ruins. Modern society has fallen and humanity's existence, or preservation of that very ideal, limps to continue with a renegade crew struggling to agree as shipmates and survivors. What we find is a world not much different from our own—*a world that is more vulnerable to our choices than ever before.*

Blame BP and forget the problem. The Deepwater Horizon oil spill gave us a villain to blame, like they were some sort of rogue marksman. The narrative was crafted by government, media, and oil companies alike.

The next year oil giant Gazprom tows the Prirazlomnaya into the Arctic Circle, and Royal Dutch Shell sets its eyes on Alaska (both are now partners in the development of shale oil and Arctic offshore oil projects). Meanwhile, the cleanup efforts and investigations surrounding the Deepwater Horizon oil spill continue.

The *Exxon Valdez* has been dwarfed by the BP Gulf spill, a reenactment of Love Canal takes place in Appalachia as the coal industry contaminates the water supply, and genocide continues as fracking and tar-sands development poison indigenous peoples and their lands. History repeats, and low-income communities and communities of color take the brunt of the damage.

Three of us hunker down in a 7 x 4–foot ledge blocking a passenger vessel attempting a shift change. There's no way to get comfortable on this thing, hanging sixty feet up the steel skirt of an oil rig. Orders come, and frustrated workers start the fire hoses.

Hours pass.

The hosing is relentless, and hypothermia presents itself for the first time. A cast-iron ballast ball is dropped and crashes into the rig beside us. Tensions are growing . . .

A week later I return home. There were no arrests. Gazprom cancels the start of oil production for the season due to safety concerns. The Arctic Sunrise *continues north, where it'll document the lowest sea-ice level ever recorded.*

Seasons change, my family's concerns wane, I marry a woman who puts me on the far right in comparison, and the seesaw effect of working for a big green continues. Shit happens, life goes on.

The *Kapital* combs the seas in search of its missing sister ship, *The Massive*. Fighting, wandering, remembering . . . What the fuck are they doing? In some ways, I hate Wood for taking stories of hard-hitting direct action and turning them inside out. But it may be what I need. There's too much at stake to be stuck in any one group, people, place of privilege, ideology, or movement. And Wood makes me grapple with it. *The Massive* doesn't hesitate to throw you into the struggle and our common fate headfirst. It's a fine line between fiction, reality, and identity.

September 18, 2013: A year later, the Arctic Sunrise *returns to the Pechora Sea to peacefully protest drilling in the Arctic. Russian military seize the ship, crew, and accompanying journalists with Kalashnikovs in hand. All are taken to Russia, detained, and charged with piracy, which is later replaced by hooliganism. They face seven years in prison.*

December 25, 2013: The twenty-eight activists and two freelance journalists are granted amnesty by the Russian government following burgeoning pressure from the international community. It's Christmas. The Arctic 30 are free.

Two days later Gazprom announces that it has produced the first quantities of commercial oil, and Russia plans for the Olympics.

June 6, 2014: The Russian Investigative Committee releases the Arctic Sunrise *back to Greenpeace.*

The Massive is not about the death of our planet. The world will go on without us. That's the irony of a post-everything world. It reminds us what's at stake— everything. The *reality* of *The Massive* lies in its fiction, and I sure as hell don't want to live in a sovereign nation of oil platforms destined for collapse. Life goes on, but the fight is not over.

Basil Tsimoyianis works as a training coordinator for Greenpeace USA's Action Team. In his spare time he maintains RopeGuerrilla.org—a project dedicated to climbing and rigging for activists, rebels, and radicals in the vertical world. He lives in Oakland, CA.

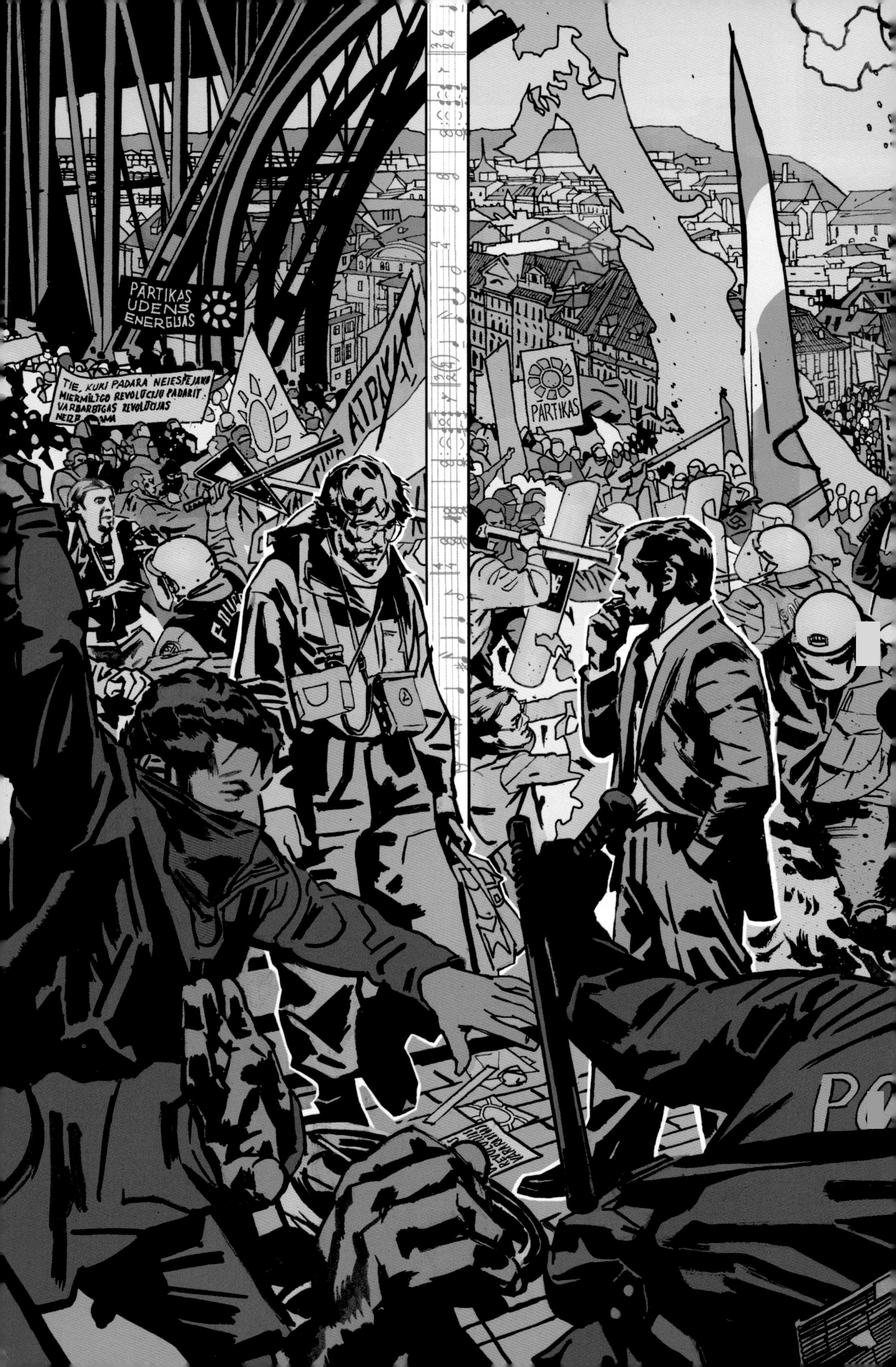
PĀRTIKAS
UDENS
ENERGIJAS
TIE, KURI PADARA NEIESPĒJAMU
MIERMĪLĪGO REVOLŪCIJU PADARĪT
VARDARBĪGAS REVOLŪCIJAS
PĀRTIKAS

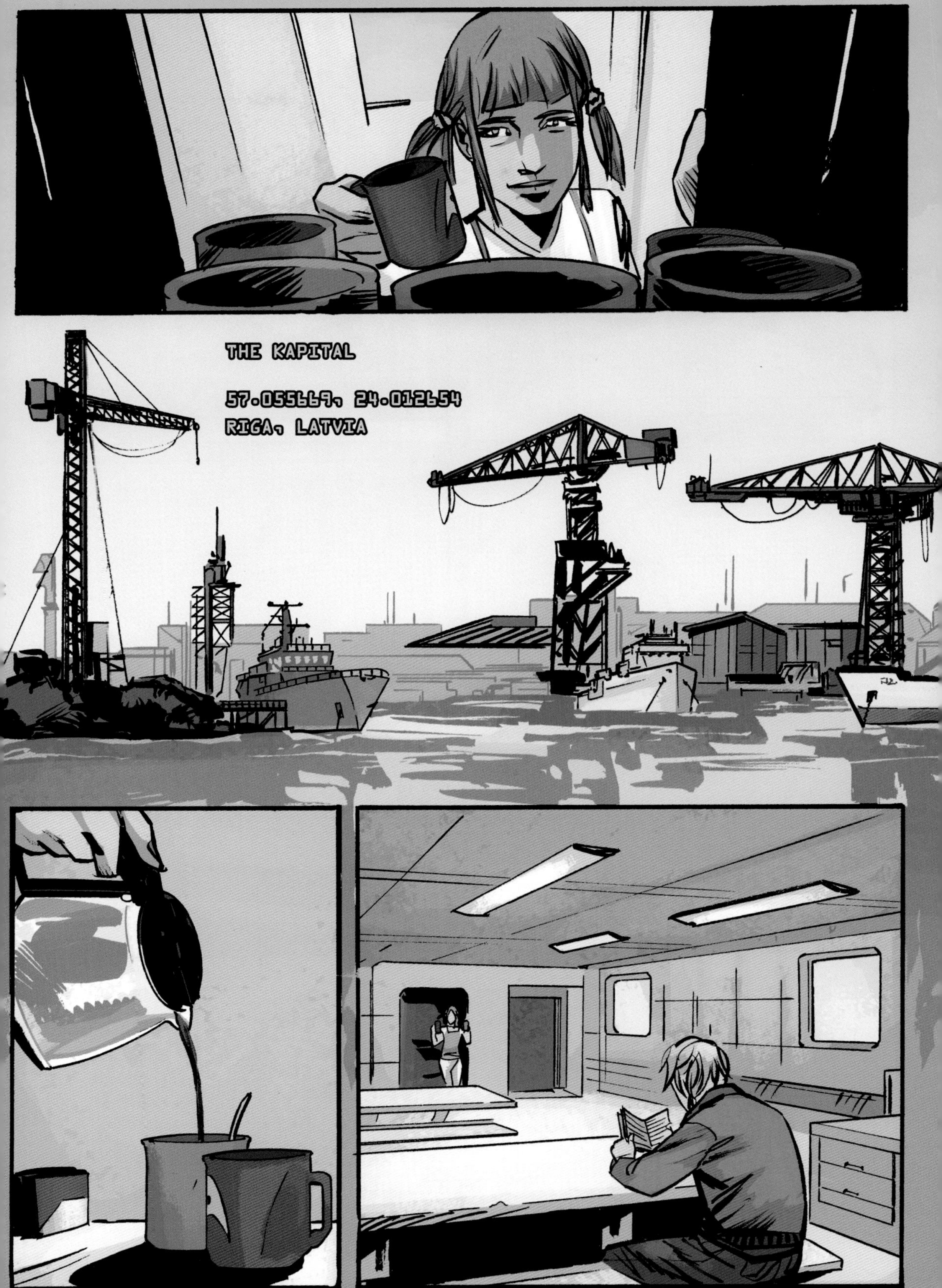
THE KAPITAL
57.055669, 24.012654
RIGA, LATVIA

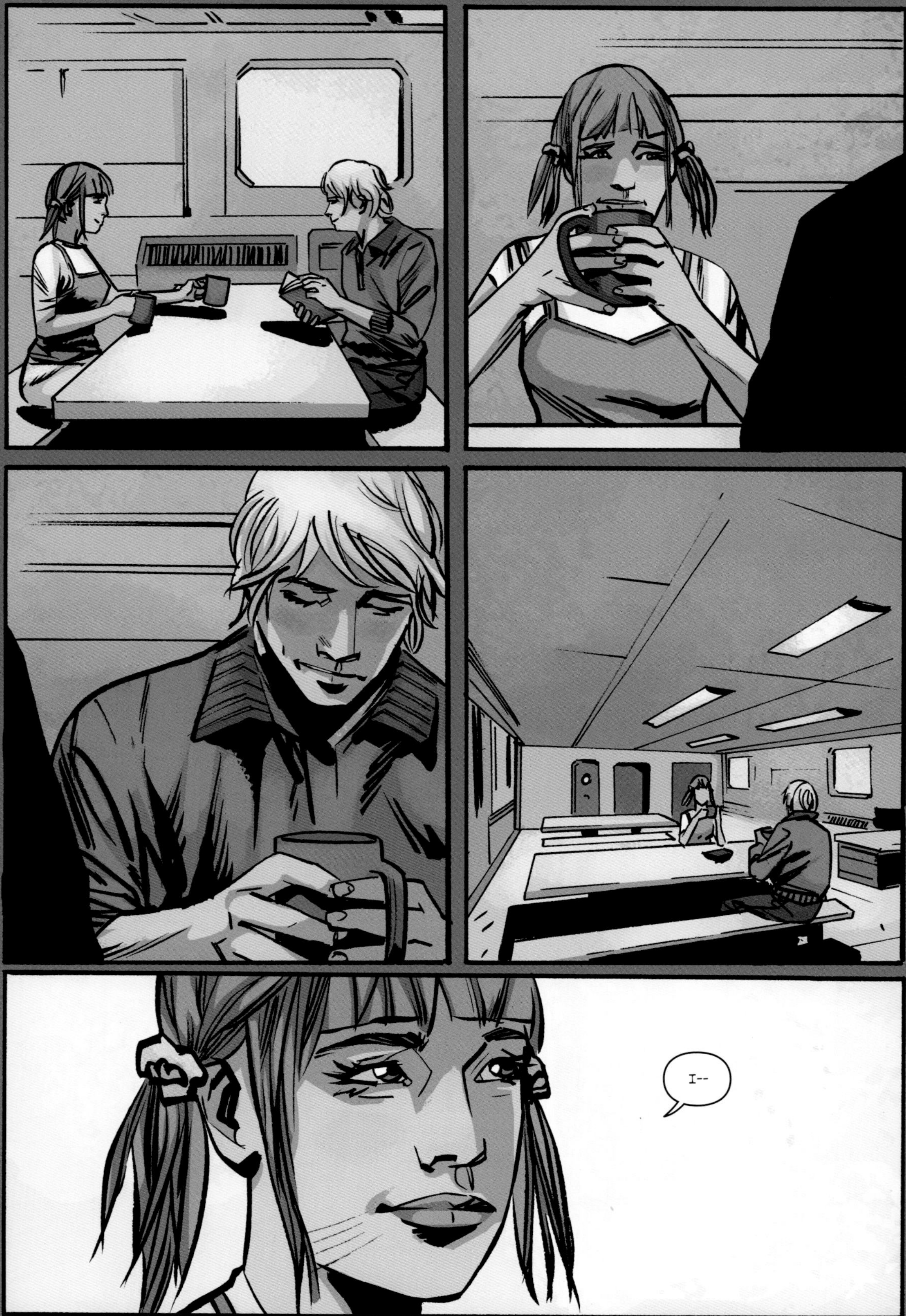
I--

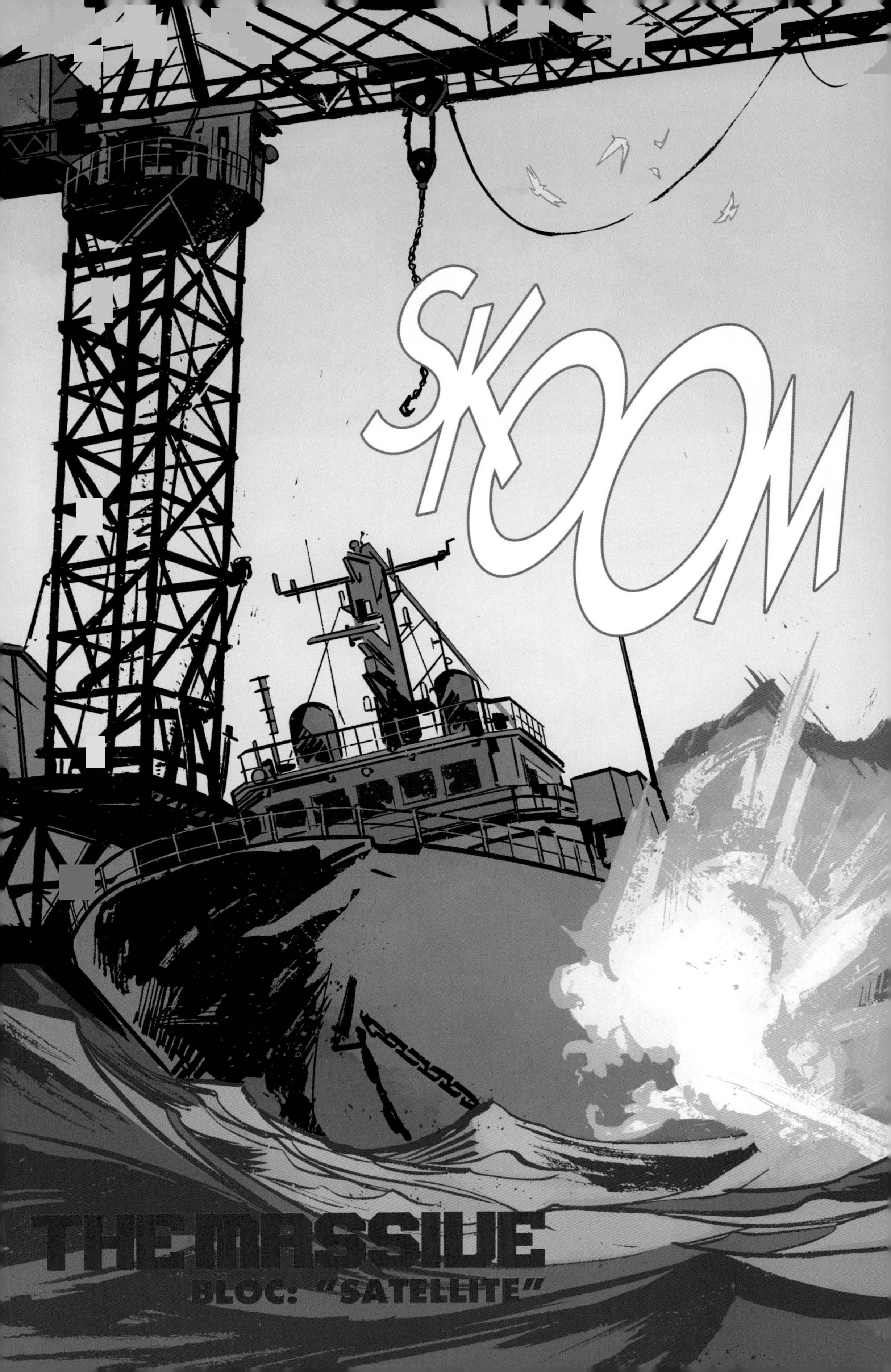
SKOOM
THE MASSIVE
BLOC: "SATELLITE"

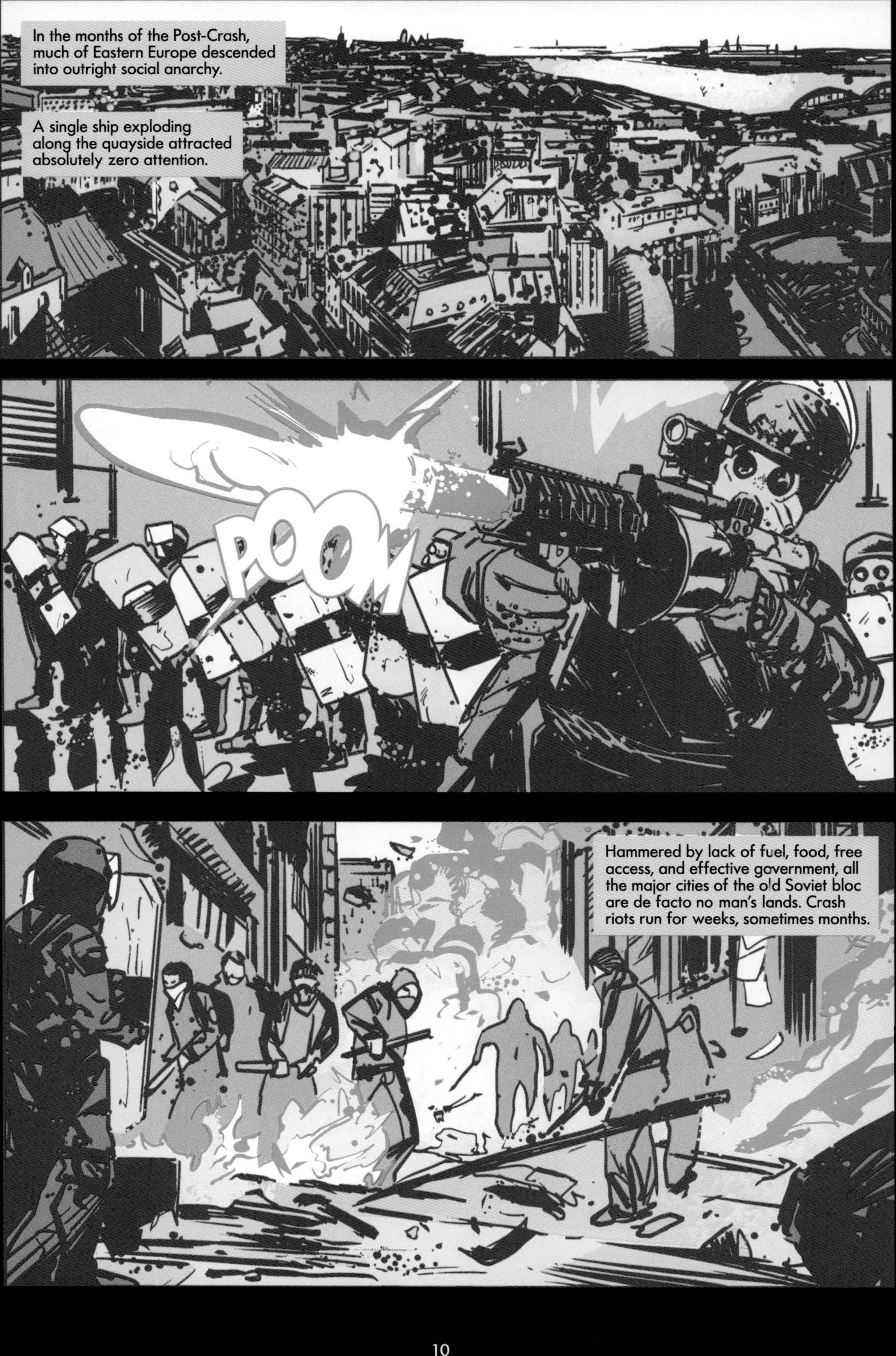
In the months of the Post-Crash, much of Eastern Europe descended into outright social anarchy.
A single ship exploding along the quayside attracted absolutely zero attention.
POOM
Hammered by lack of fuel, food, free access, and effective government, all the major cities of the old Soviet bloc are de facto no man's lands. Crash riots run for weeks, sometimes months.

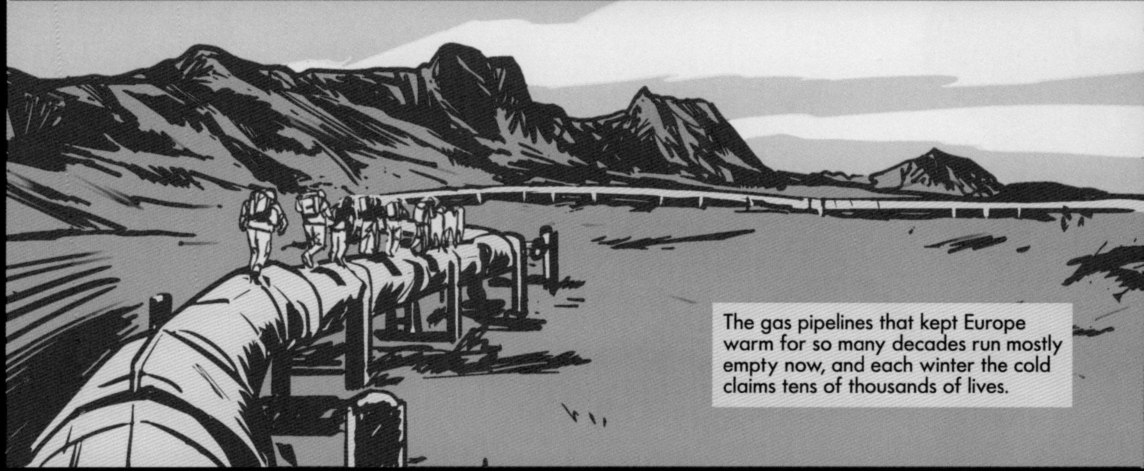
The gas pipelines that kept Europe warm for so many decades run mostly empty now, and each winter the cold claims tens of thousands of lives.

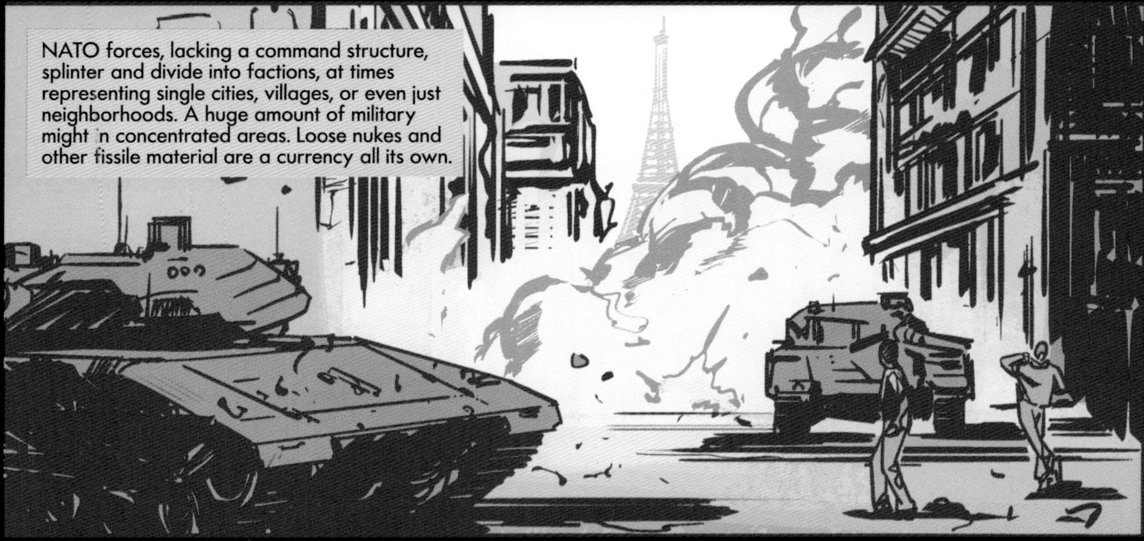
NATO forces, lacking a command structure, splinter and divide into factions, at times representing single cities, villages, or even just neighborhoods. A huge amount of military might in concentrated areas. Loose nukes and other fissile material are a currency all its own.

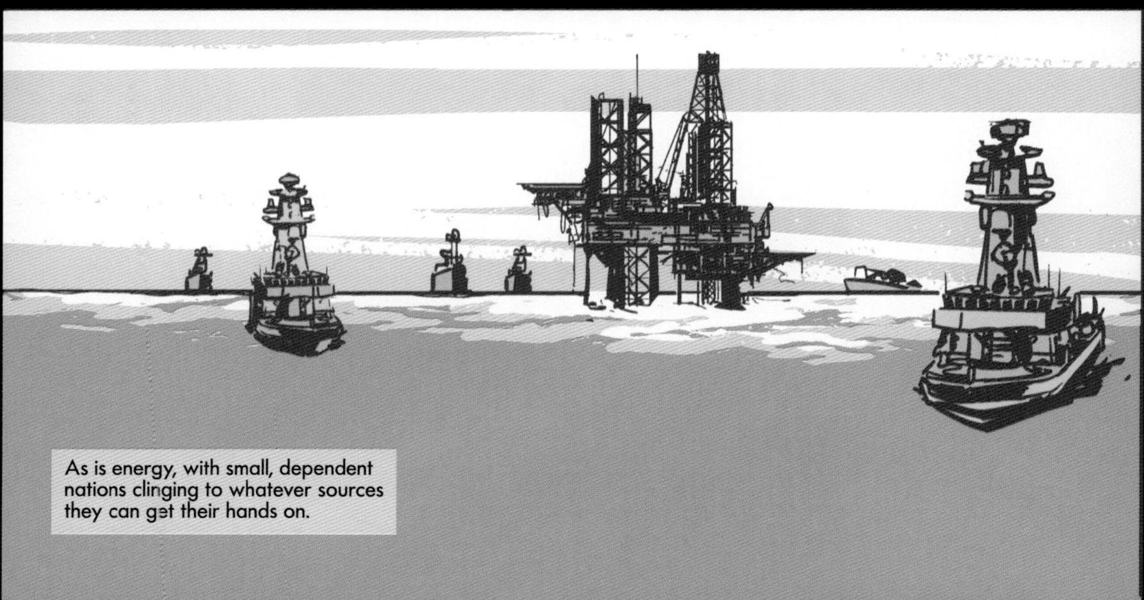
As is energy, with small, dependent nations clinging to whatever sources they can get their hands on.

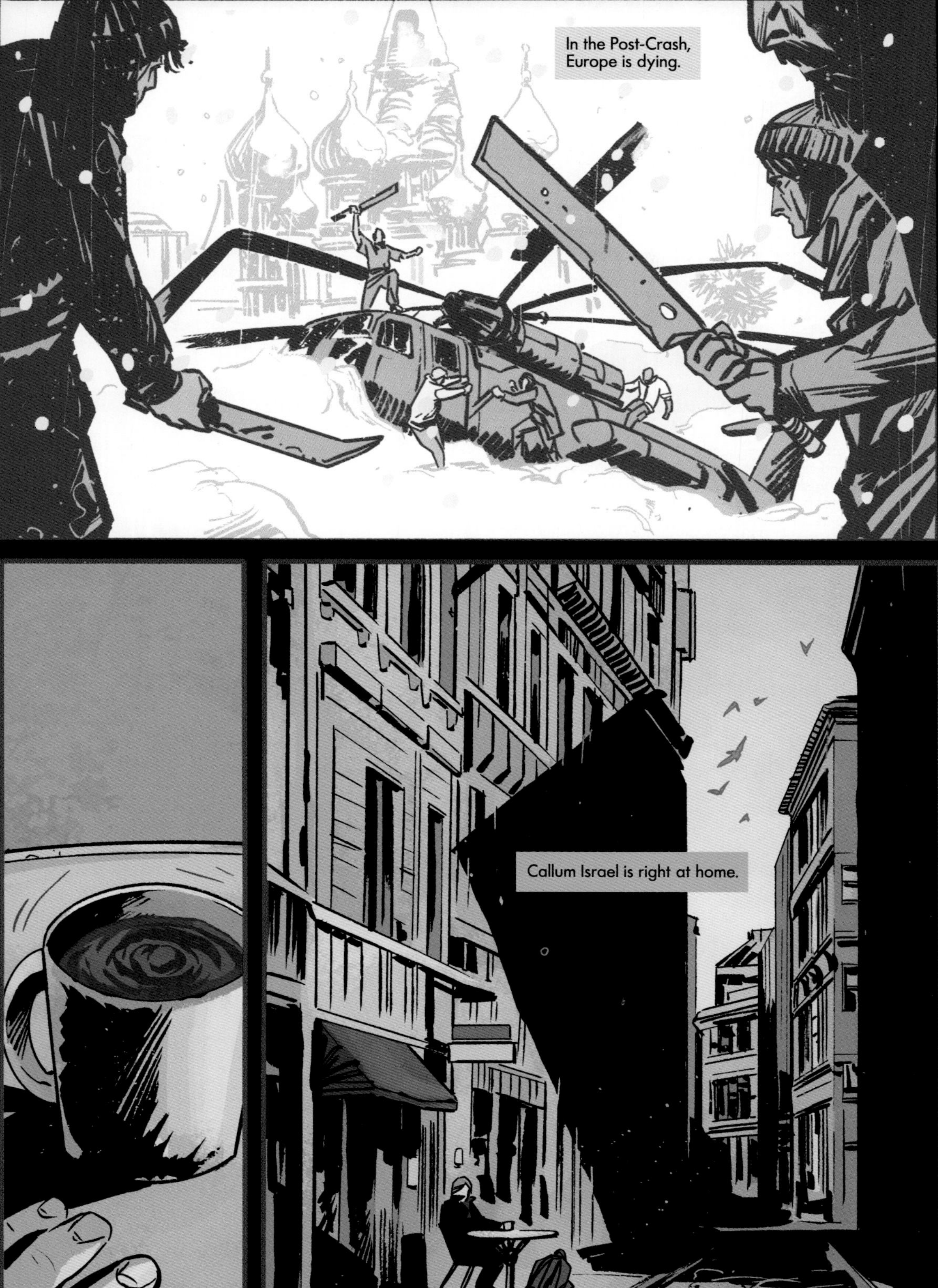
In the Post-Crash, Europe is dying.
Callum Israel is right at home.

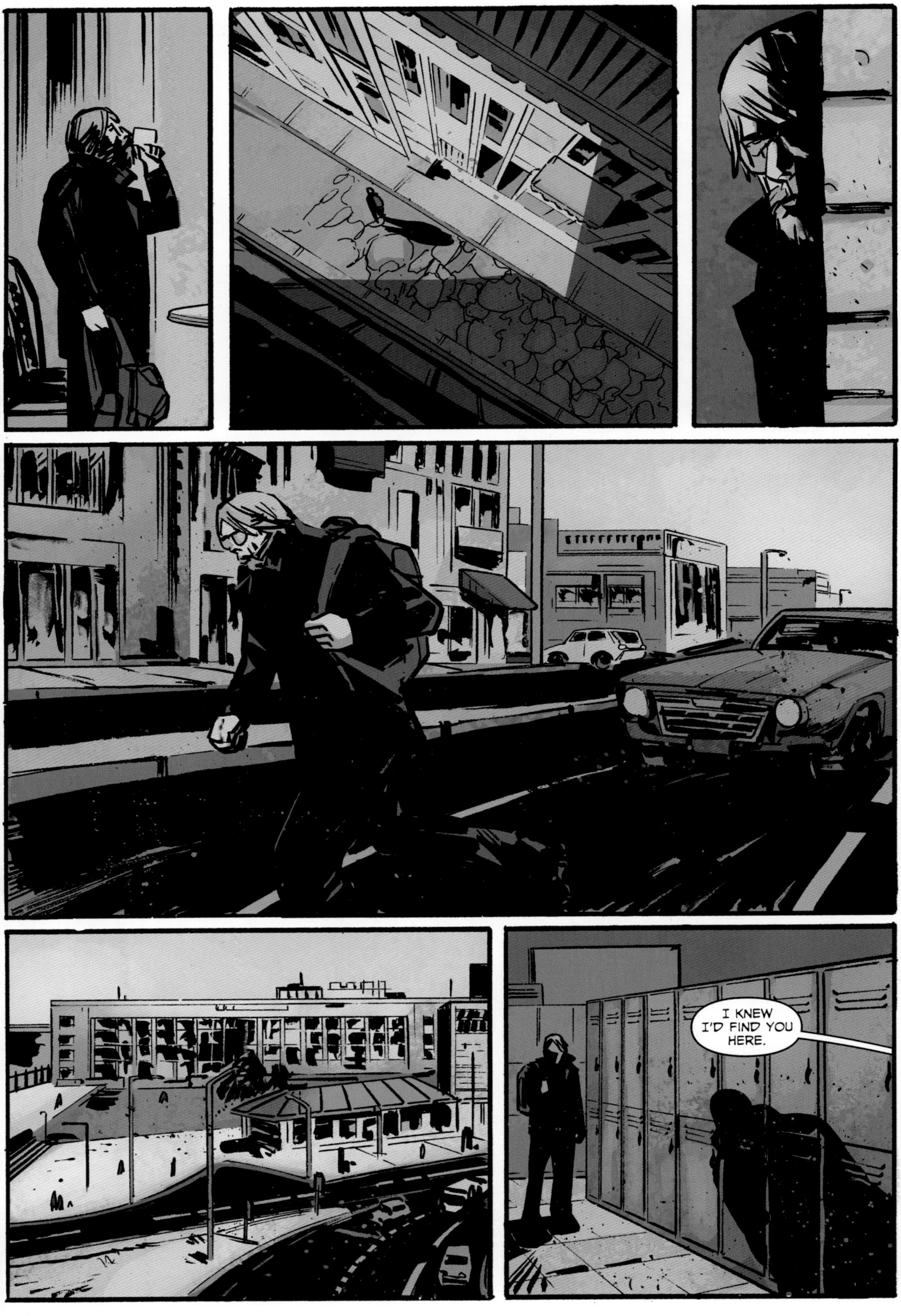
I KNEW I'D FIND YOU HERE.

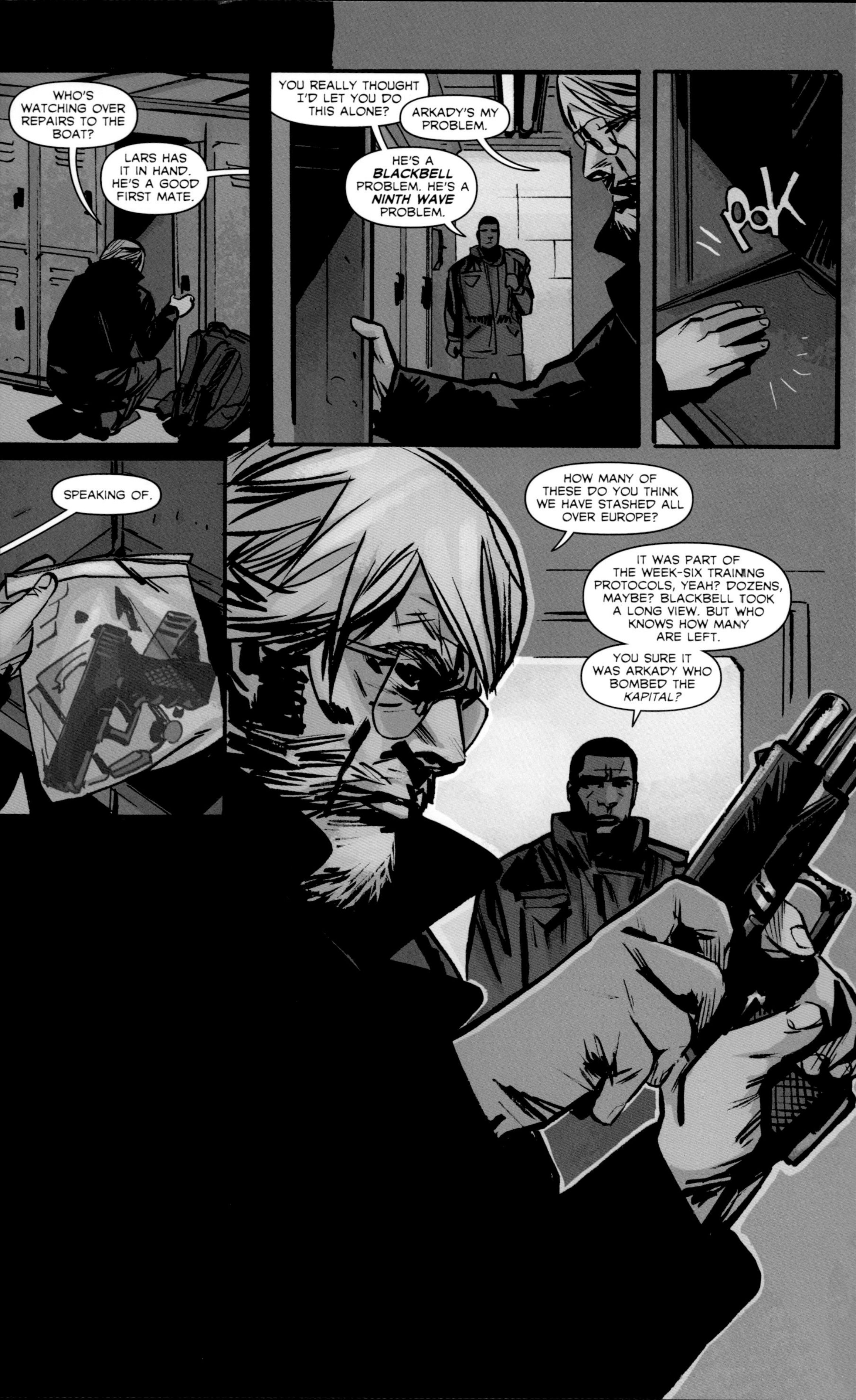
WHO'S WATCHING OVER REPAIRS TO THE BOAT?
LARS HAS IT IN HAND. HE'S A GOOD FIRST MATE.
YOU REALLY THOUGHT I'D LET YOU DO THIS ALONE?
ARKADY'S MY PROBLEM.
HE'S A **BLACKBELL** PROBLEM. HE'S A **NINTH WAVE** PROBLEM.
POK
SPEAKING OF.
HOW MANY OF THESE DO YOU THINK WE HAVE STASHED ALL OVER EUROPE?
IT WAS PART OF THE WEEK-SIX TRAINING PROTOCOLS, YEAH? DOZENS, MAYBE? BLACKBELL TOOK A LONG VIEW. BUT WHO KNOWS HOW MANY ARE LEFT.
YOU SURE IT WAS ARKADY WHO BOMBED THE *KAPITAL?*

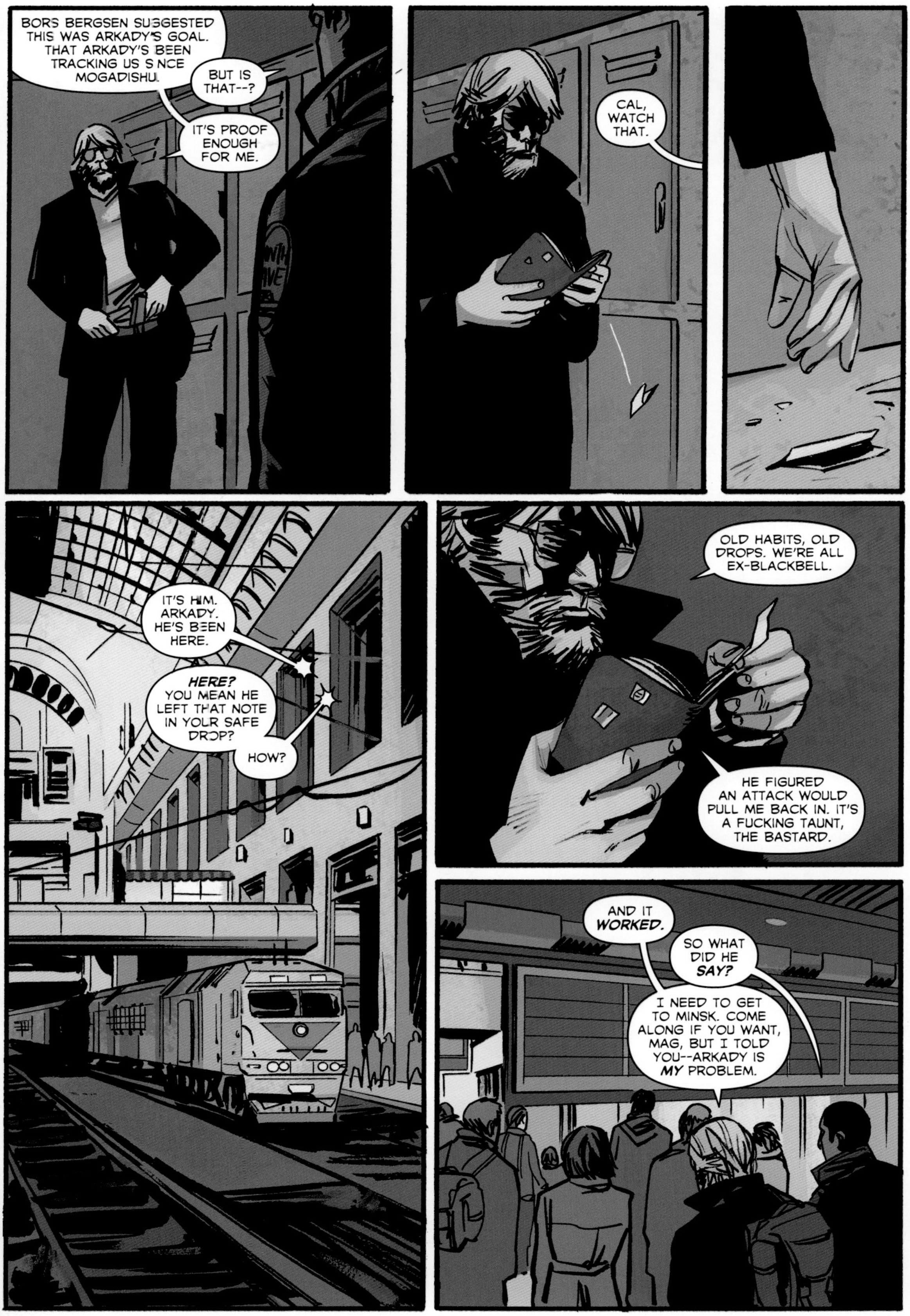
BORS BERGSEN SUGGESTED THIS WAS ARKADY'S GOAL. THAT ARKADY'S BEEN TRACKING US SINCE MOGADISHU.
BUT IS THAT--?
IT'S PROOF ENOUGH FOR ME.
CAL, WATCH THAT.
IT'S HIM. ARKADY. HE'S BEEN HERE.
HERE? YOU MEAN HE LEFT THAT NOTE IN YOUR SAFE DROP?
HOW?
OLD HABITS, OLD DROPS. WE'RE ALL EX-BLACKBELL.
HE FIGURED AN ATTACK WOULD PULL ME BACK IN. IT'S A FUCKING TAUNT, THE BASTARD.
AND IT *WORKED.*
SO WHAT DID HE *SAY?*
I NEED TO GET TO MINSK. COME ALONG IF YOU WANT, MAG, BUT I TOLD YOU--ARKADY IS *MY* PROBLEM.

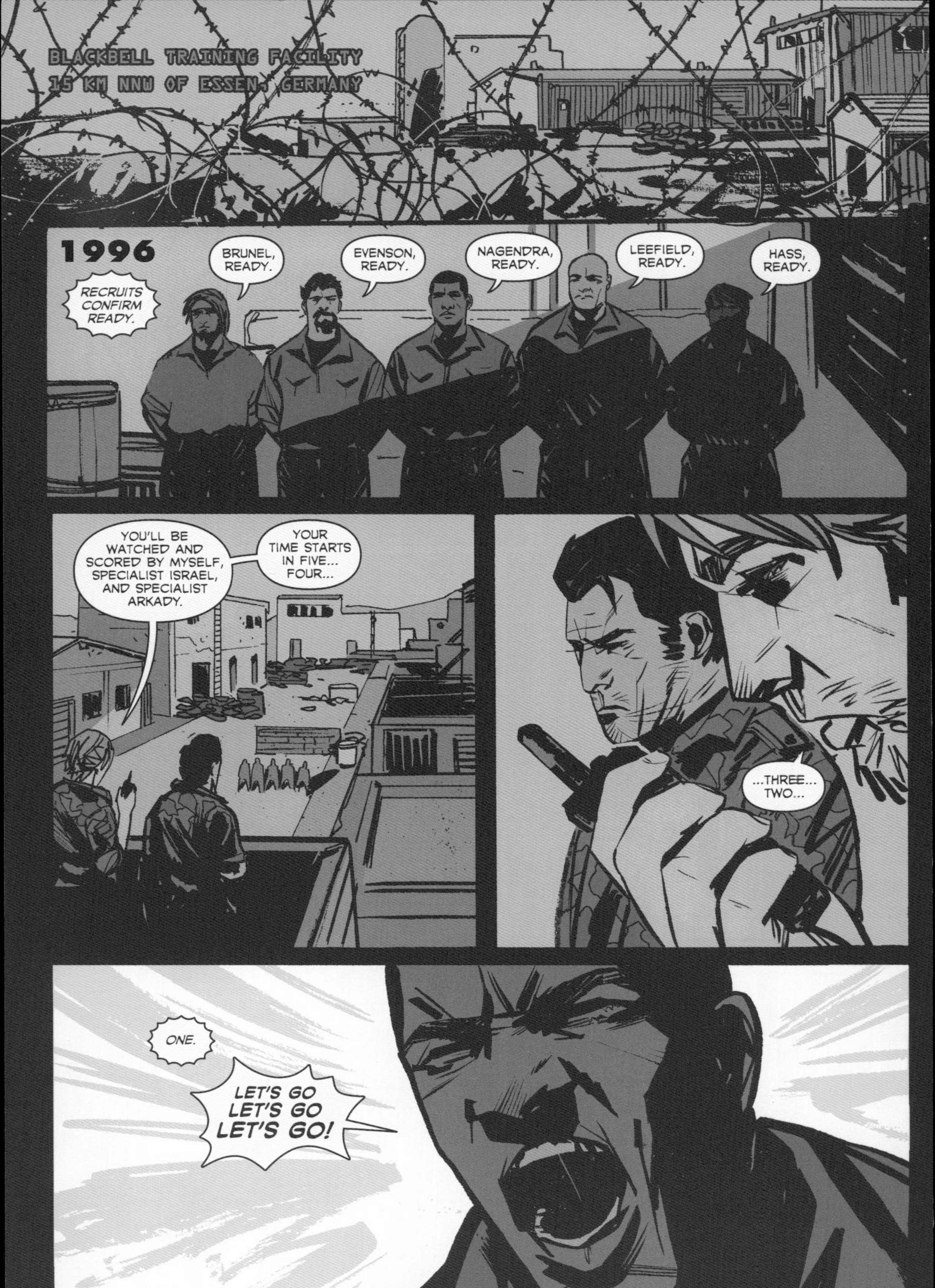
BLACKBELL TRAINING FACILITY
15 KM NNW OF ESSEN, GERMANY
1996
RECRUITS CONFIRM READY.
BRUNEL, READY.
EVENSON, READY.
NAGENDRA, READY.
LEEFIELD, READY.
HASS, READY.
YOU'LL BE WATCHED AND SCORED BY MYSELF, SPECIALIST ISRAEL, AND SPECIALIST ARKADY.
YOUR TIME STARTS IN FIVE... FOUR...
...THREE... TWO...
ONE.
LET'S GO LET'S GO LET'S GO!

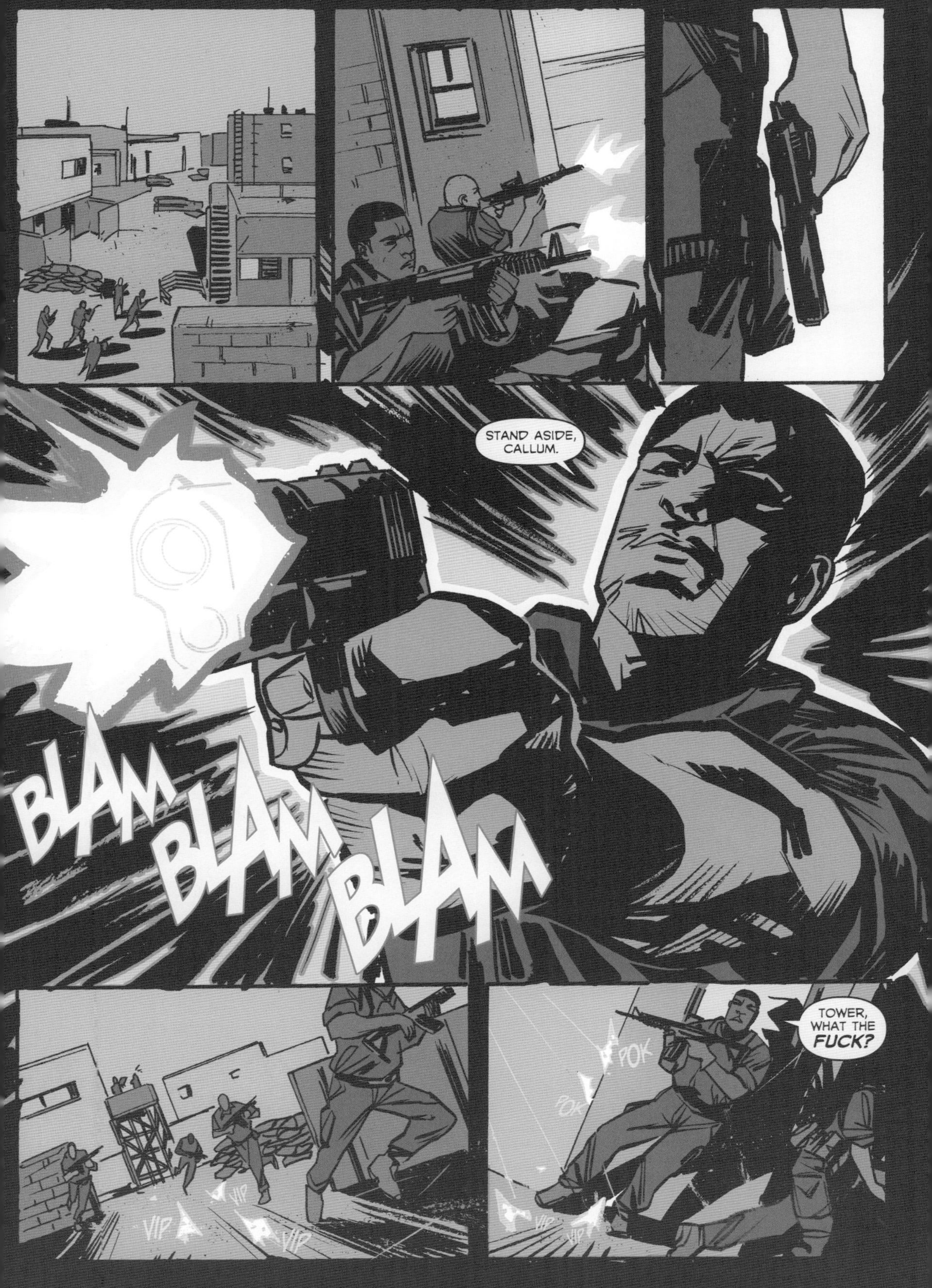
STAND ASIDE, CALLUM.
BLAM BLAM BLAM
VIP VIP VIP VIP
POK POK
TOWER, WHAT THE **FUCK?**
VIP VIP

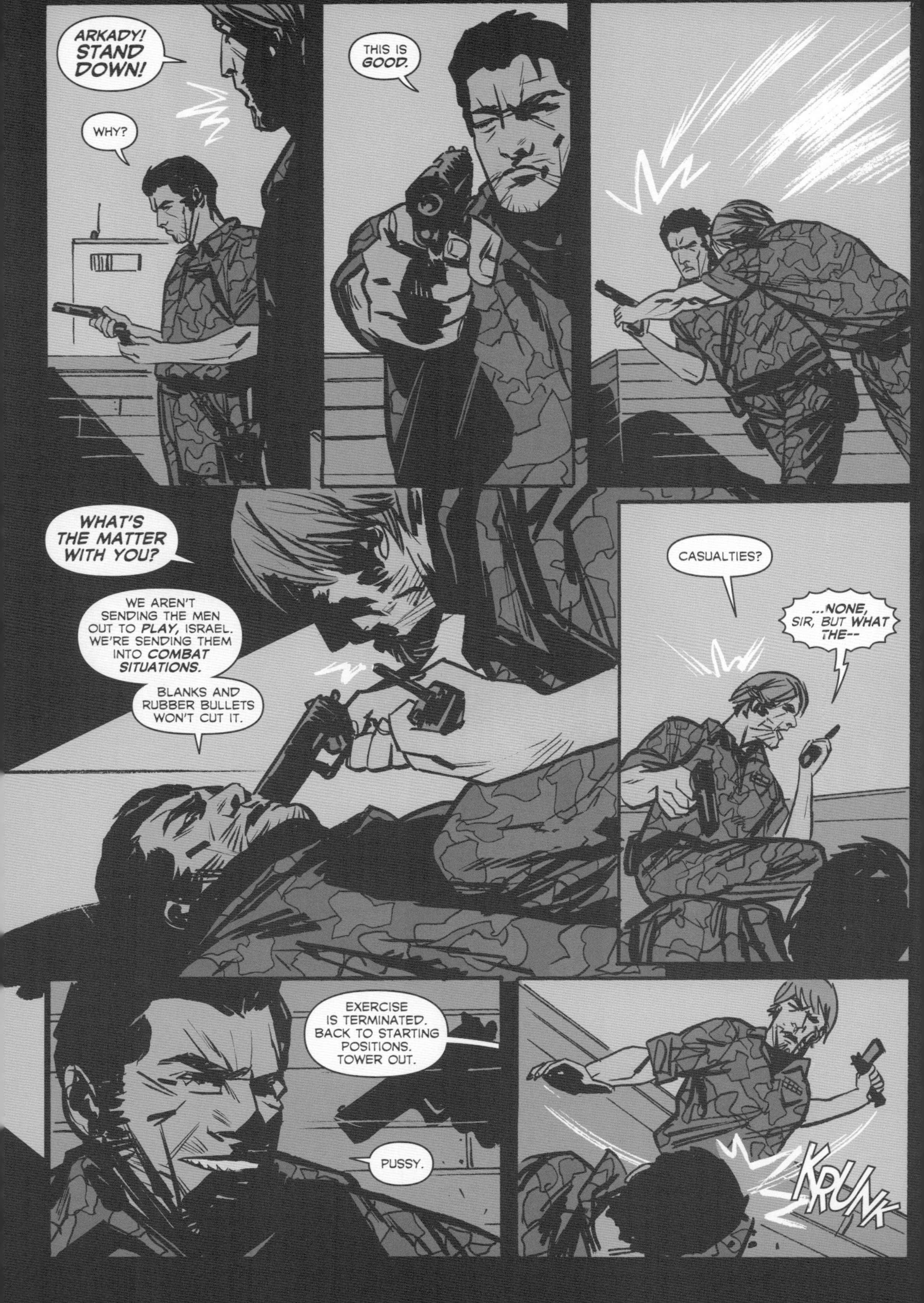
ARKADY! STAND DOWN!
WHY?
THIS IS GOOD.
WHAT'S THE MATTER WITH YOU?
WE AREN'T SENDING THE MEN OUT TO PLAY, ISRAEL. WE'RE SENDING THEM INTO COMBAT SITUATIONS.
BLANKS AND RUBBER BULLETS WON'T CUT IT.
CASUALTIES?
...NONE, SIR, BUT WHAT THE--
EXERCISE IS TERMINATED. BACK TO STARTING POSITIONS. TOWER OUT.
PUSSY.
KRUNK

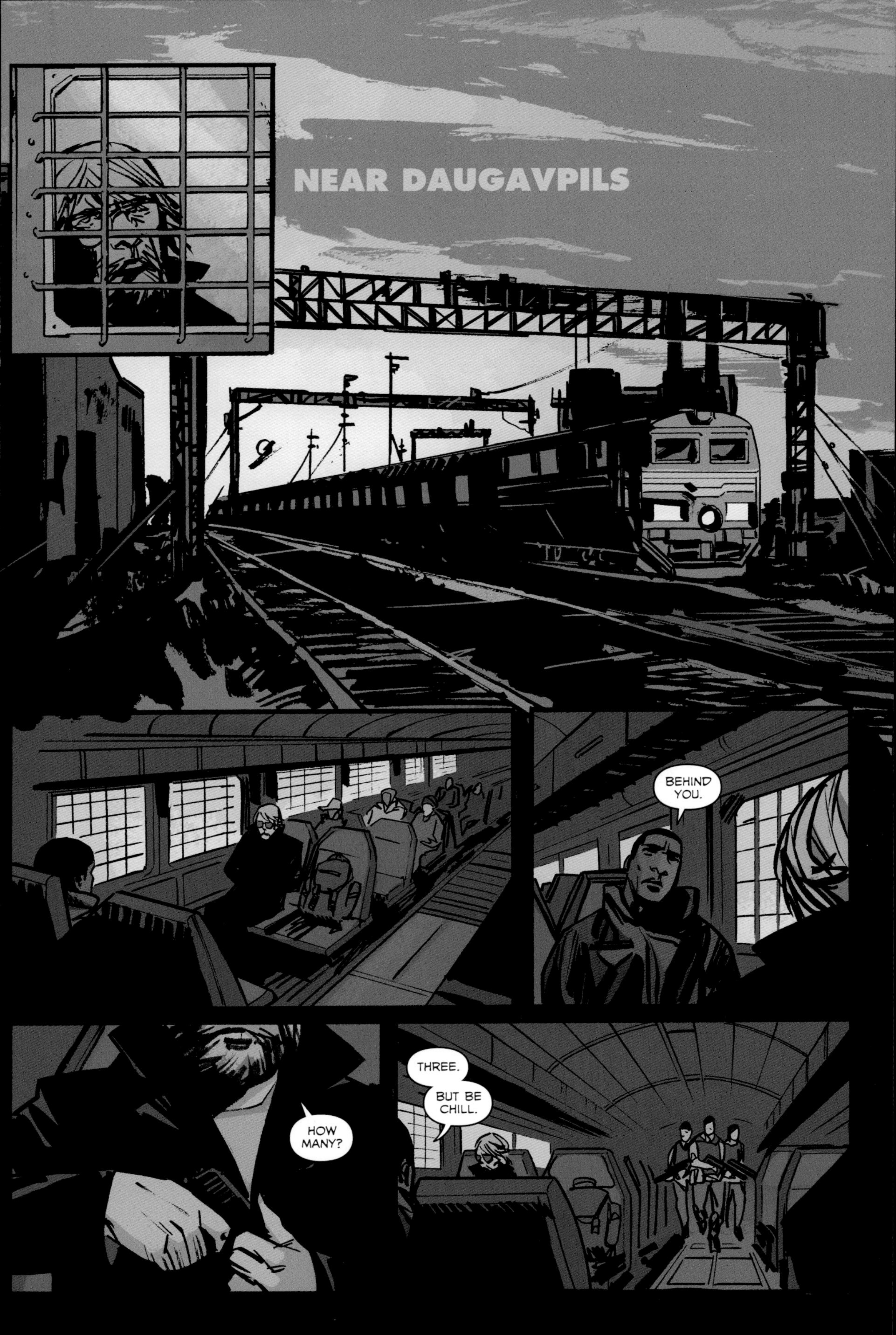
NEAR DAUGAVPILS
BEHIND YOU.
HOW MANY?
THREE.
BUT BE CHILL.

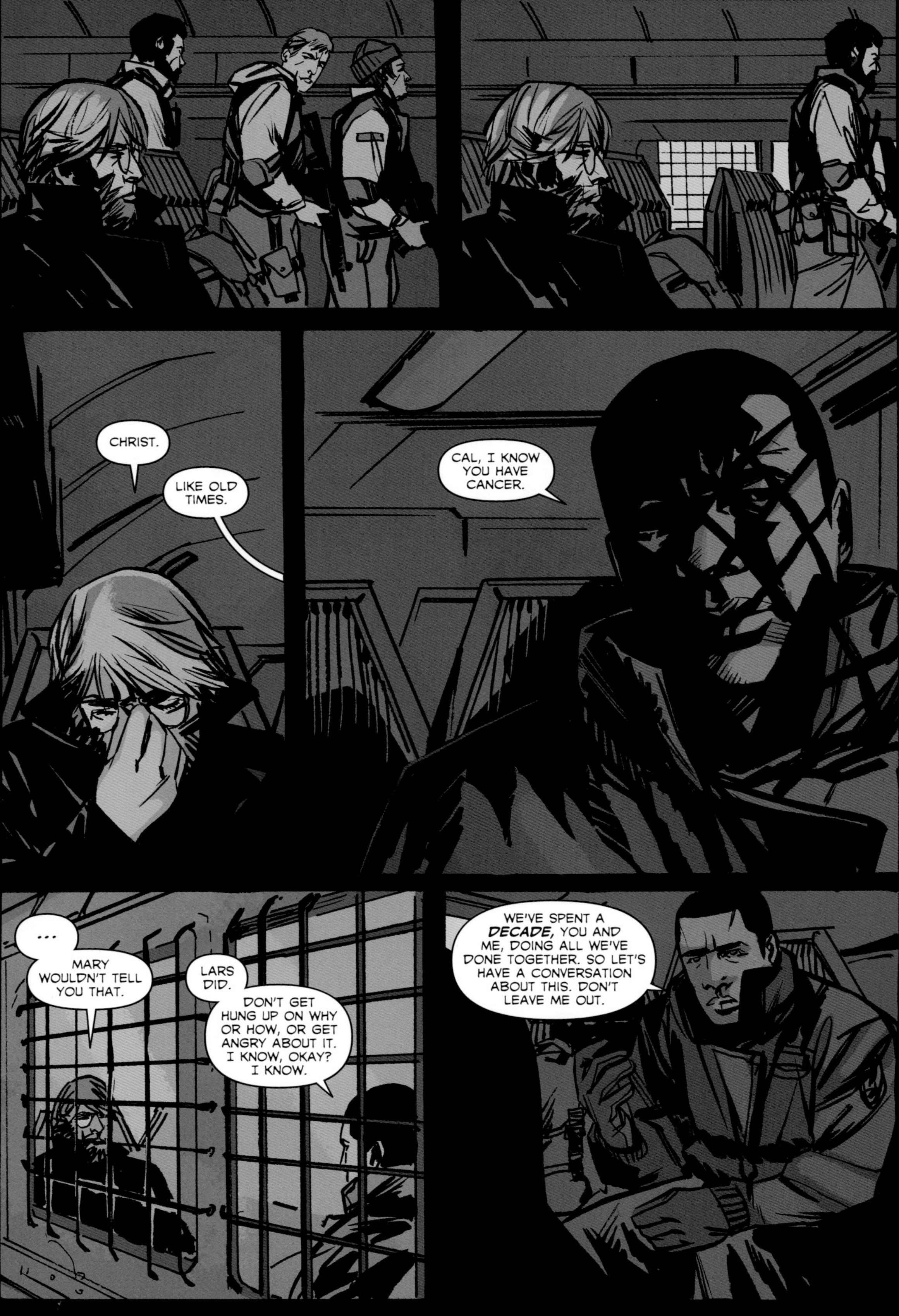
CHRIST.
LIKE OLD TIMES.
CAL, I KNOW YOU HAVE CANCER.
...
MARY WOULDN'T TELL YOU THAT.
LARS DID.
DON'T GET HUNG UP ON WHY OR HOW, OR GET ANGRY ABOUT IT. I KNOW, OKAY? I KNOW.
WE'VE SPENT A ***DECADE,*** YOU AND ME, DOING ALL WE'VE DONE TOGETHER. SO LET'S HAVE A CONVERSATION ABOUT THIS. DON'T LEAVE ME OUT.

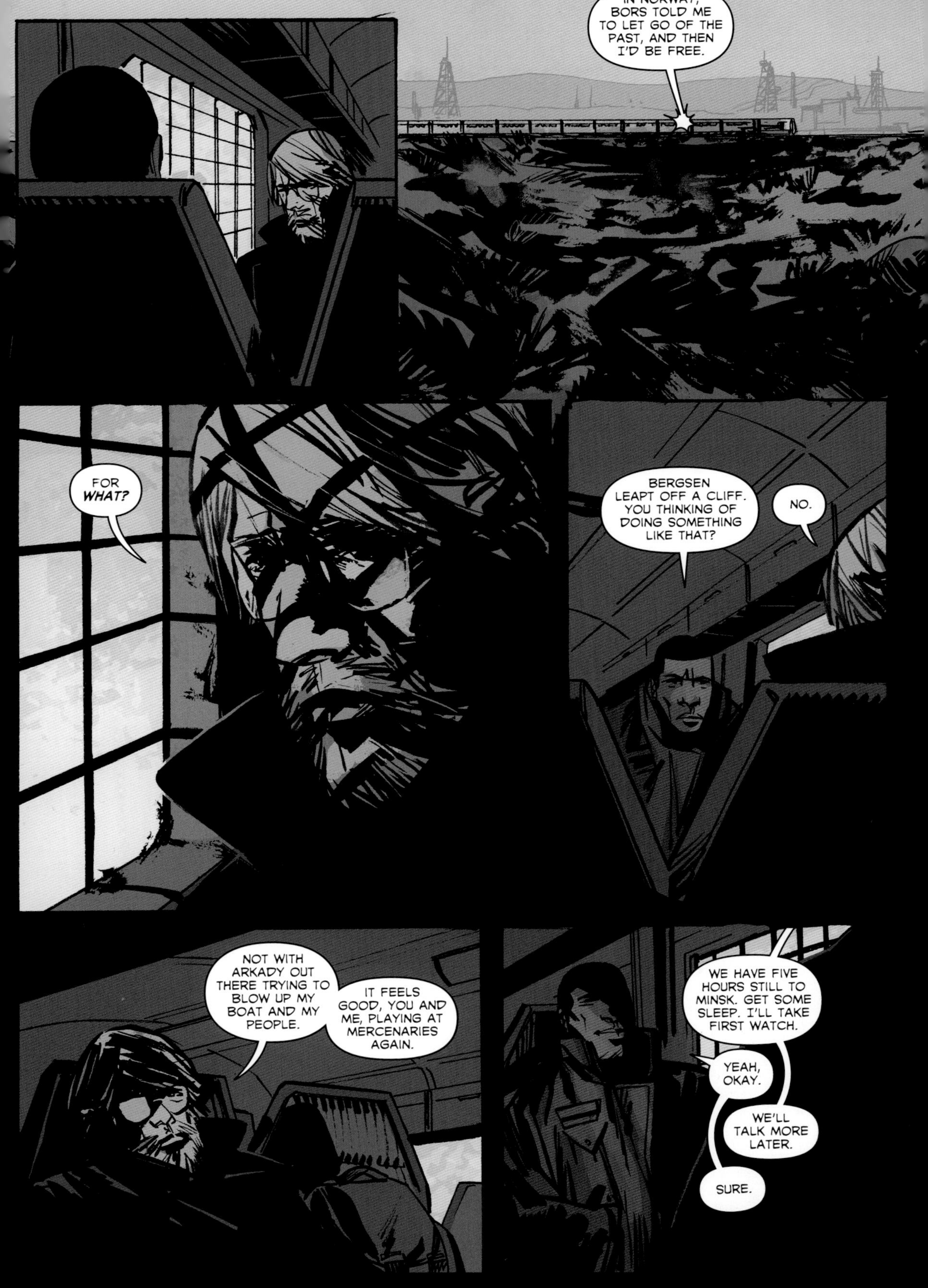

IN NORWAY, BORS TOLD ME TO LET GO OF THE PAST, AND THEN I'D BE FREE.
FOR *WHAT?*
BERGSEN LEAPT OFF A CLIFF. YOU THINKING OF DOING SOMETHING LIKE THAT?
NO.
NOT WITH ARKADY OUT THERE TRYING TO BLOW UP MY BOAT AND MY PEOPLE.
IT FEELS GOOD, YOU AND ME, PLAYING AT MERCENARIES AGAIN.
WE HAVE FIVE HOURS STILL TO MINSK. GET SOME SLEEP. I'LL TAKE FIRST WATCH.
YEAH, OKAY.
WE'LL TALK MORE LATER.
SURE.

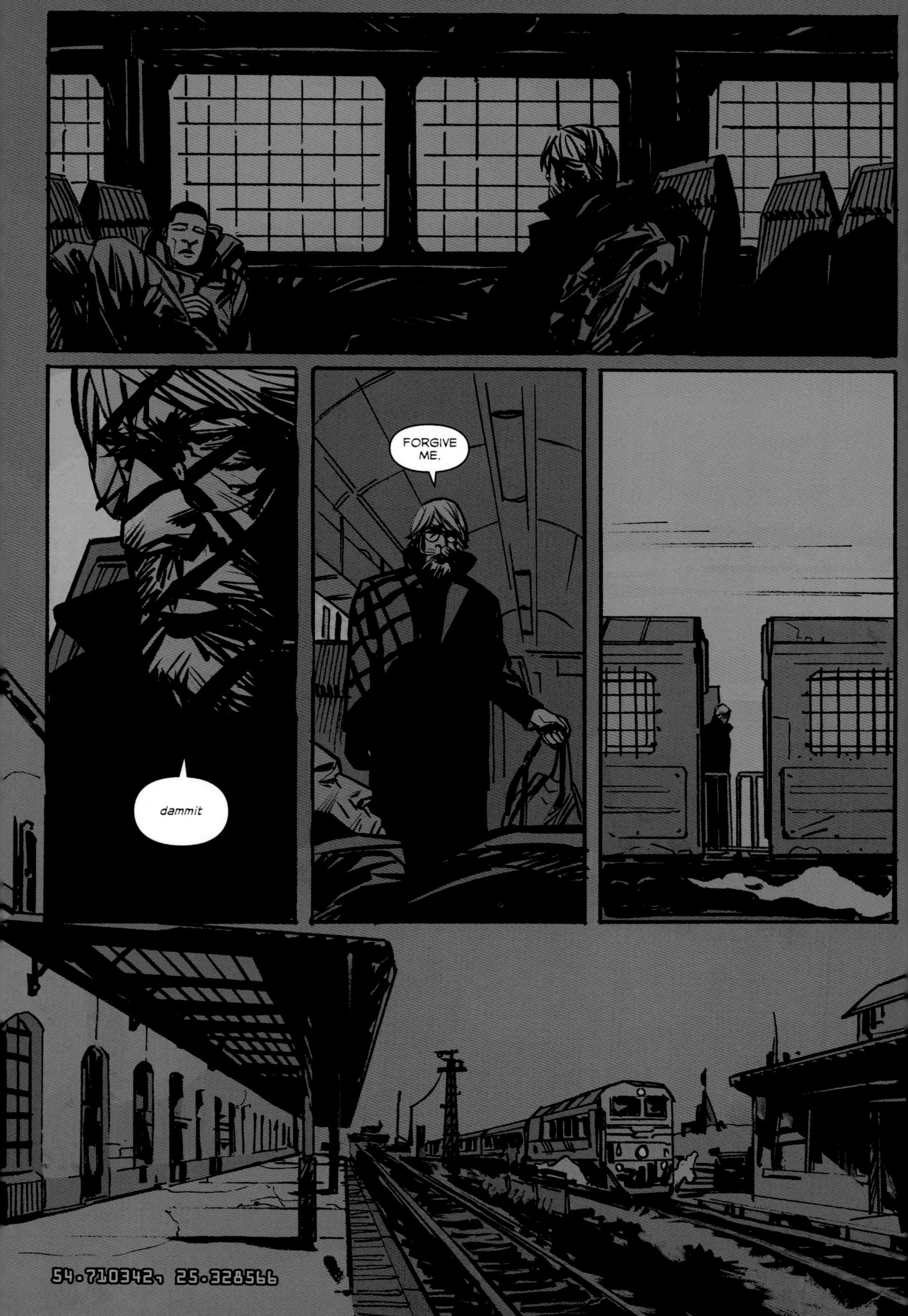
dammit
FORGIVE ME.
54.710342, 25.328566

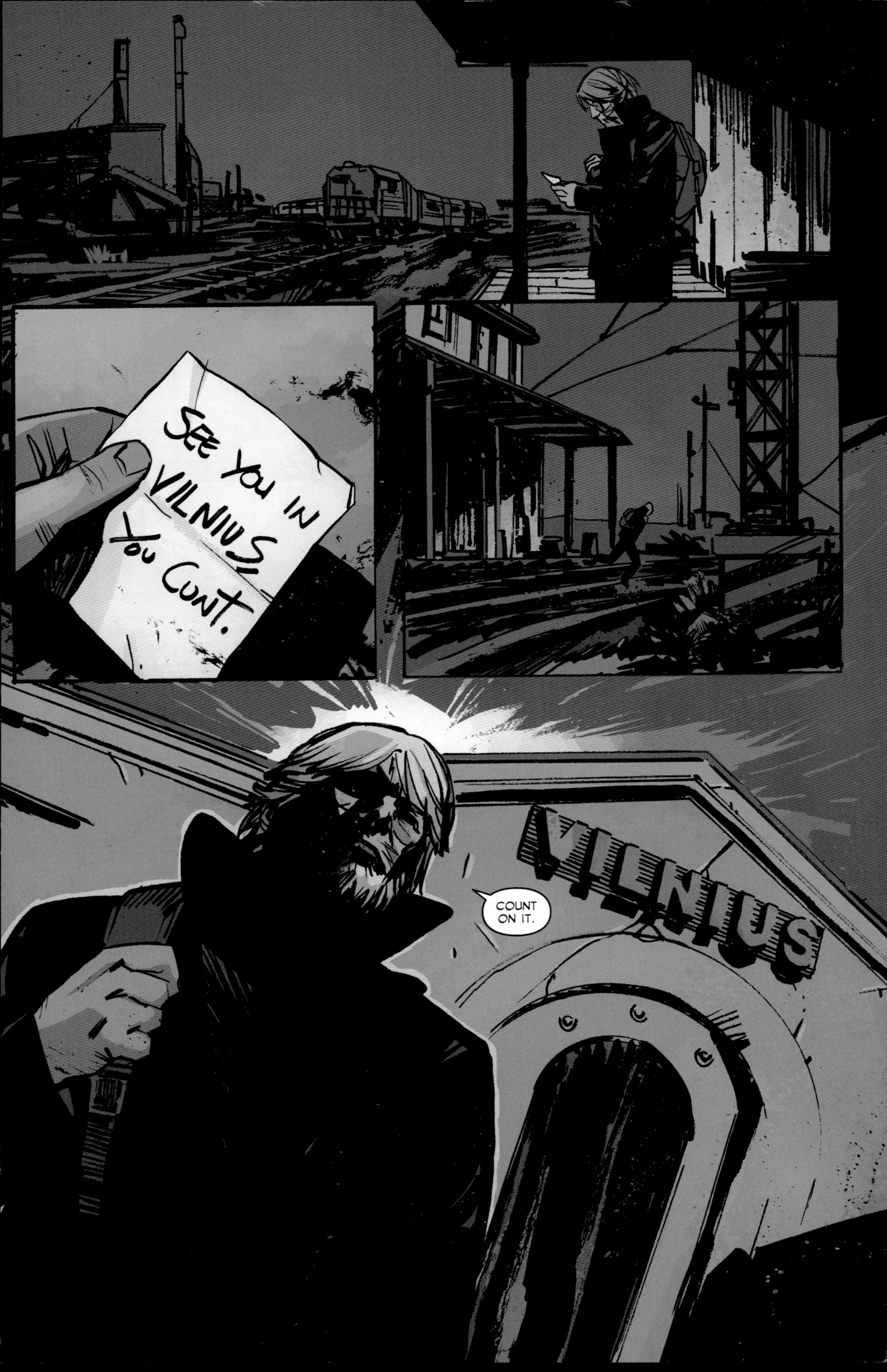
SEE YOU IN VILNIUS, YOU CUNT.
VILNIUS
COUNT ON IT.

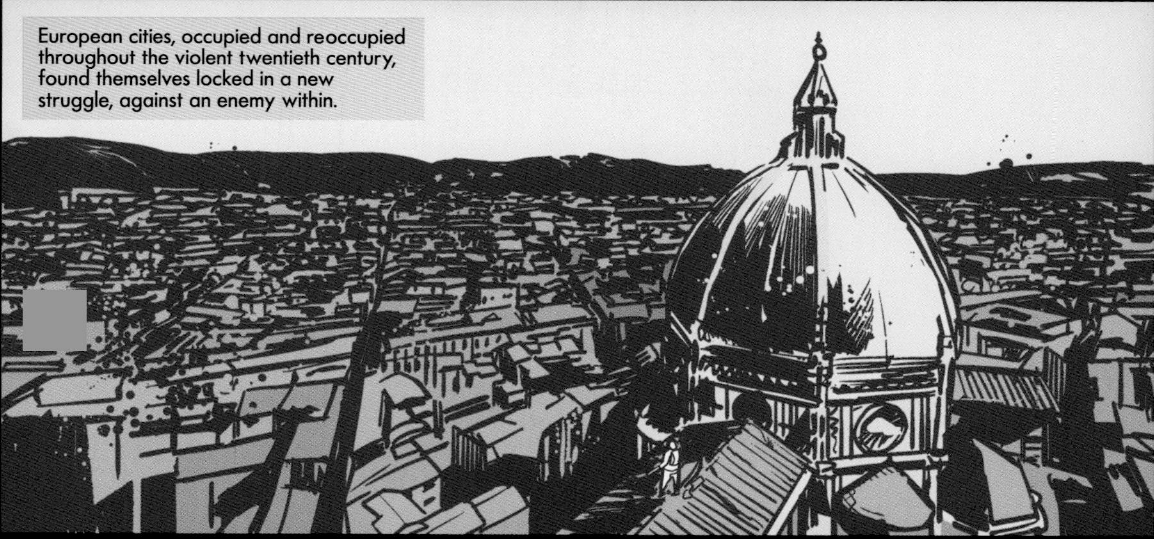
European cities, occupied and reoccupied throughout the violent twentieth century, found themselves locked in a new struggle, against an enemy within.

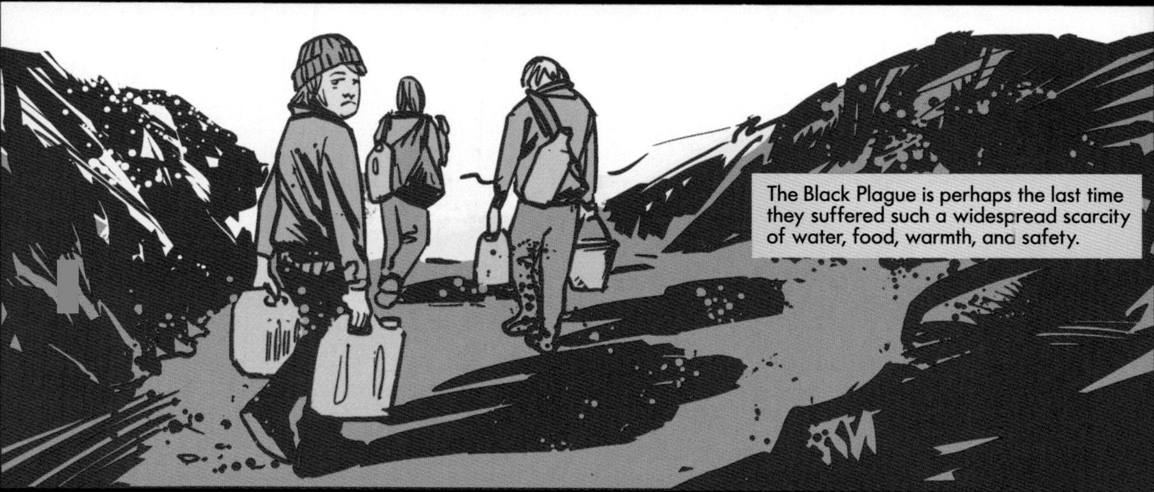
The Black Plague is perhaps the last time they suffered such a widespread scarcity of water, food, warmth, anc safety.

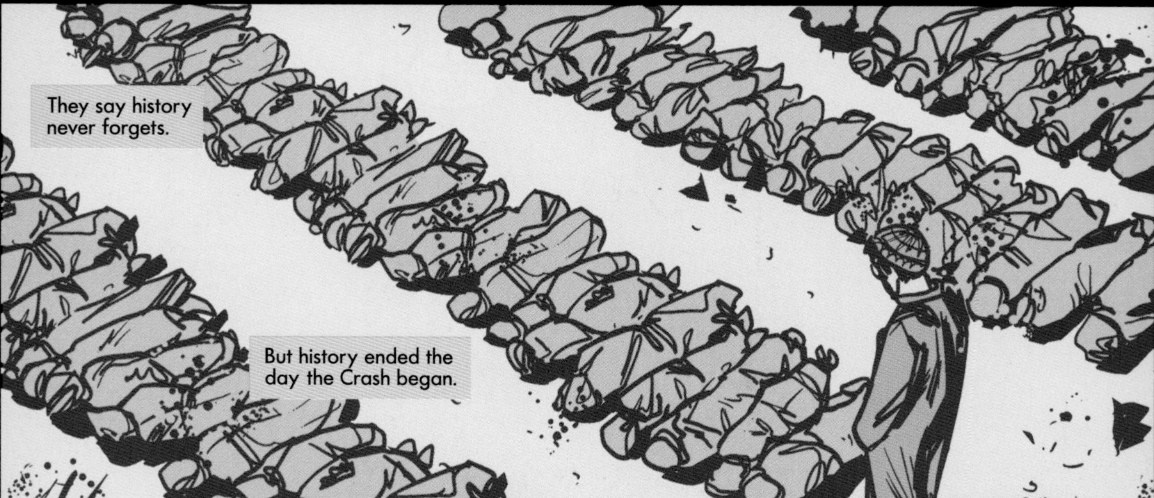
They say history never forgets.
But history ended the day the Crash began.

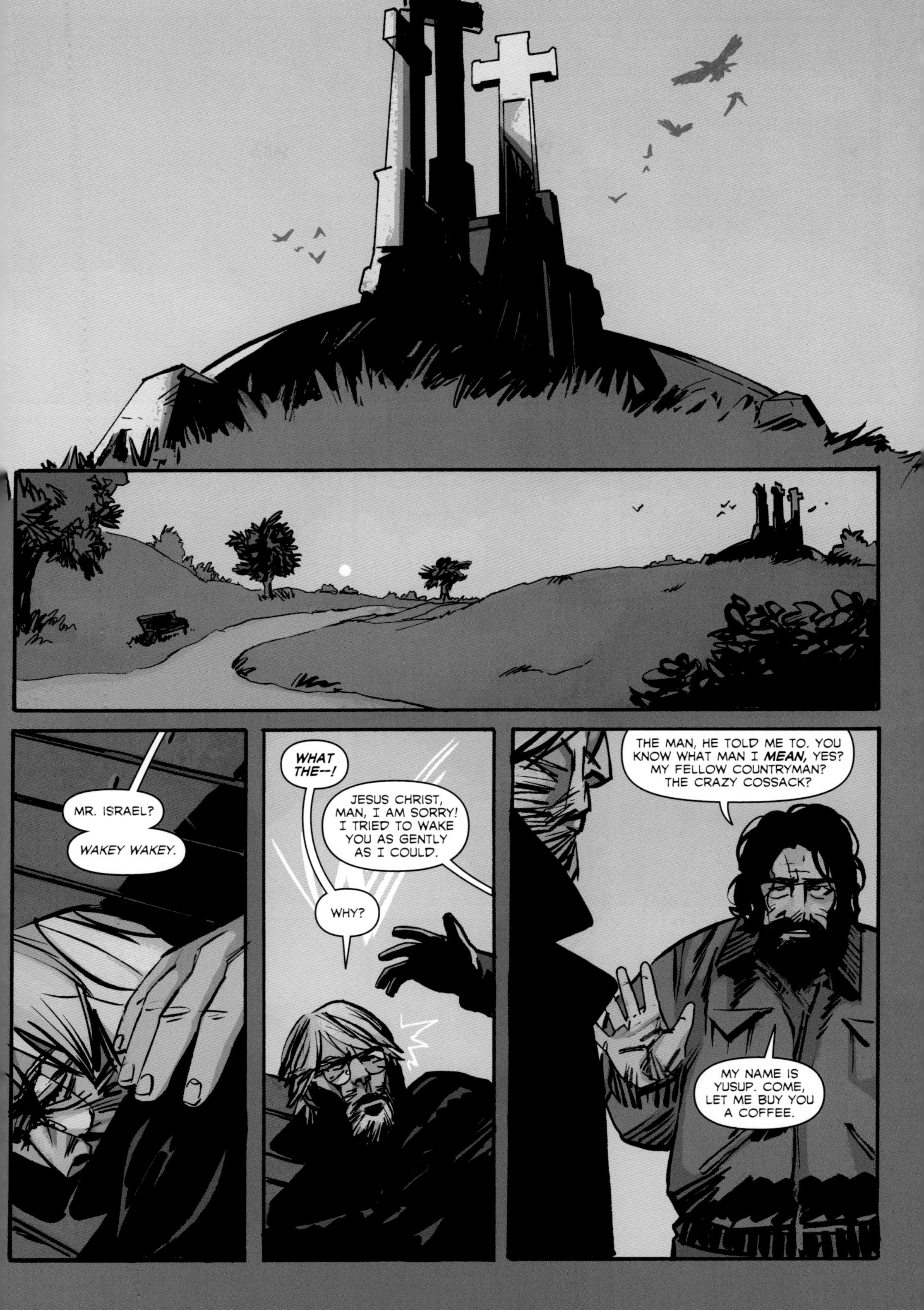
MR. ISRAEL?
WAKEY WAKEY.
WHAT THE--!
JESUS CHRIST, MAN, I AM SORRY! I TRIED TO WAKE YOU AS GENTLY AS I COULD.
WHY?
THE MAN, HE TOLD ME TO. YOU KNOW WHAT MAN I MEAN, YES? MY FELLOW COUNTRYMAN? THE CRAZY COSSACK?
MY NAME IS YUSUP. COME, LET ME BUY YOU A COFFEE.

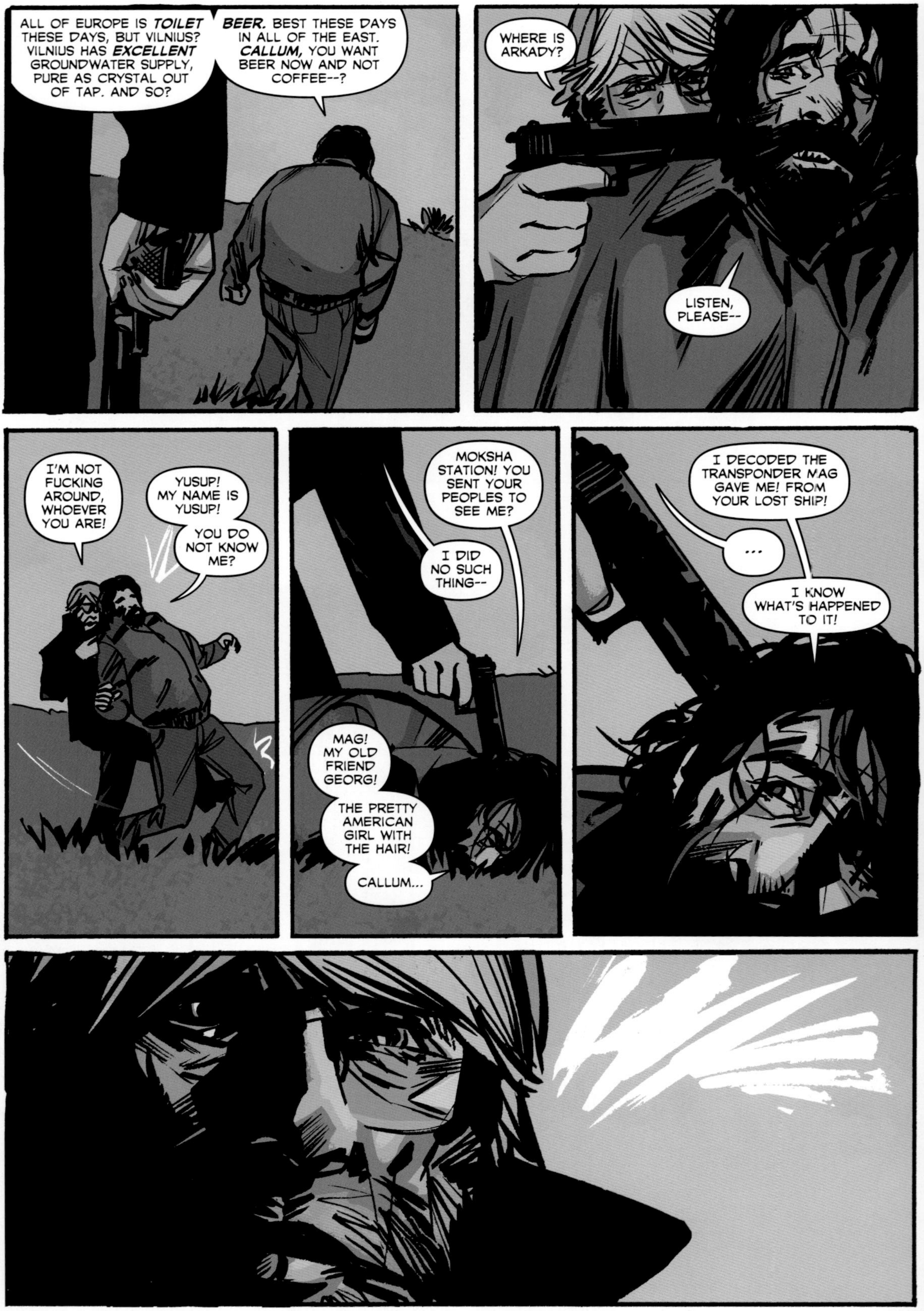
ALL OF EUROPE IS TOILET THESE DAYS, BUT VILNIUS? VILNIUS HAS EXCELLENT GROUNDWATER SUPPLY, PURE AS CRYSTAL OUT OF TAP. AND SO?
BEER. BEST THESE DAYS IN ALL OF THE EAST. CALLUM, YOU WANT BEER NOW AND NOT COFFEE--?
WHERE IS ARKADY?
LISTEN, PLEASE--
I'M NOT FUCKING AROUND, WHOEVER YOU ARE!
YUSUP! MY NAME IS YUSUP!
YOU DO NOT KNOW ME?
MOKSHA STATION! YOU SENT YOUR PEOPLES TO SEE ME?
I DID NO SUCH THING--
MAG! MY OLD FRIEND GEORG!
THE PRETTY AMERICAN GIRL WITH THE HAIR!
CALLUM...
I DECODED THE TRANSPONDER MAG GAVE ME! FROM YOUR LOST SHIP!
...
I KNOW WHAT'S HAPPENED TO IT!

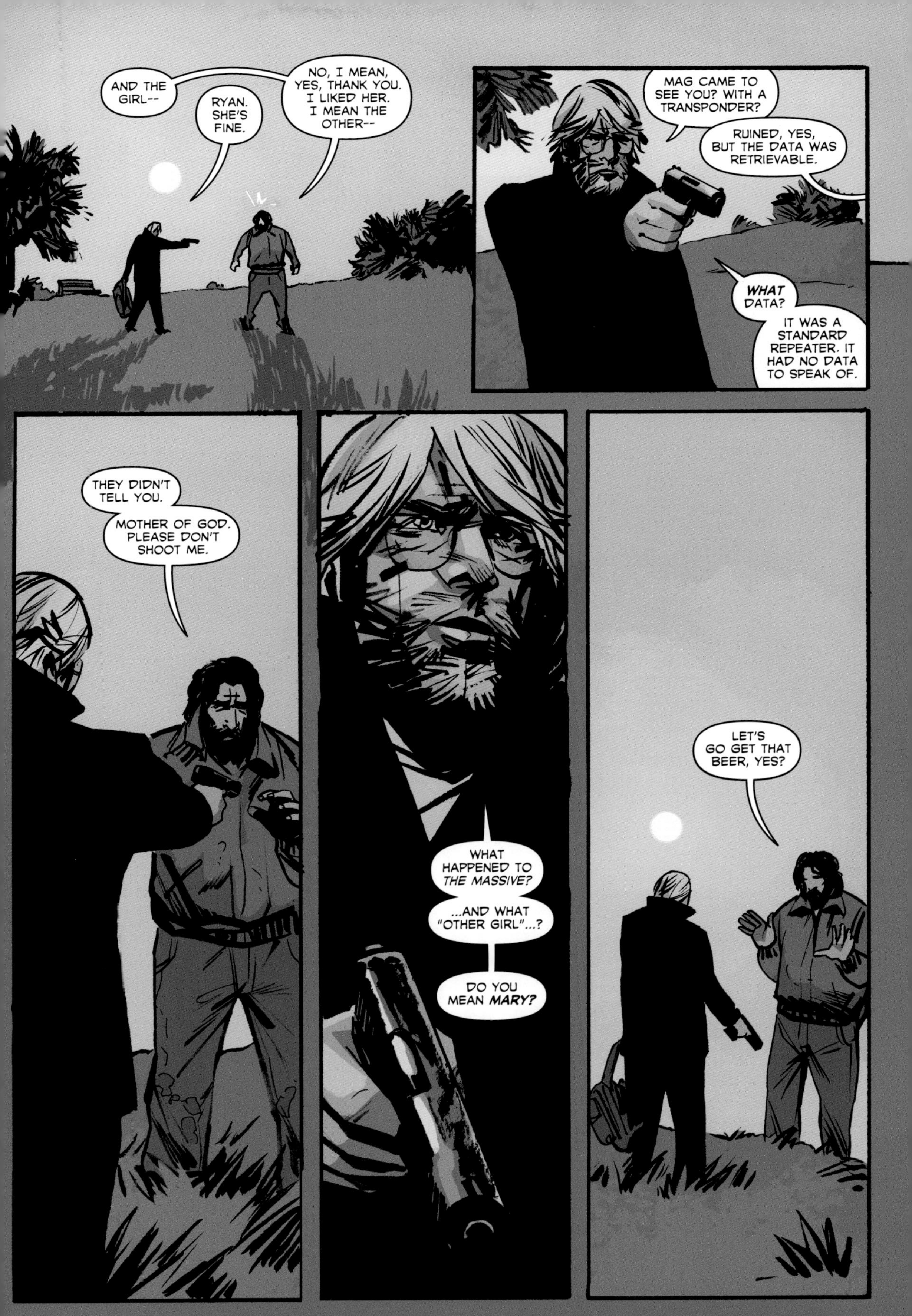
AND THE GIRL--
RYAN. SHE'S FINE.
NO, I MEAN, YES, THANK YOU. I LIKED HER. I MEAN THE OTHER--
MAG CAME TO SEE YOU? WITH A TRANSPONDER?
RUINED, YES, BUT THE DATA WAS RETRIEVABLE.
WHAT DATA?
IT WAS A STANDARD REPEATER. IT HAD NO DATA TO SPEAK OF.
THEY DIDN'T TELL YOU.
MOTHER OF GOD. PLEASE DON'T SHOOT ME.
WHAT HAPPENED TO *THE MASSIVE?*
...AND WHAT "OTHER GIRL"...?
DO YOU MEAN *MARY?*
LET'S GO GET THAT BEER, YES?

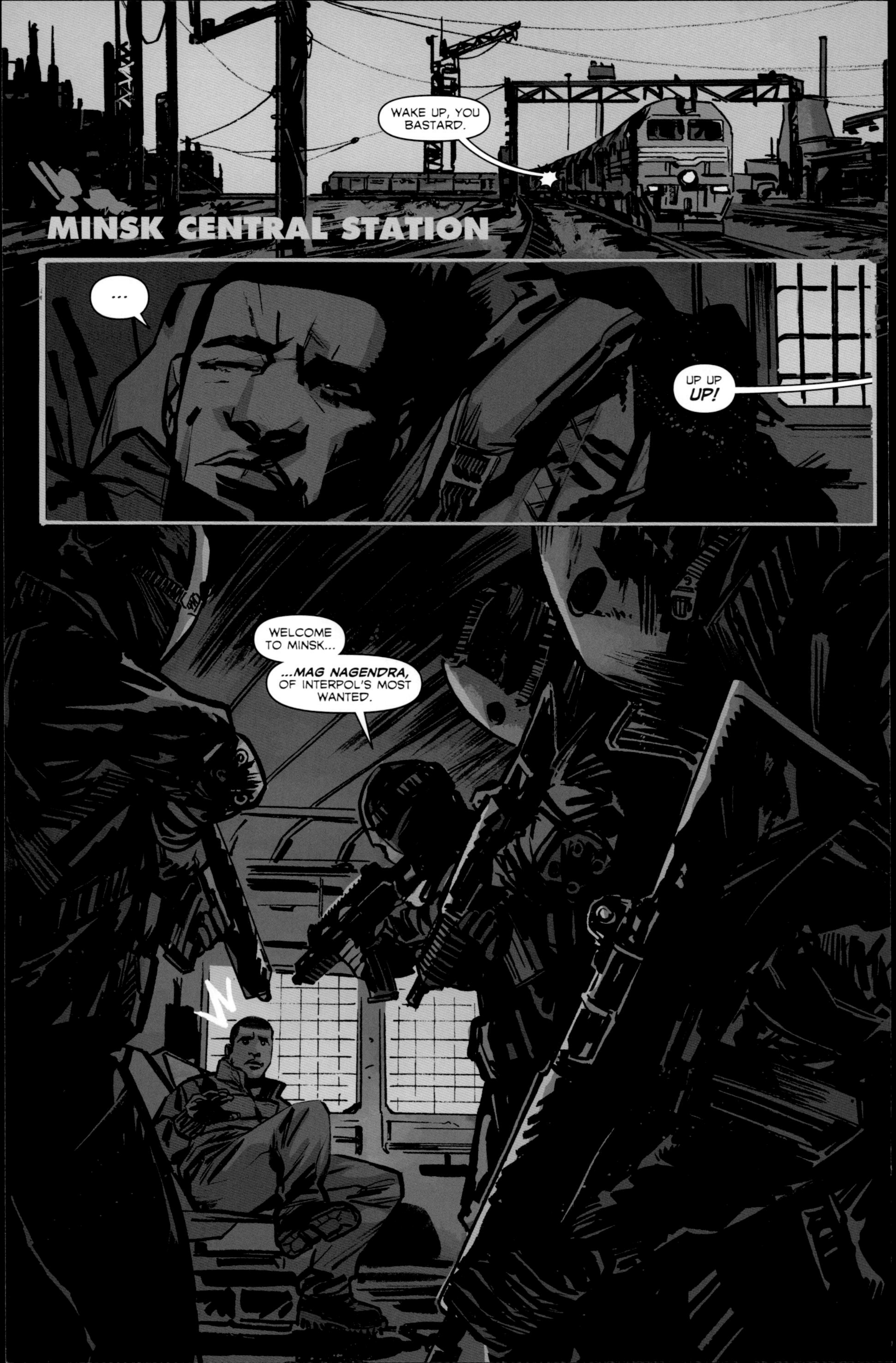
MINSK CENTRAL STATION
WAKE UP, YOU BASTARD.
...
UP UP *UP!*
WELCOME TO MINSK...
...MAG NAGENDRA, OF INTERPOL'S MOST WANTED.

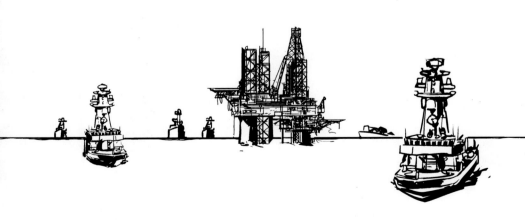

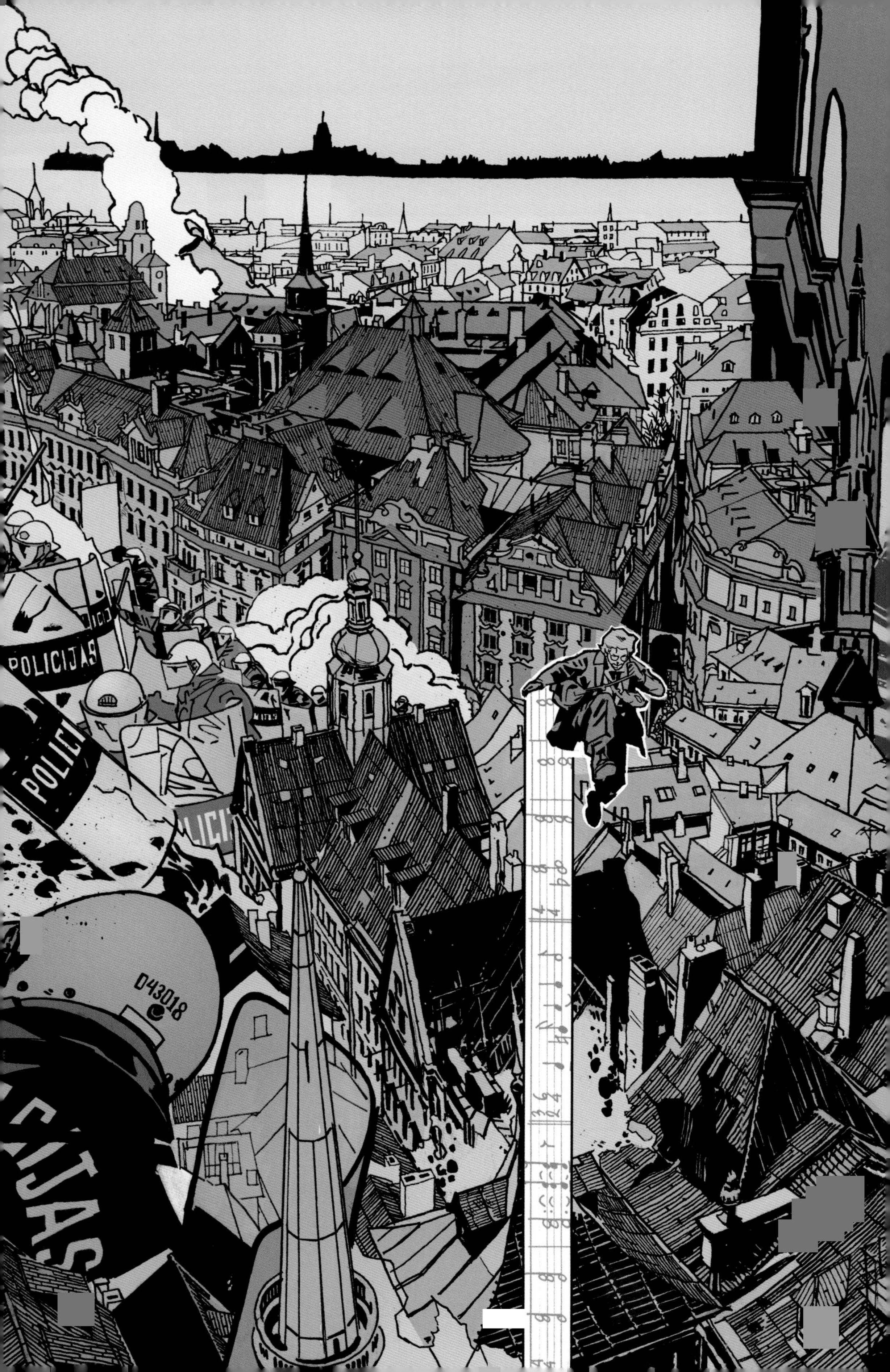
POLICIJAS
D43018

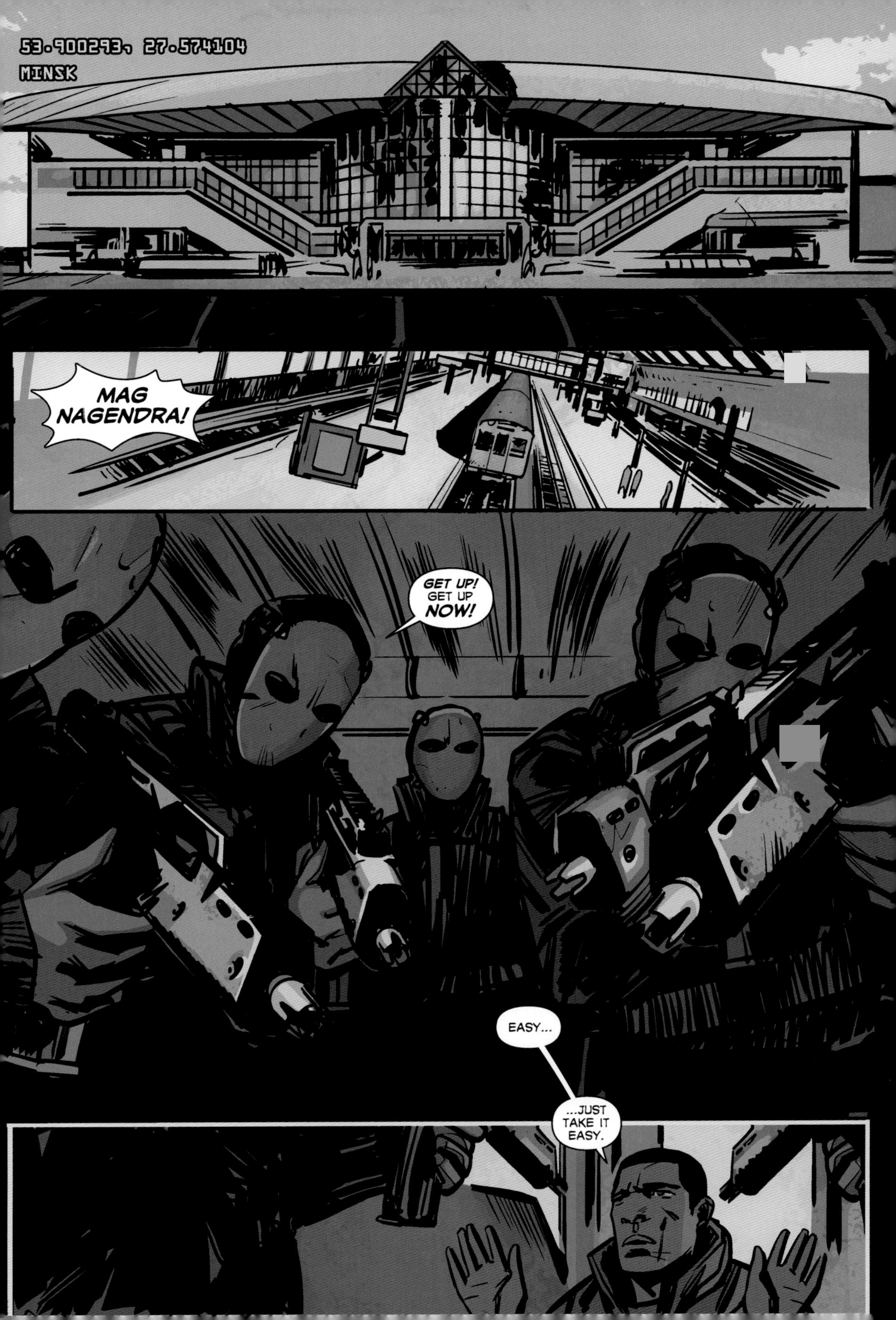
53.900293, 27.574104
MINSK
MAG NAGENDRA!
GET UP! GET UP NOW!
EASY...
...JUST TAKE IT EASY.

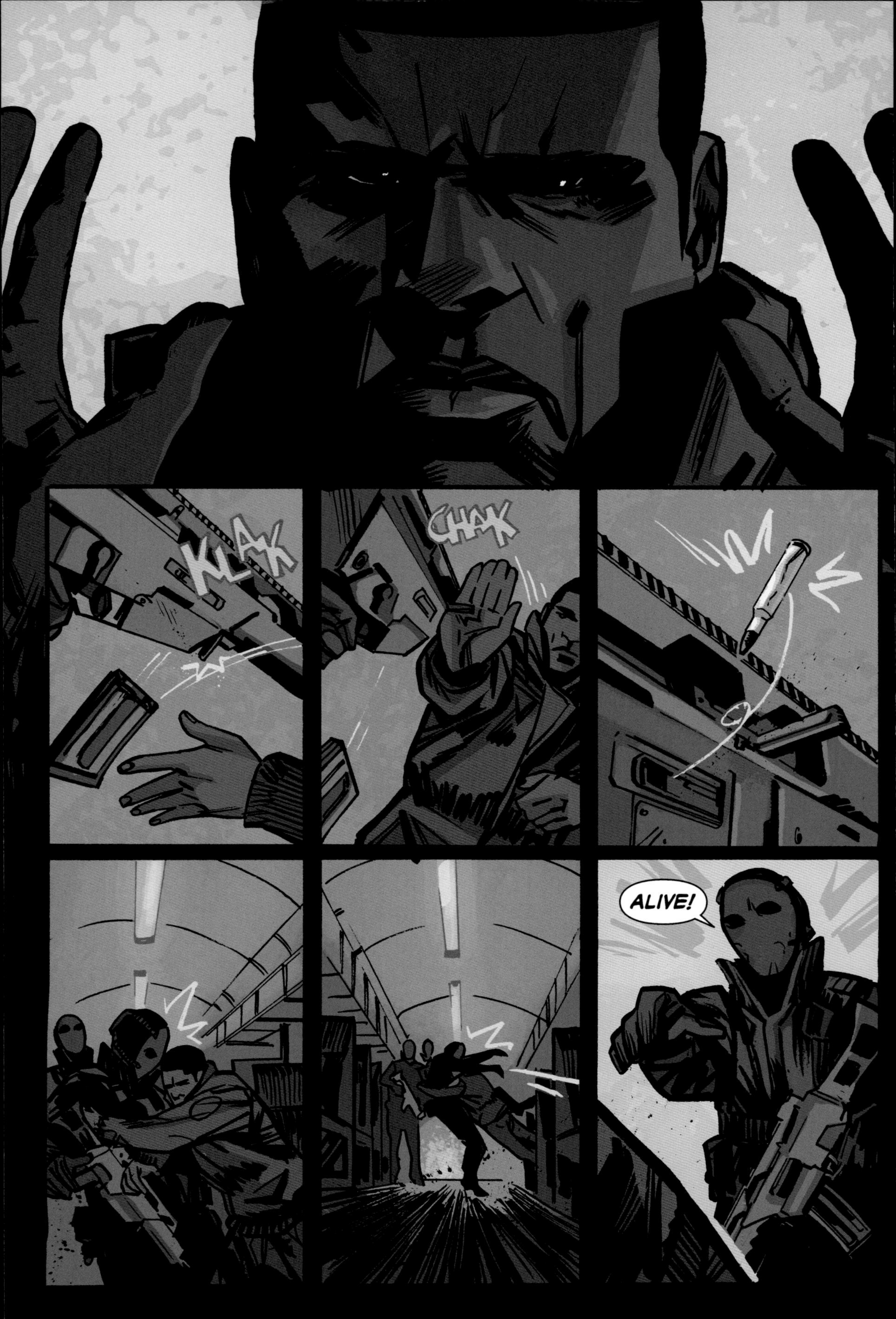
KLAK
CHAK
ALIVE!

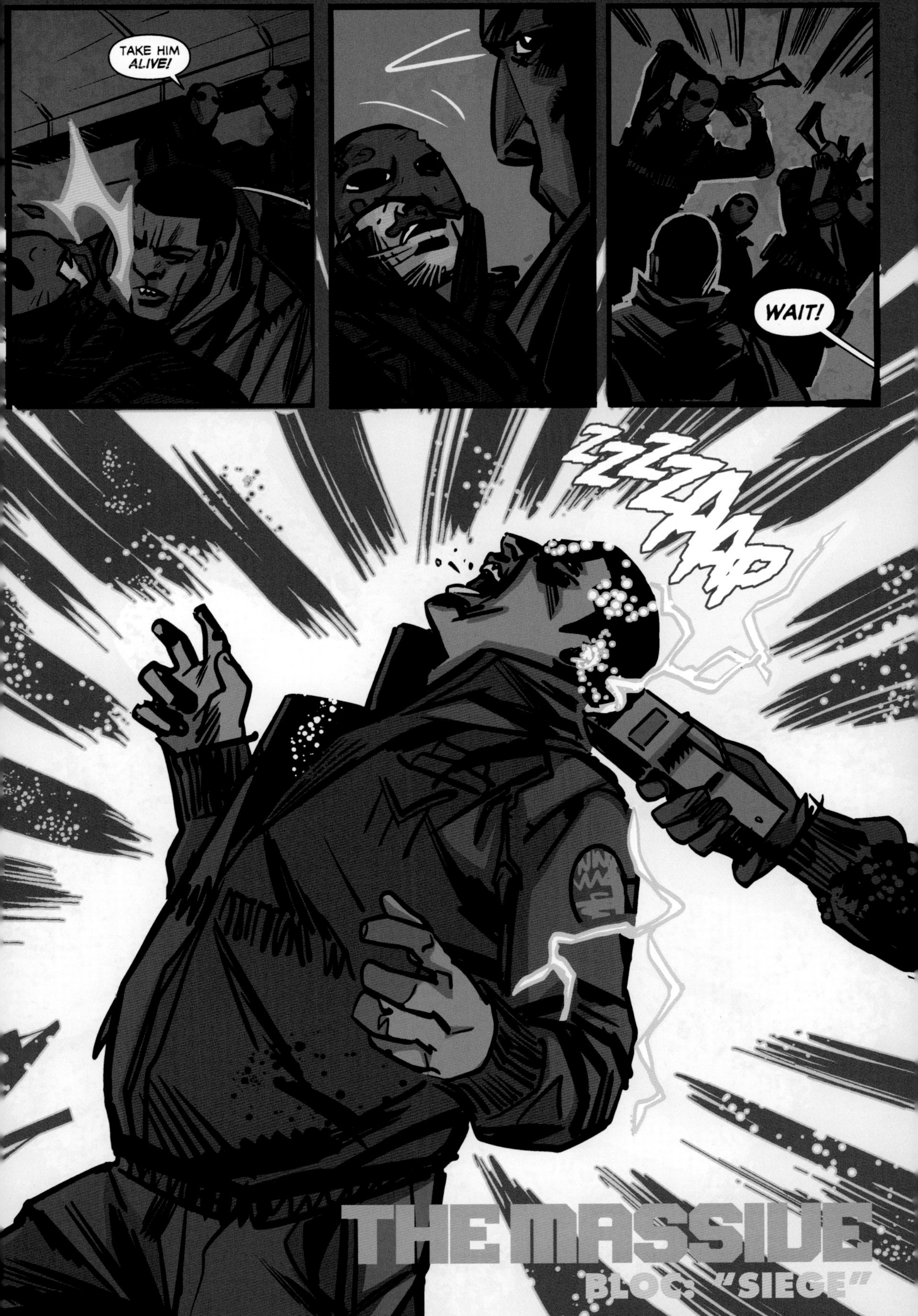
TAKE HIM ALIVE!
WAIT!
ZZZZAAP
THE MASSIVE
BLOC: "SIEGE"

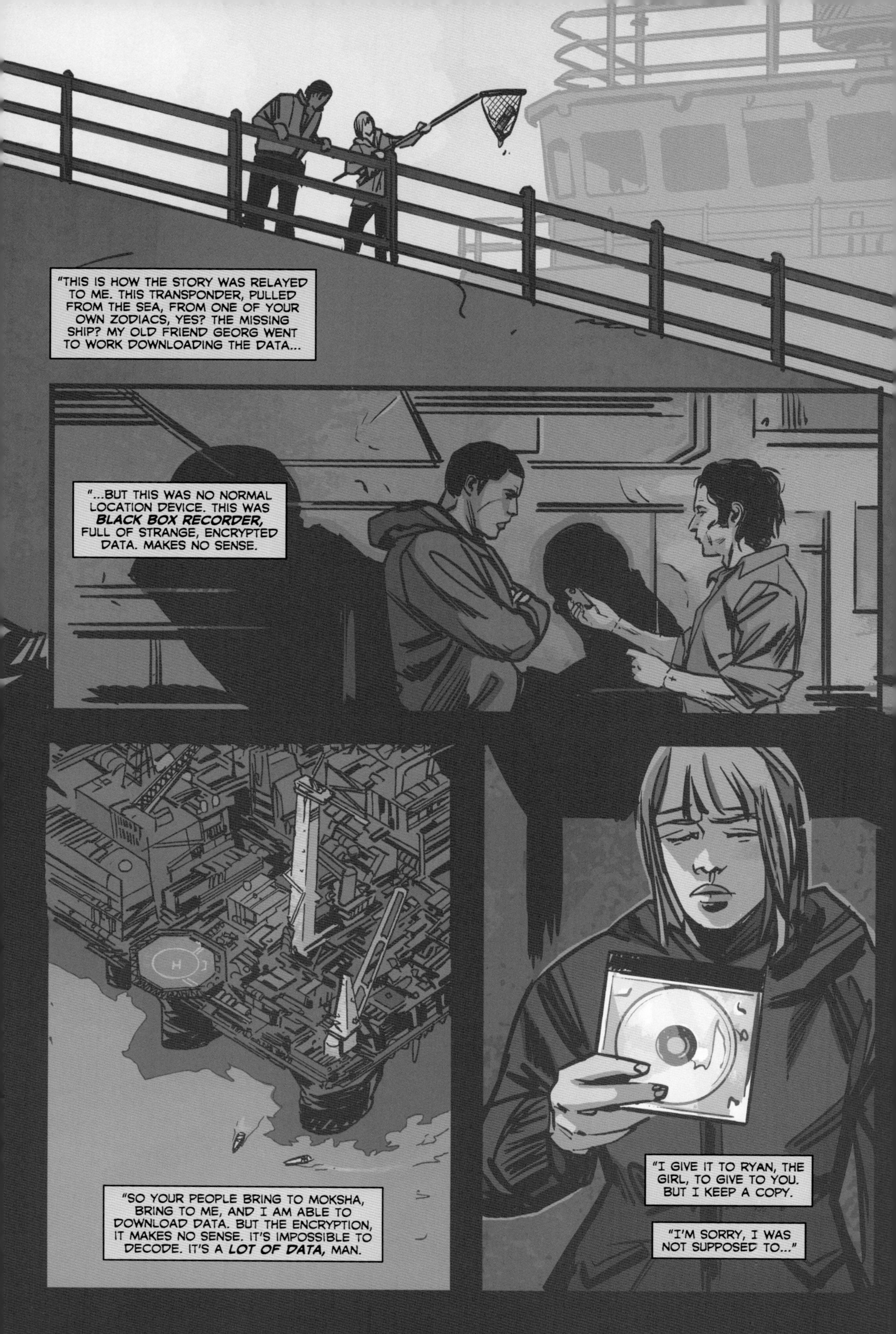
"THIS IS HOW THE STORY WAS RELAYED TO ME. THIS TRANSPONDER, PULLED FROM THE SEA, FROM ONE OF YOUR OWN ZODIACS, YES? THE MISSING SHIP? MY OLD FRIEND GEORG WENT TO WORK DOWNLOADING THE DATA...
"...BUT THIS WAS NO NORMAL LOCATION DEVICE. THIS WAS BLACK BOX RECORDER, FULL OF STRANGE, ENCRYPTED DATA. MAKES NO SENSE.
"SO YOUR PEOPLE BRING TO MOKSHA, BRING TO ME, AND I AM ABLE TO DOWNLOAD DATA. BUT THE ENCRYPTION, IT MAKES NO SENSE. IT'S IMPOSSIBLE TO DECODE. IT'S A LOT OF DATA, MAN.
"I GIVE IT TO RYAN, THE GIRL, TO GIVE TO YOU. BUT I KEEP A COPY.
"I'M SORRY, I WAS NOT SUPPOSED TO..."

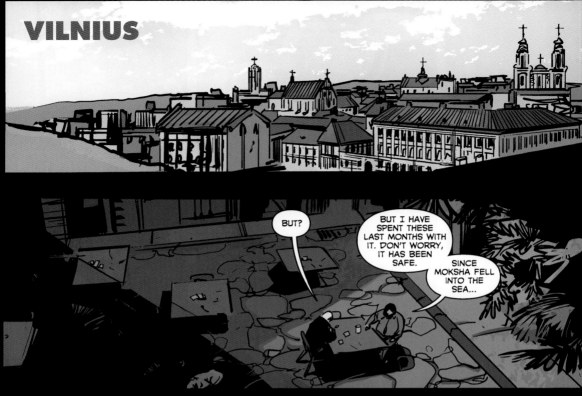

BUT?

BUT I HAVE SPENT THESE LAST MONTHS WITH IT. DON'T WORRY, IT HAS BEEN SAFE.

SINCE MOKSHA FELL INTO THE SEA...

...I HAVE DRIFTED. IT HAS BEEN DIFFICULT, LIKE FOR EVERYONE, BUT THIS CODE, I HAVE KEPT IT WITH ME. IT HAS NEVER LEFT MY MIND.

AND THEN I MEET ARKADY.

YOU MET HIM, JUST LIKE THAT?

SOMETIMES IT HAPPENS JUST LIKE THAT, COINCIDENCE. YOU ARE IN A STRANGE PLACE, YOU HEAR FAMILIAR ACCENT OR A MOTHER TONGUE...

...YOU GET HIRED TO BETRAY A MAN.

CALLUM, BY THE TIME I REALIZE WHO THIS ARKADY IS TO YOU AND YOUR PEOPLE, IT IS ALREADY TOO LATE. HE HAS HOOKS INTO ME.

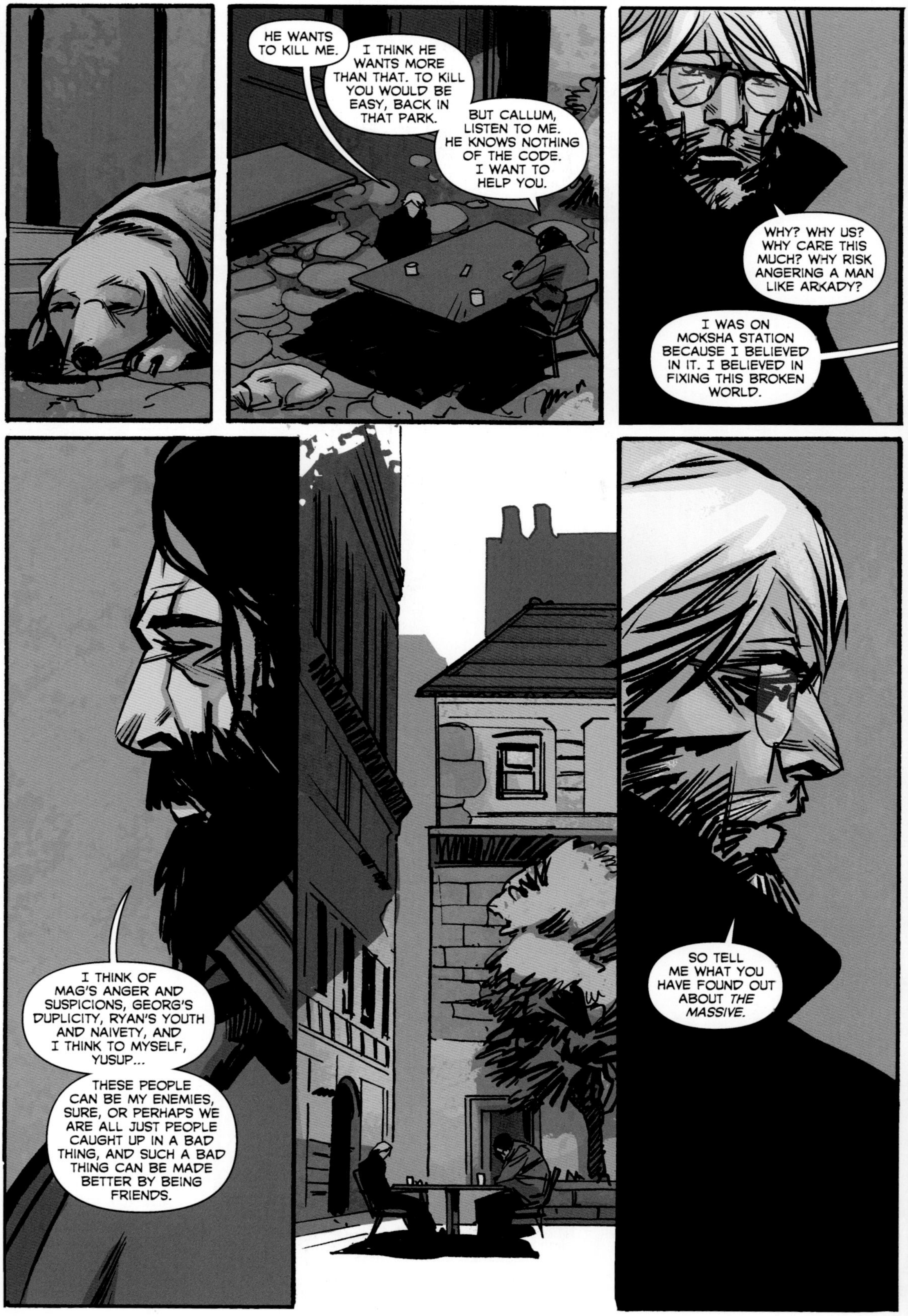
HE WANTS TO KILL ME.
I THINK HE WANTS MORE THAN THAT. TO KILL YOU WOULD BE EASY, BACK IN THAT PARK.
BUT CALLUM, LISTEN TO ME. HE KNOWS NOTHING OF THE CODE. I WANT TO HELP YOU.
WHY? WHY US? WHY CARE THIS MUCH? WHY RISK ANGERING A MAN LIKE ARKADY?
I WAS ON MOKSHA STATION BECAUSE I BELIEVED IN IT. I BELIEVED IN FIXING THIS BROKEN WORLD.
I THINK OF MAG'S ANGER AND SUSPICIONS, GEORG'S DUPLICITY, RYAN'S YOUTH AND NAIVETY, AND I THINK TO MYSELF, YUSUP...
THESE PEOPLE CAN BE MY ENEMIES, SURE, OR PERHAPS WE ARE ALL JUST PEOPLE CAUGHT UP IN A BAD THING, AND SUCH A BAD THING CAN BE MADE BETTER BY BEING FRIENDS.
SO TELL ME WHAT YOU HAVE FOUND OUT ABOUT *THE MASSIVE.*

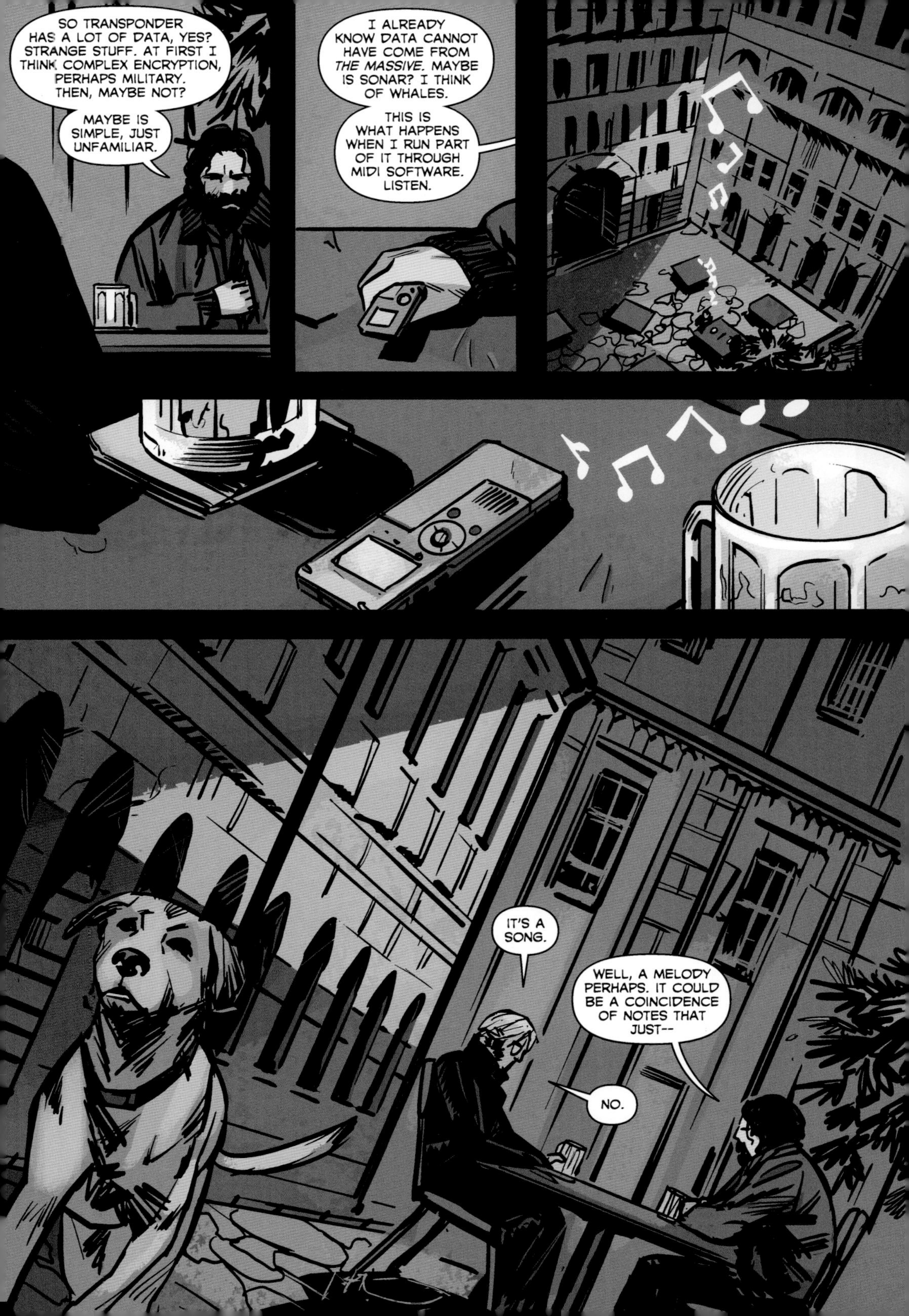
SO TRANSPONDER HAS A LOT OF DATA, YES? STRANGE STUFF. AT FIRST I THINK COMPLEX ENCRYPTION, PERHAPS MILITARY. THEN, MAYBE NOT?
MAYBE IS SIMPLE, JUST UNFAMILIAR.
I ALREADY KNOW DATA CANNOT HAVE COME FROM *THE MASSIVE.* MAYBE IS SONAR? I THINK OF WHALES.
THIS IS WHAT HAPPENS WHEN I RUN PART OF IT THROUGH MIDI SOFTWARE. LISTEN.
IT'S A SONG.
WELL, A MELODY PERHAPS. IT COULD BE A COINCIDENCE OF NOTES THAT JUST--
NO.

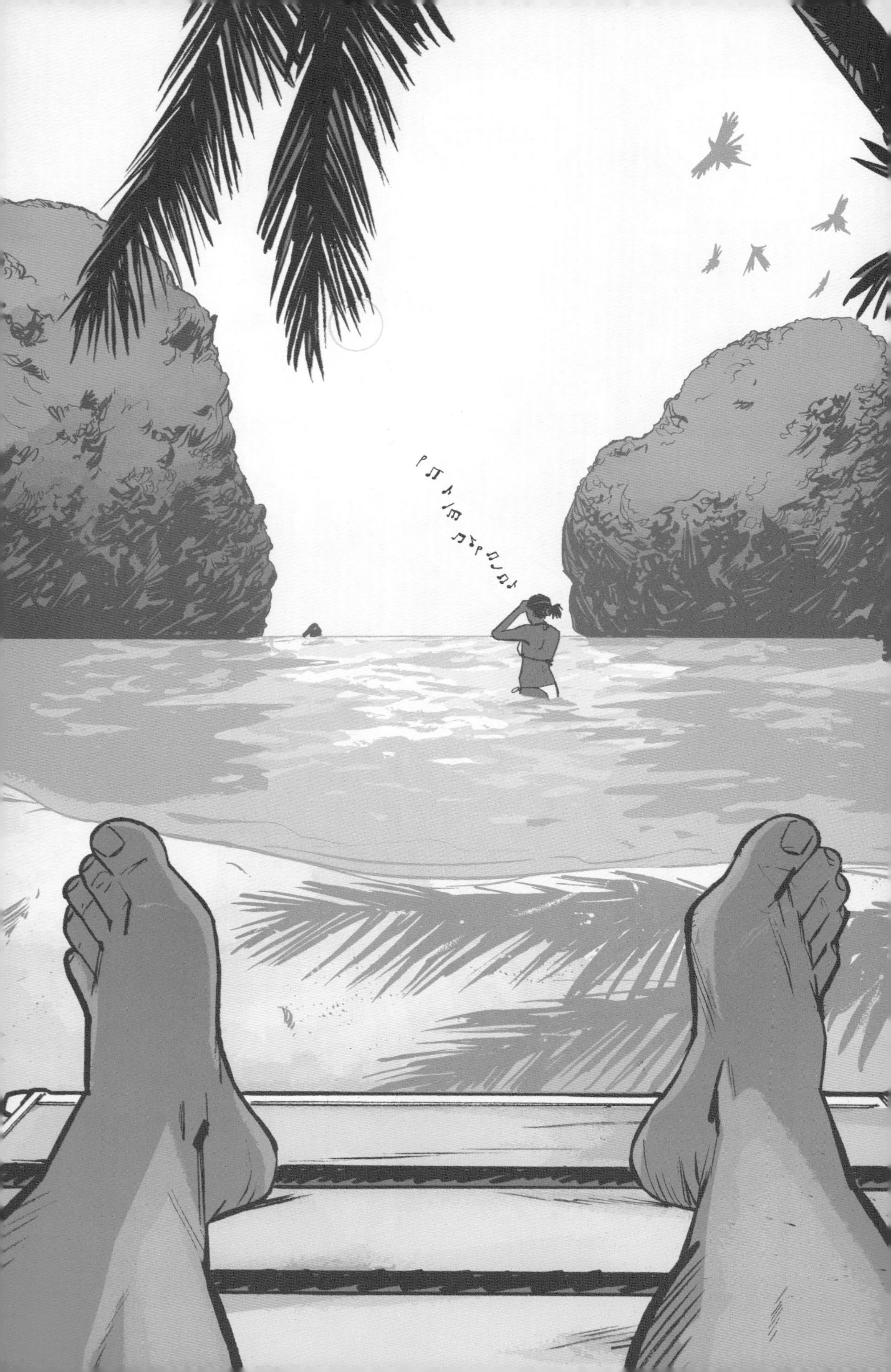

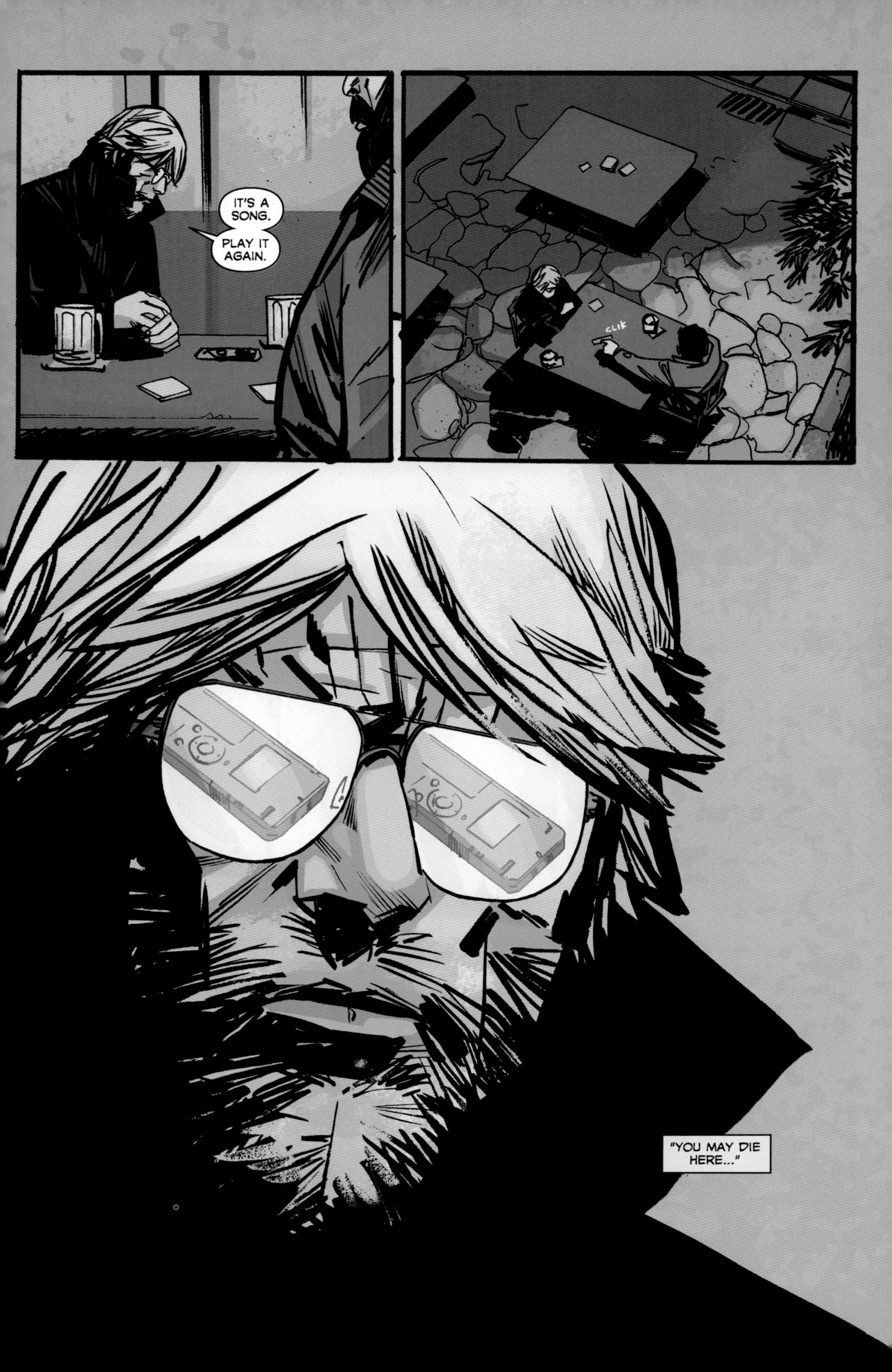
IT'S A SONG.
PLAY IT AGAIN.
CLIK
"YOU MAY DIE HERE..."

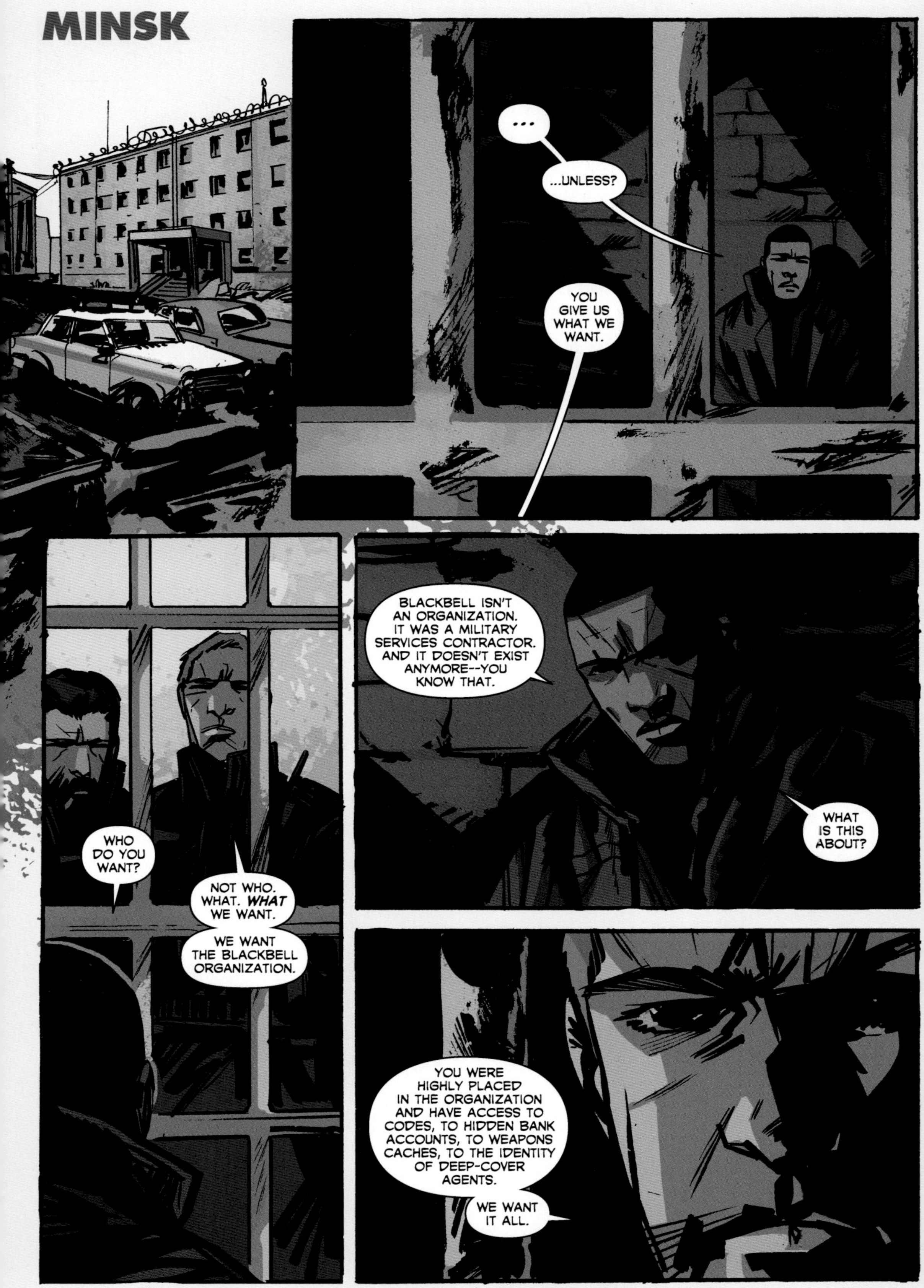
MINSK
...
...UNLESS?
YOU GIVE US WHAT WE WANT.
WHO DO YOU WANT?
NOT WHO. WHAT. *WHAT* WE WANT.
WE WANT THE BLACKBELL ORGANIZATION.
BLACKBELL ISN'T AN ORGANIZATION. IT WAS A MILITARY SERVICES CONTRACTOR. AND IT DOESN'T EXIST ANYMORE--YOU KNOW THAT.
WHAT IS THIS ABOUT?
YOU WERE HIGHLY PLACED IN THE ORGANIZATION AND HAVE ACCESS TO CODES, TO HIDDEN BANK ACCOUNTS, TO WEAPONS CACHES, TO THE IDENTITY OF DEEP-COVER AGENTS.
WE WANT IT ALL.

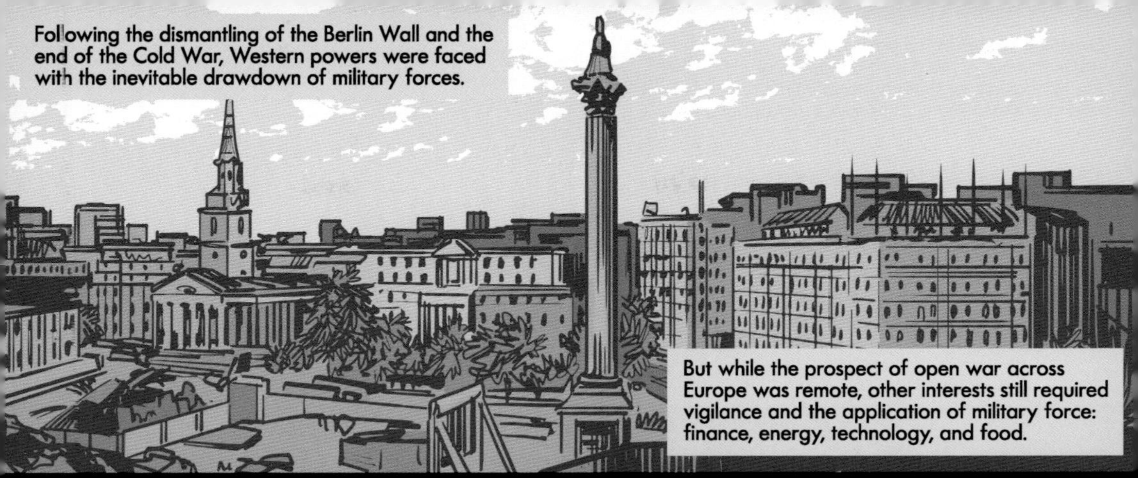
Following the dismantling of the Berlin Wall and the end of the Cold War, Western powers were faced with the inevitable drawdown of military forces.
But while the prospect of open war across Europe was remote, other interests still required vigilance and the application of military force: finance, energy, technology, and food.

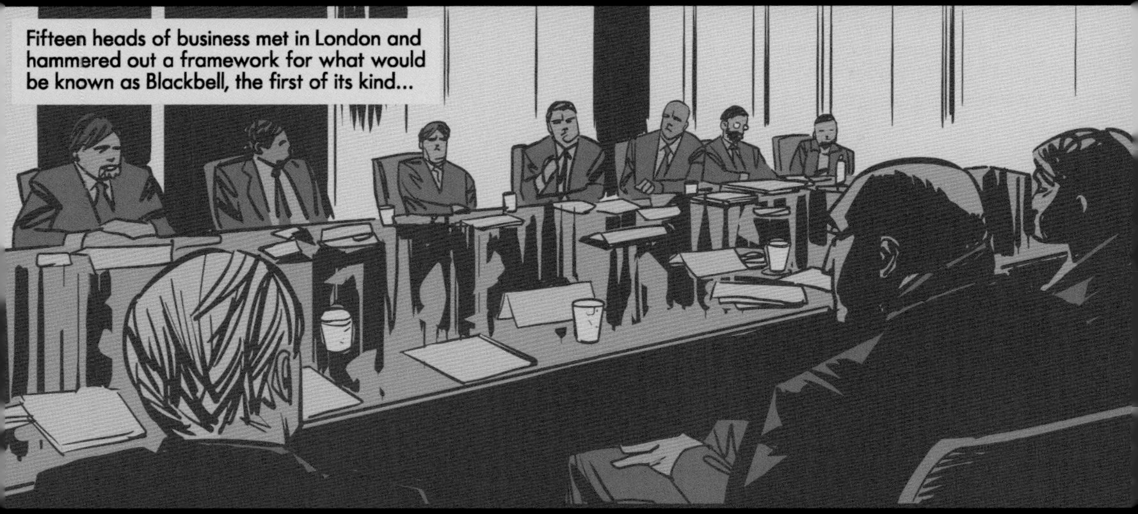
Fifteen heads of business met in London and hammered out a framework for what would be known as Blackbell, the first of its kind...

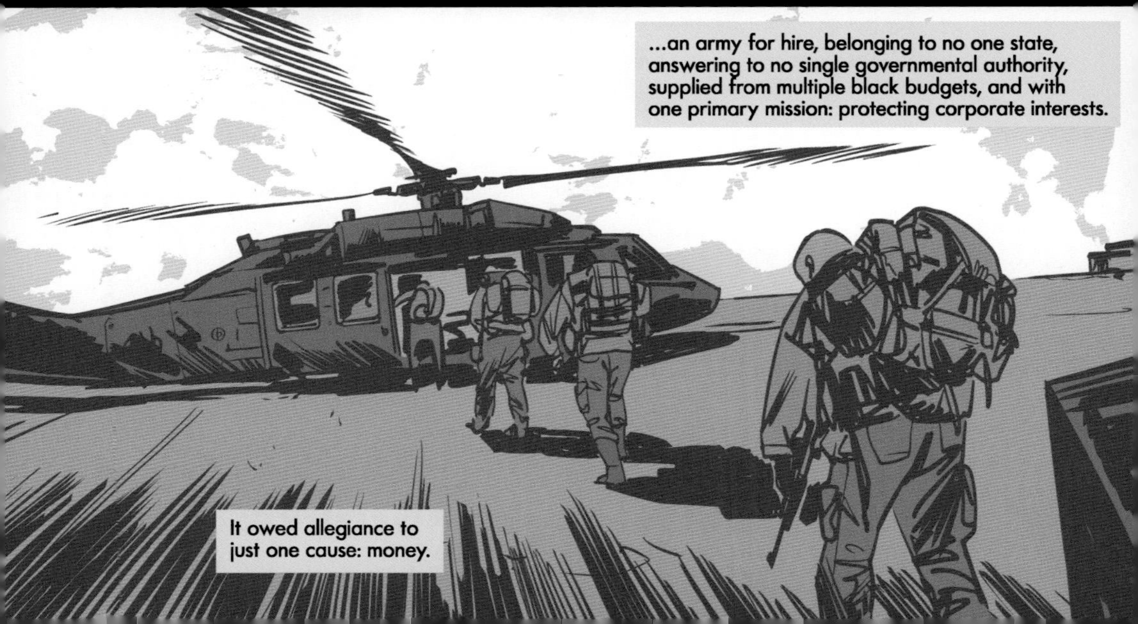
...an army for hire, belonging to no one state, answering to no single governmental authority, supplied from multiple black budgets, and with one primary mission: protecting corporate interests.
It owed allegiance to just one cause: money.

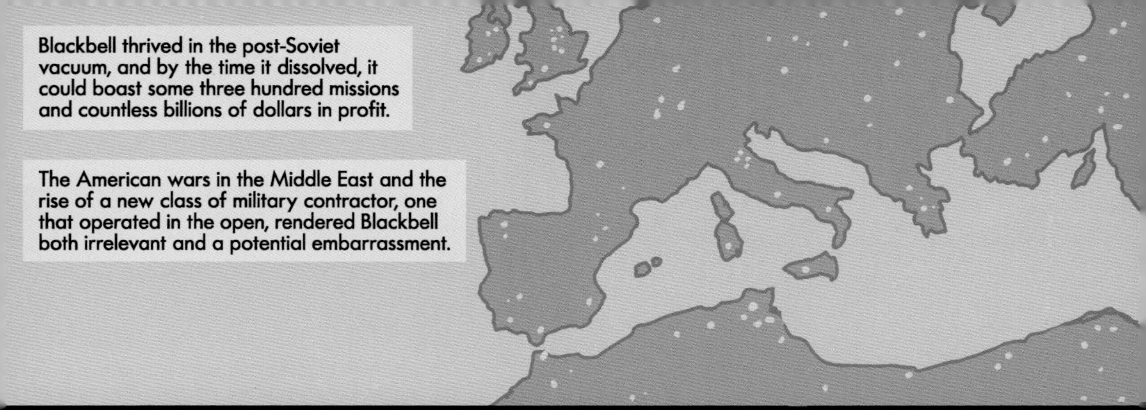
Blackbell thrived in the post-Soviet vacuum, and by the time it dissolved, it could boast some three hundred missions and countless billions of dollars in profit.
The American wars in the Middle East and the rise of a new class of military contractor, one that operated in the open, rendered Blackbell both irrelevant and a potential embarrassment.

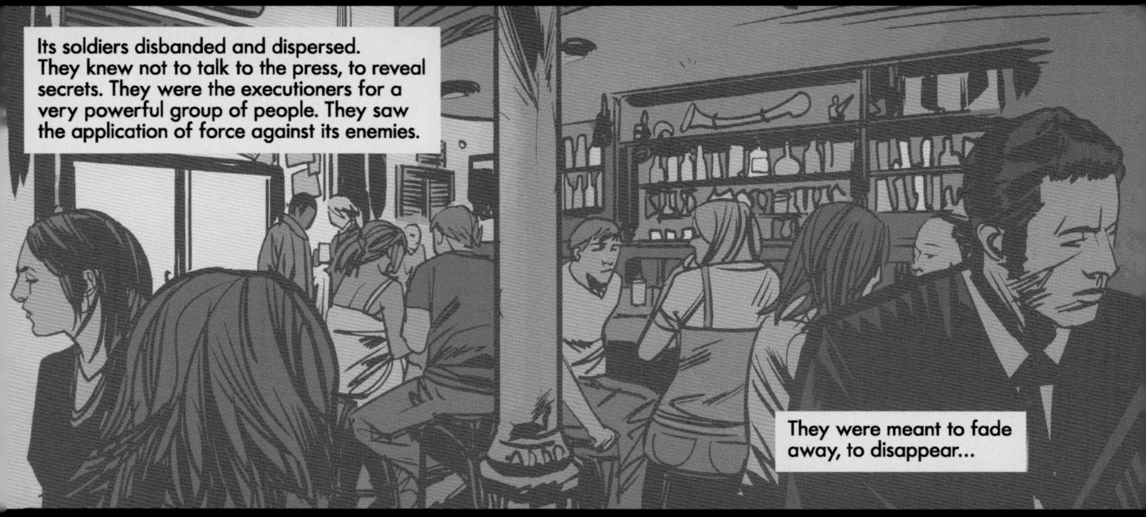
Its soldiers disbanded and dispersed. They knew not to talk to the press, to reveal secrets. They were the executioners for a very powerful group of people. They saw the application of force against its enemies.
They were meant to fade away, to disappear...

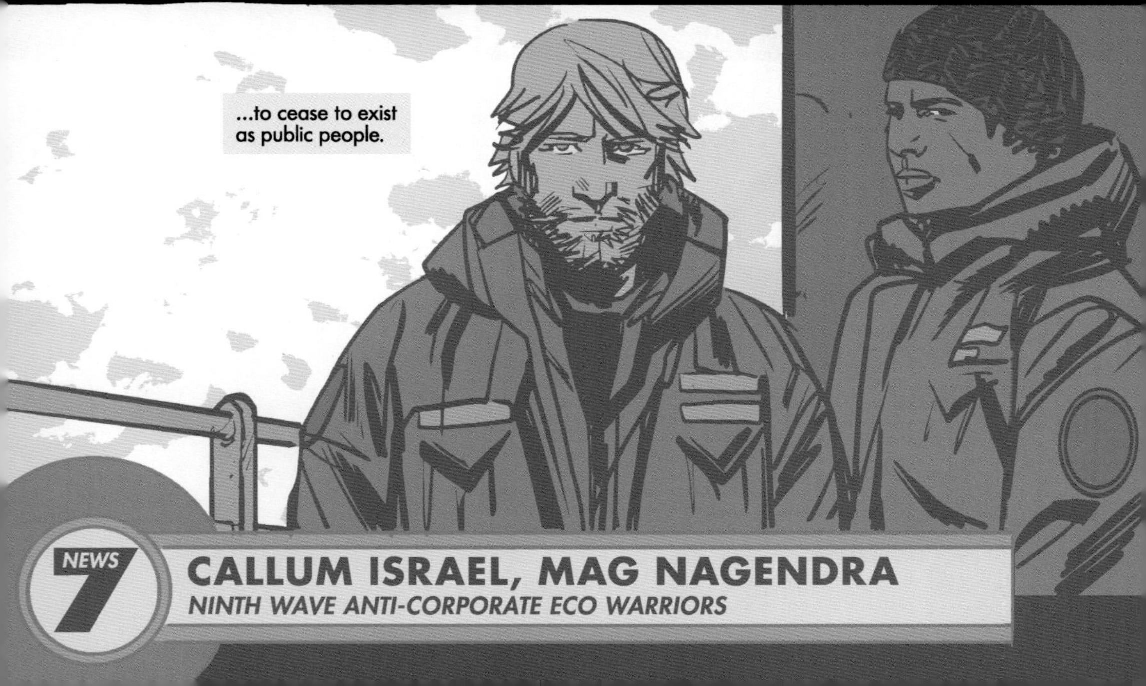
...to cease to exist as public people.
NEWS 7
CALLUM ISRAEL, MAG NAGENDRA
NINTH WAVE ANTI-CORPORATE ECO WARRIORS

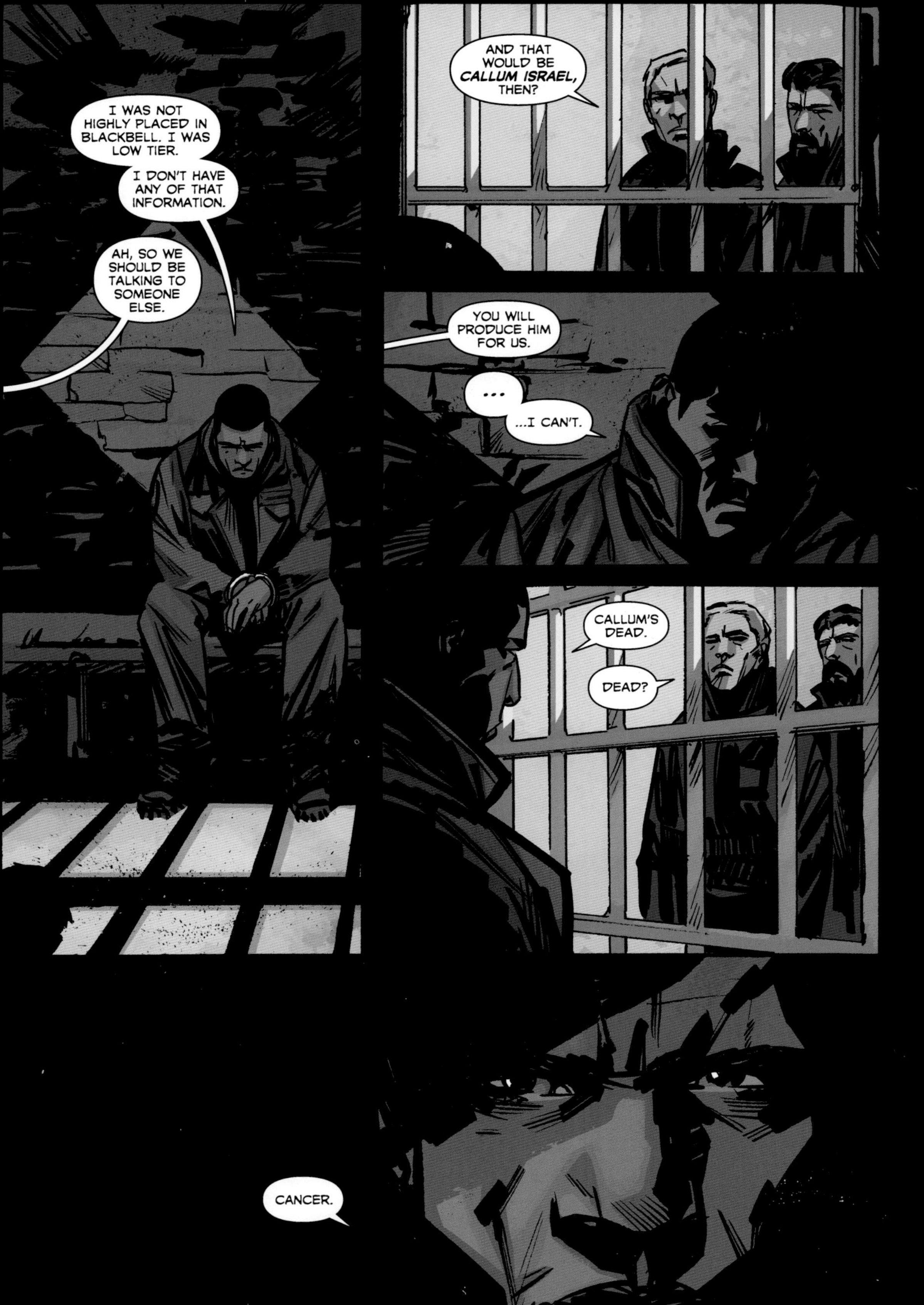
I WAS NOT HIGHLY PLACED IN BLACKBELL. I WAS LOW TIER.
I DON'T HAVE ANY OF THAT INFORMATION.
AH, SO WE SHOULD BE TALKING TO SOMEONE ELSE.
AND THAT WOULD BE *CALLUM ISRAEL,* THEN?
YOU WILL PRODUCE HIM FOR US.
...
...I CAN'T.
CALLUM'S DEAD.
DEAD?
CANCER.

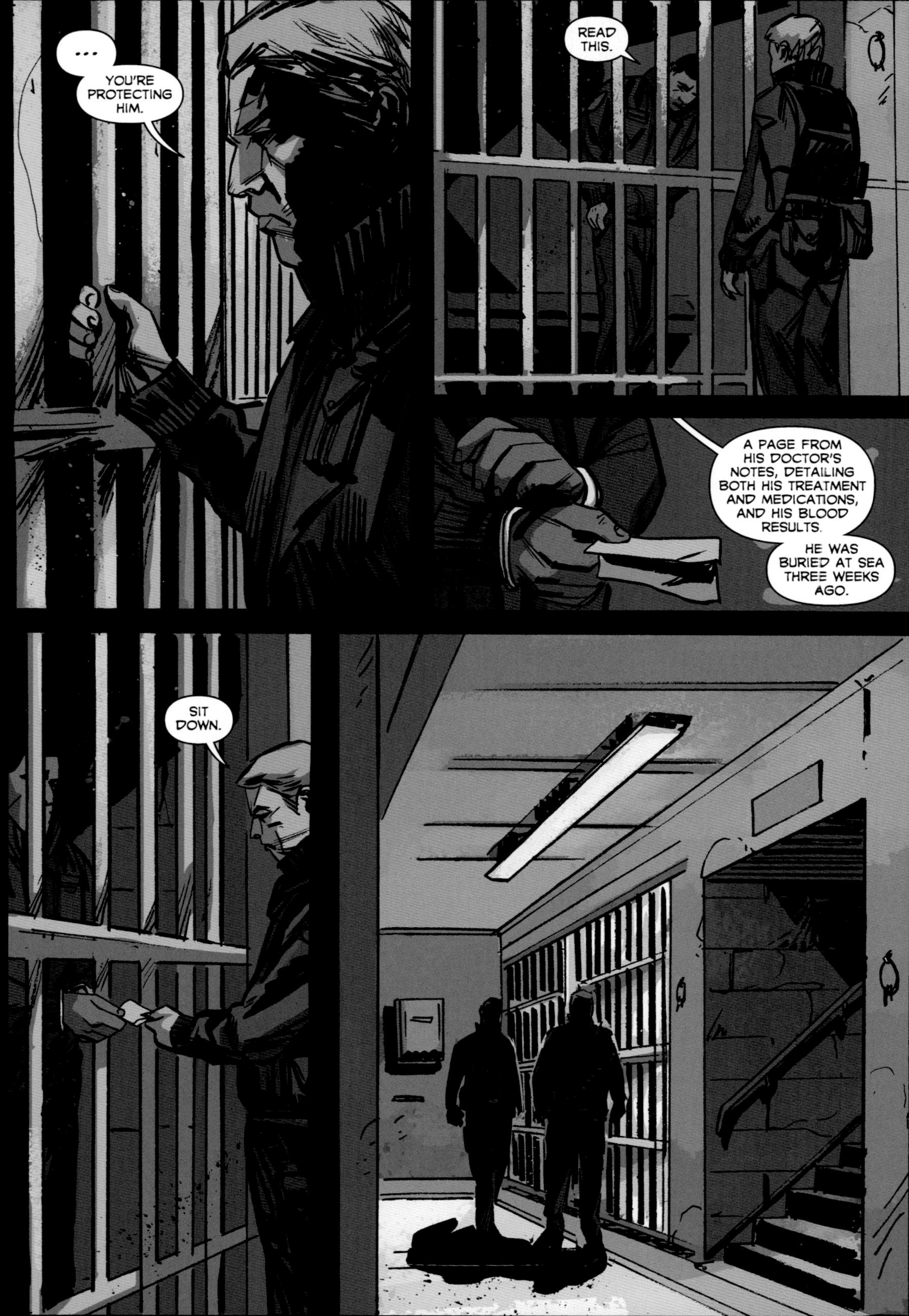
...
YOU'RE PROTECTING HIM.
READ THIS.
A PAGE FROM HIS DOCTOR'S NOTES, DETAILING BOTH HIS TREATMENT AND MEDICATIONS, AND HIS BLOOD RESULTS.
HE WAS BURIED AT SEA THREE WEEKS AGO.
SIT DOWN.

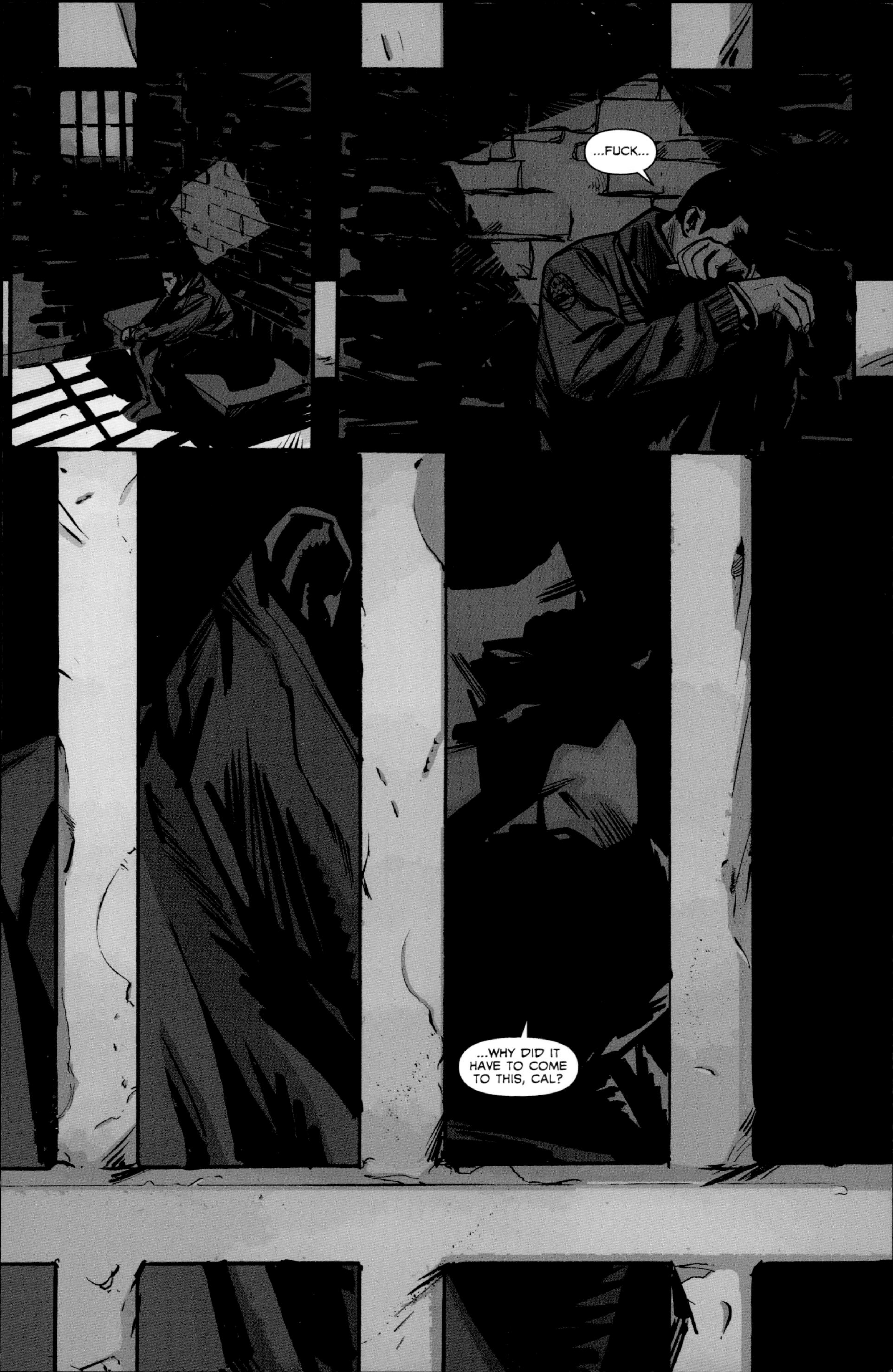
...FUCK...
...WHY DID IT HAVE TO COME TO THIS, CAL?

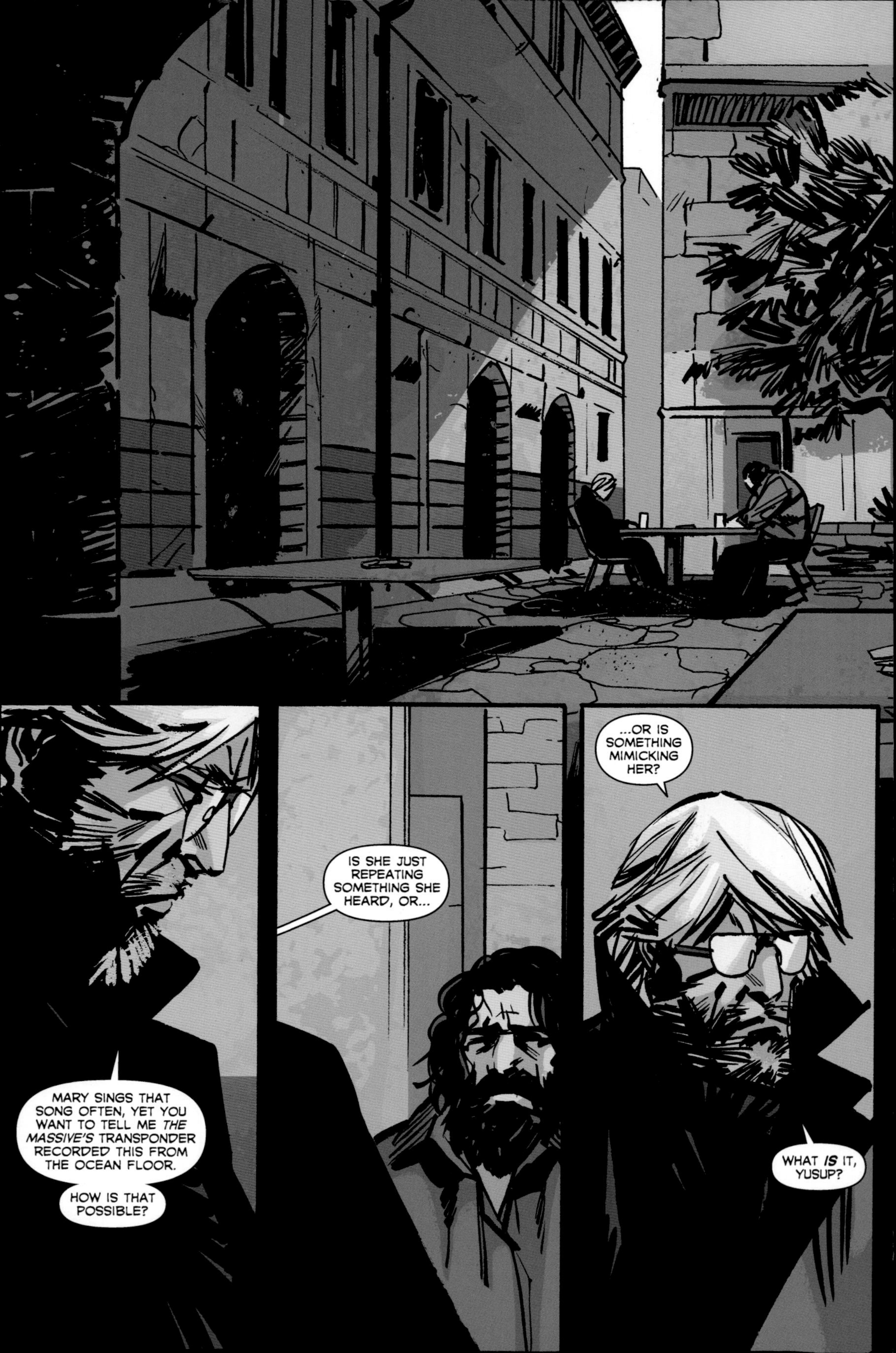
MARY SINGS THAT SONG OFTEN, YET YOU WANT TO TELL ME *THE MASSIVE'S* TRANSPONDER RECORDED THIS FROM THE OCEAN FLOOR.
HOW IS THAT POSSIBLE?
IS SHE JUST REPEATING SOMETHING SHE HEARD, OR...
...OR IS SOMETHING MIMICKING HER?
WHAT ***IS*** IT, YUSUP?

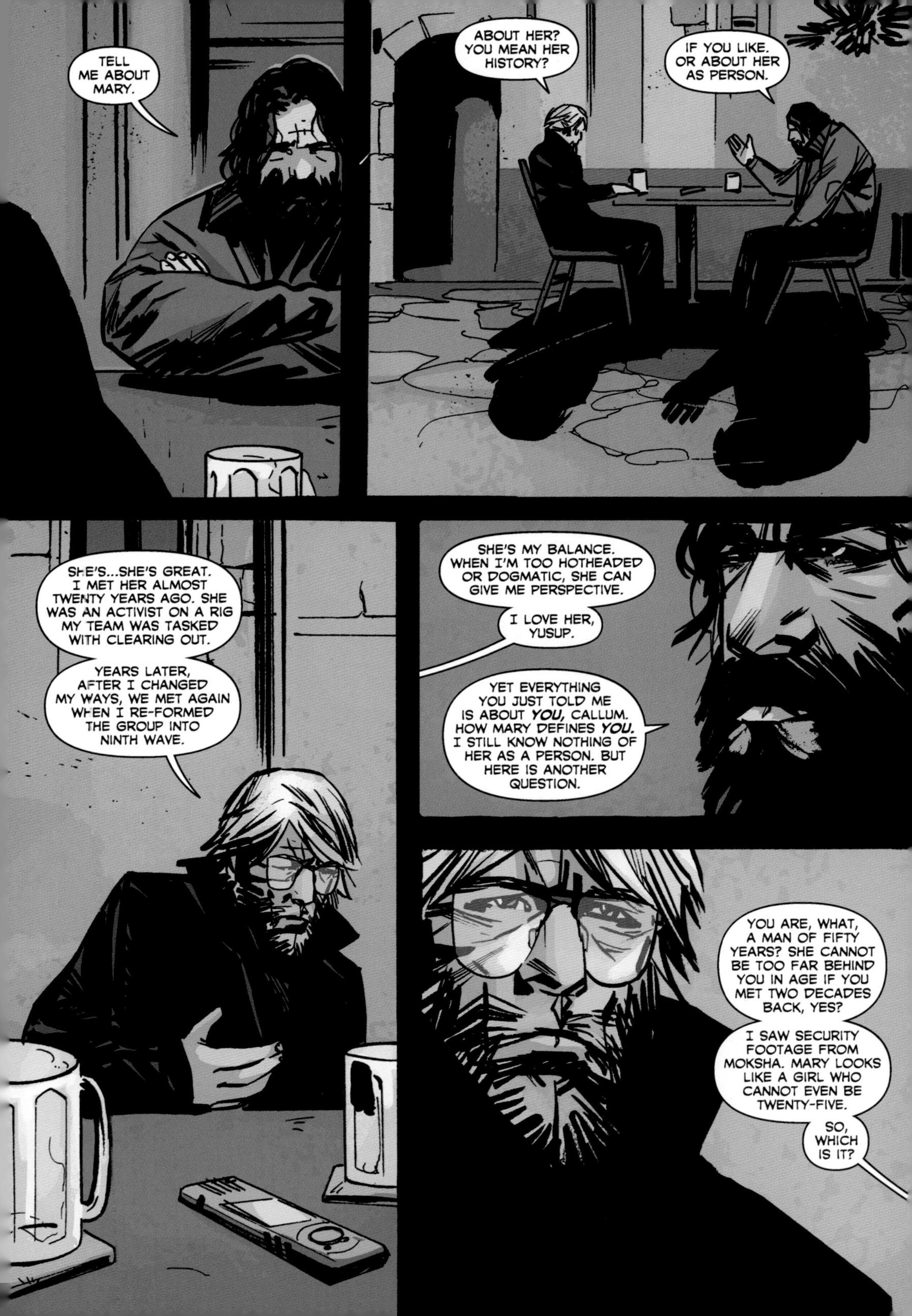
TELL ME ABOUT MARY.
ABOUT HER? YOU MEAN HER HISTORY?
IF YOU LIKE. OR ABOUT HER AS PERSON.
SHE'S...SHE'S GREAT. I MET HER ALMOST TWENTY YEARS AGO. SHE WAS AN ACTIVIST ON A RIG MY TEAM WAS TASKED WITH CLEARING OUT.
YEARS LATER, AFTER I CHANGED MY WAYS, WE MET AGAIN WHEN I RE-FORMED THE GROUP INTO NINTH WAVE.
SHE'S MY BALANCE. WHEN I'M TOO HOTHEADED OR DOGMATIC, SHE CAN GIVE ME PERSPECTIVE.
I LOVE HER, YUSUP.
YET EVERYTHING YOU JUST TOLD ME IS ABOUT *YOU,* CALLUM. HOW MARY DEFINES *YOU.* I STILL KNOW NOTHING OF HER AS A PERSON. BUT HERE IS ANOTHER QUESTION.
YOU ARE, WHAT, A MAN OF FIFTY YEARS? SHE CANNOT BE TOO FAR BEHIND YOU IN AGE IF YOU MET TWO DECADES BACK, YES?
I SAW SECURITY FOOTAGE FROM MOKSHA. MARY LOOKS LIKE A GIRL WHO CANNOT EVEN BE TWENTY-FIVE.
SO, WHICH IS IT?

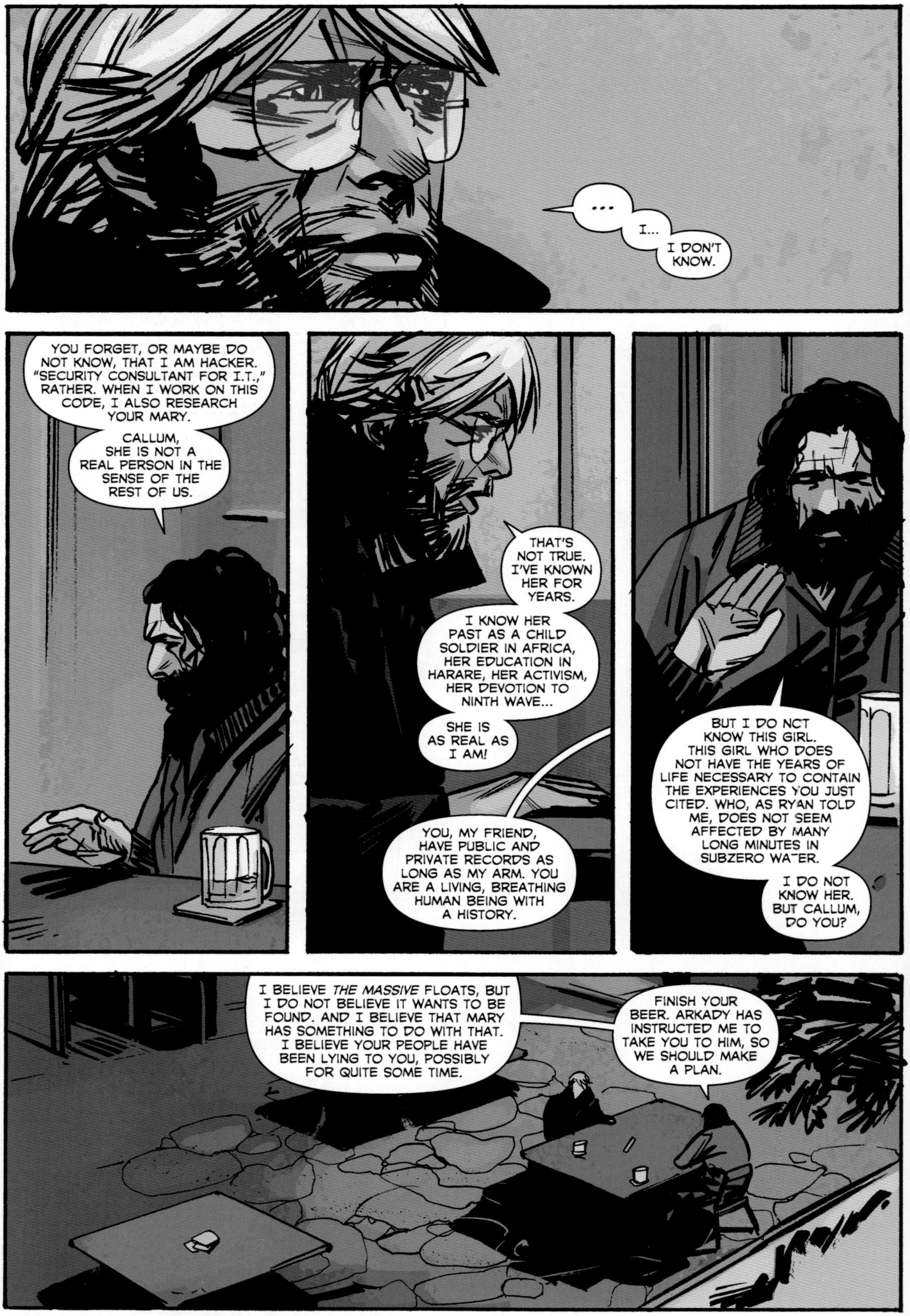
...
I...
I DON'T KNOW.
YOU FORGET, OR MAYBE DO NOT KNOW, THAT I AM HACKER. "SECURITY CONSULTANT FOR I.T.," RATHER. WHEN I WORK ON THIS CODE, I ALSO RESEARCH YOUR MARY.
CALLUM, SHE IS NOT A REAL PERSON IN THE SENSE OF THE REST OF US.
THAT'S NOT TRUE. I'VE KNOWN HER FOR YEARS.
I KNOW HER PAST AS A CHILD SOLDIER IN AFRICA, HER EDUCATION IN HARARE, HER ACTIVISM, HER DEVOTION TO NINTH WAVE...
SHE IS AS REAL AS I AM!
YOU, MY FRIEND, HAVE PUBLIC AND PRIVATE RECORDS AS LONG AS MY ARM. YOU ARE A LIVING, BREATHING HUMAN BEING WITH A HISTORY.
BUT I DO NOT KNOW THIS GIRL. THIS GIRL WHO DOES NOT HAVE THE YEARS OF LIFE NECESSARY TO CONTAIN THE EXPERIENCES YOU JUST CITED. WHO, AS RYAN TOLD ME, DOES NOT SEEM AFFECTED BY MANY LONG MINUTES IN SUBZERO WATER.
I DO NOT KNOW HER. BUT CALLUM, DO YOU?
I BELIEVE *THE MASSIVE* FLOATS, BUT I DO NOT BELIEVE IT WANTS TO BE FOUND. AND I BELIEVE THAT MARY HAS SOMETHING TO DO WITH THAT. I BELIEVE YOUR PEOPLE HAVE BEEN LYING TO YOU, POSSIBLY FOR QUITE SOME TIME.
FINISH YOUR BEER. ARKADY HAS INSTRUCTED ME TO TAKE YOU TO HIM, SO WE SHOULD MAKE A PLAN.

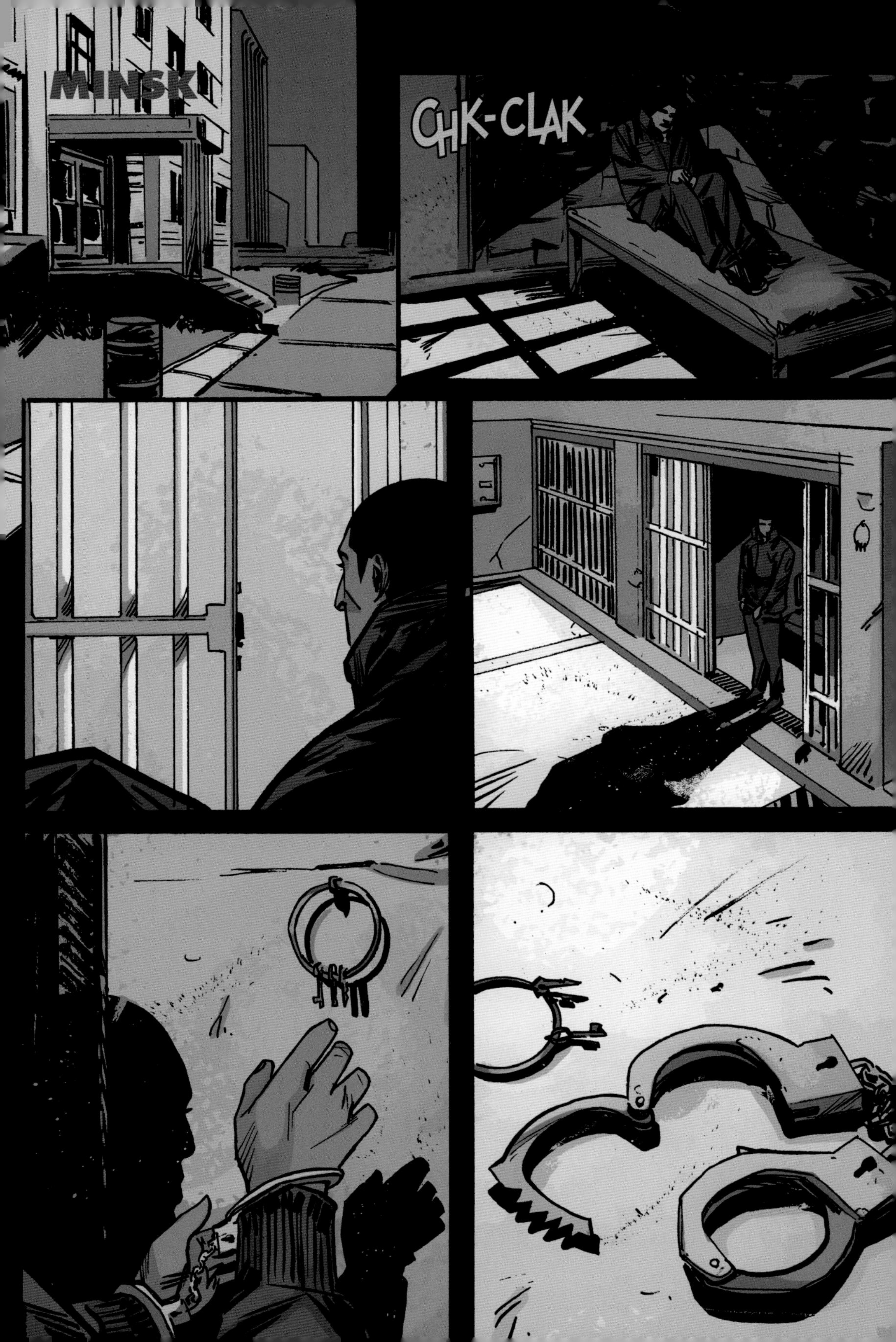
MINSK
CHK-CLAK

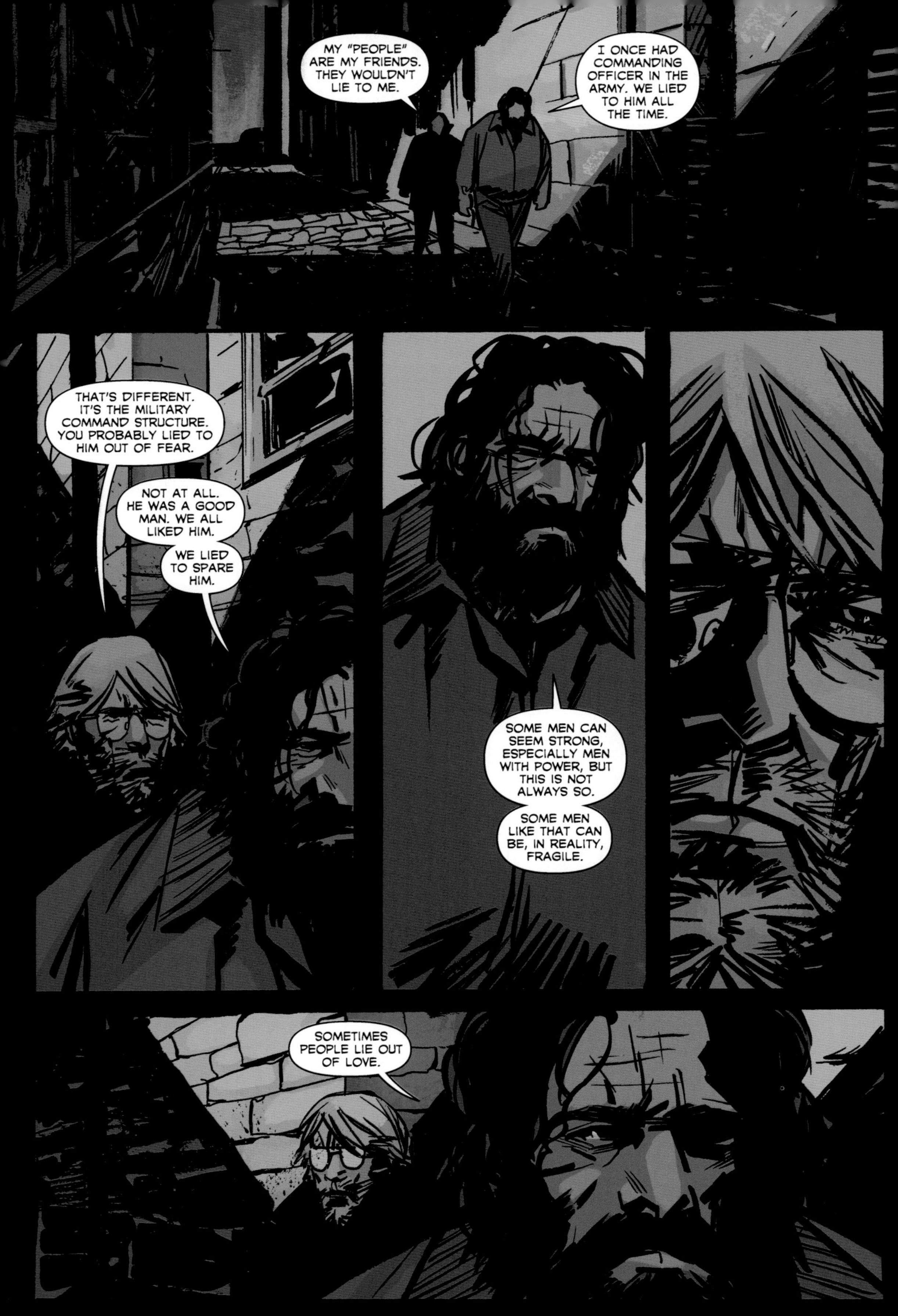
MY "PEOPLE" ARE MY FRIENDS. THEY WOULDN'T LIE TO ME.
I ONCE HAD COMMANDING OFFICER IN THE ARMY. WE LIED TO HIM ALL THE TIME.
THAT'S DIFFERENT. IT'S THE MILITARY COMMAND STRUCTURE. YOU PROBABLY LIED TO HIM OUT OF FEAR.
NOT AT ALL. HE WAS A GOOD MAN. WE ALL LIKED HIM.
WE LIED TO SPARE HIM.
SOME MEN CAN SEEM STRONG, ESPECIALLY MEN WITH POWER, BUT THIS IS NOT ALWAYS SO.
SOME MEN LIKE THAT CAN BE, IN REALITY, FRAGILE.
SOMETIMES PEOPLE LIE OUT OF LOVE.

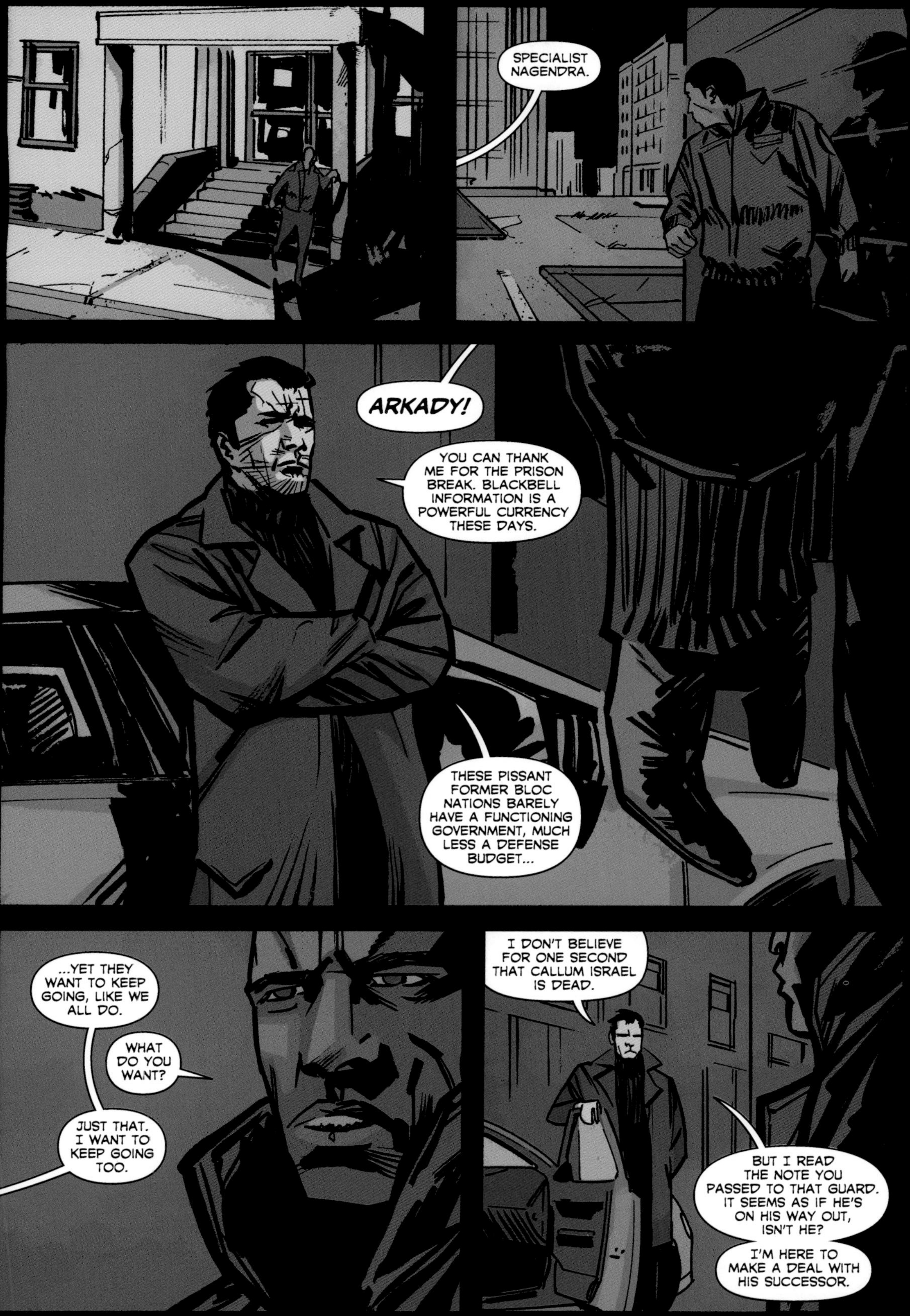
SPECIALIST NAGENDRA.
ARKADY!
YOU CAN THANK ME FOR THE PRISON BREAK. BLACKBELL INFORMATION IS A POWERFUL CURRENCY THESE DAYS.
THESE PISSANT FORMER BLOC NATIONS BARELY HAVE A FUNCTIONING GOVERNMENT, MUCH LESS A DEFENSE BUDGET...
...YET THEY WANT TO KEEP GOING, LIKE WE ALL DO.
WHAT DO YOU WANT?
JUST THAT. I WANT TO KEEP GOING TOO.
I DON'T BELIEVE FOR ONE SECOND THAT CALLUM ISRAEL IS DEAD.
BUT I READ THE NOTE YOU PASSED TO THAT GUARD. IT SEEMS AS IF HE'S ON HIS WAY OUT, ISN'T HE?
I'M HERE TO MAKE A DEAL WITH HIS SUCCESSOR.

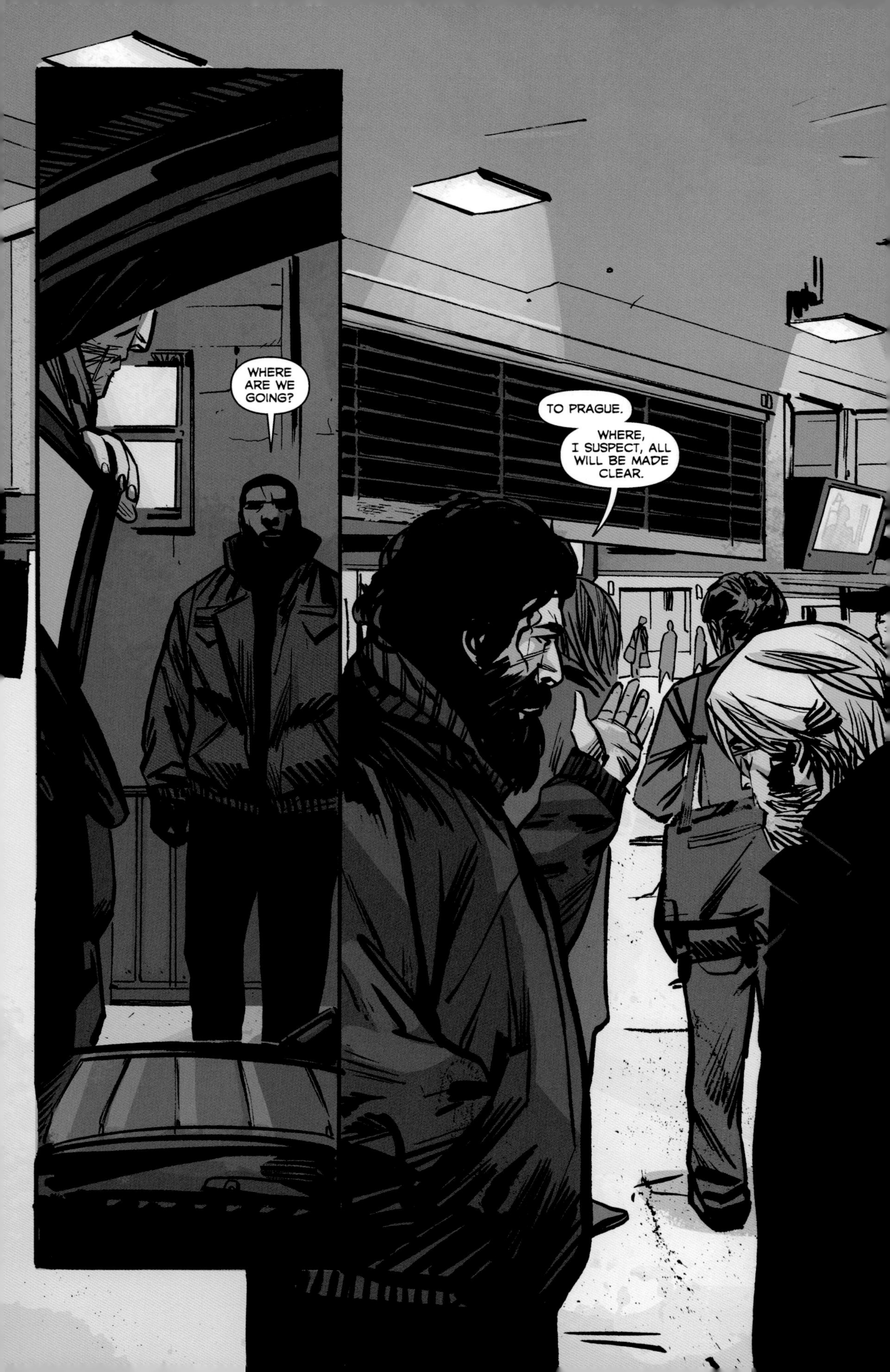
WHERE ARE WE GOING?
TO PRAGUE.
WHERE, I SUSPECT, ALL WILL BE MADE CLEAR.

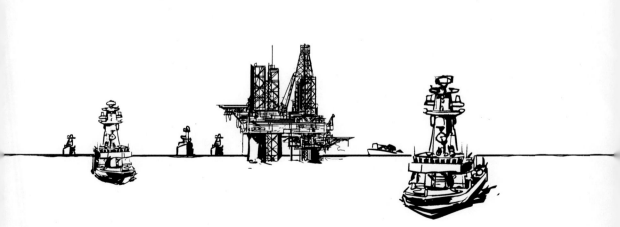

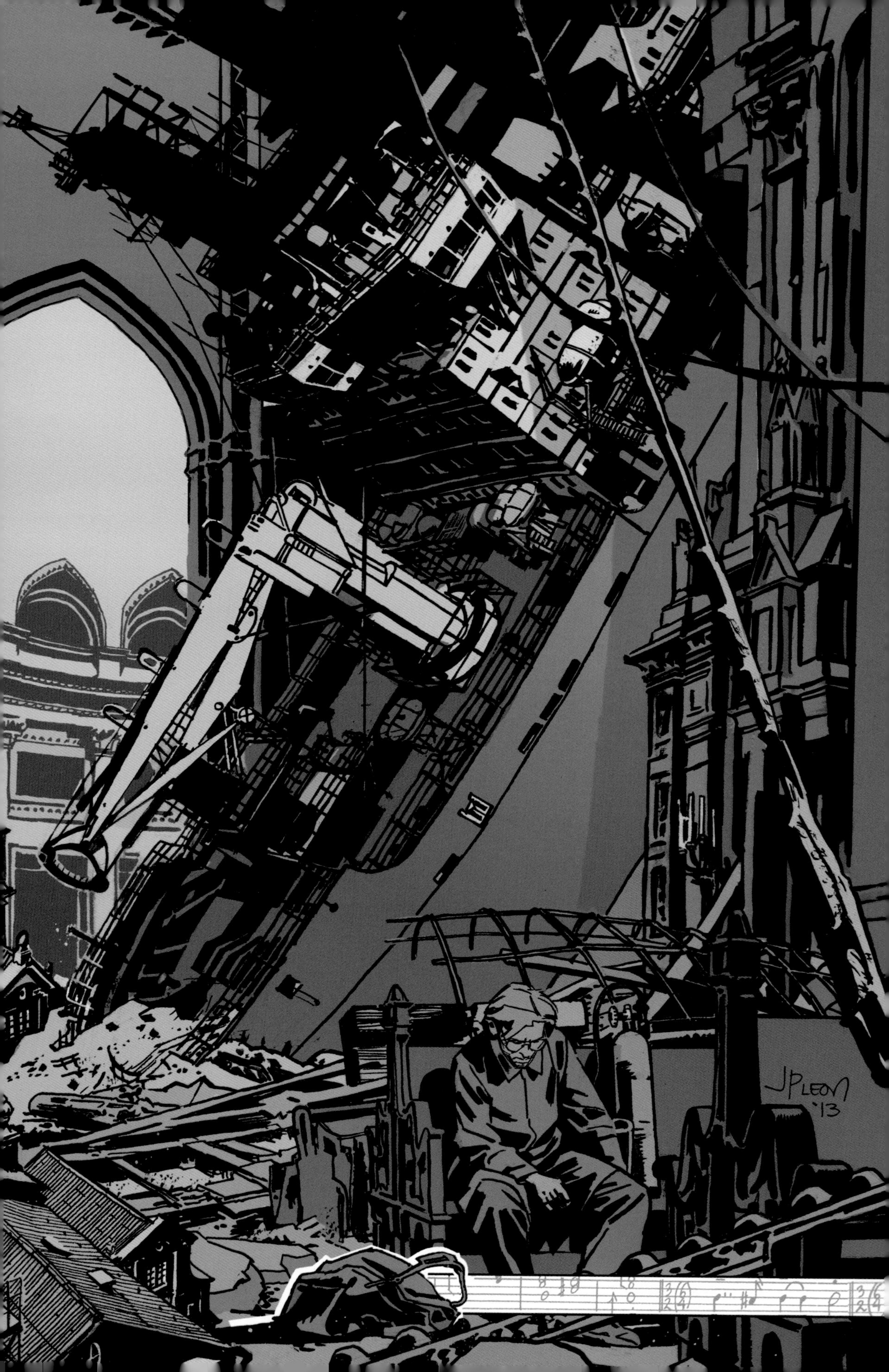
JP LEON
'13

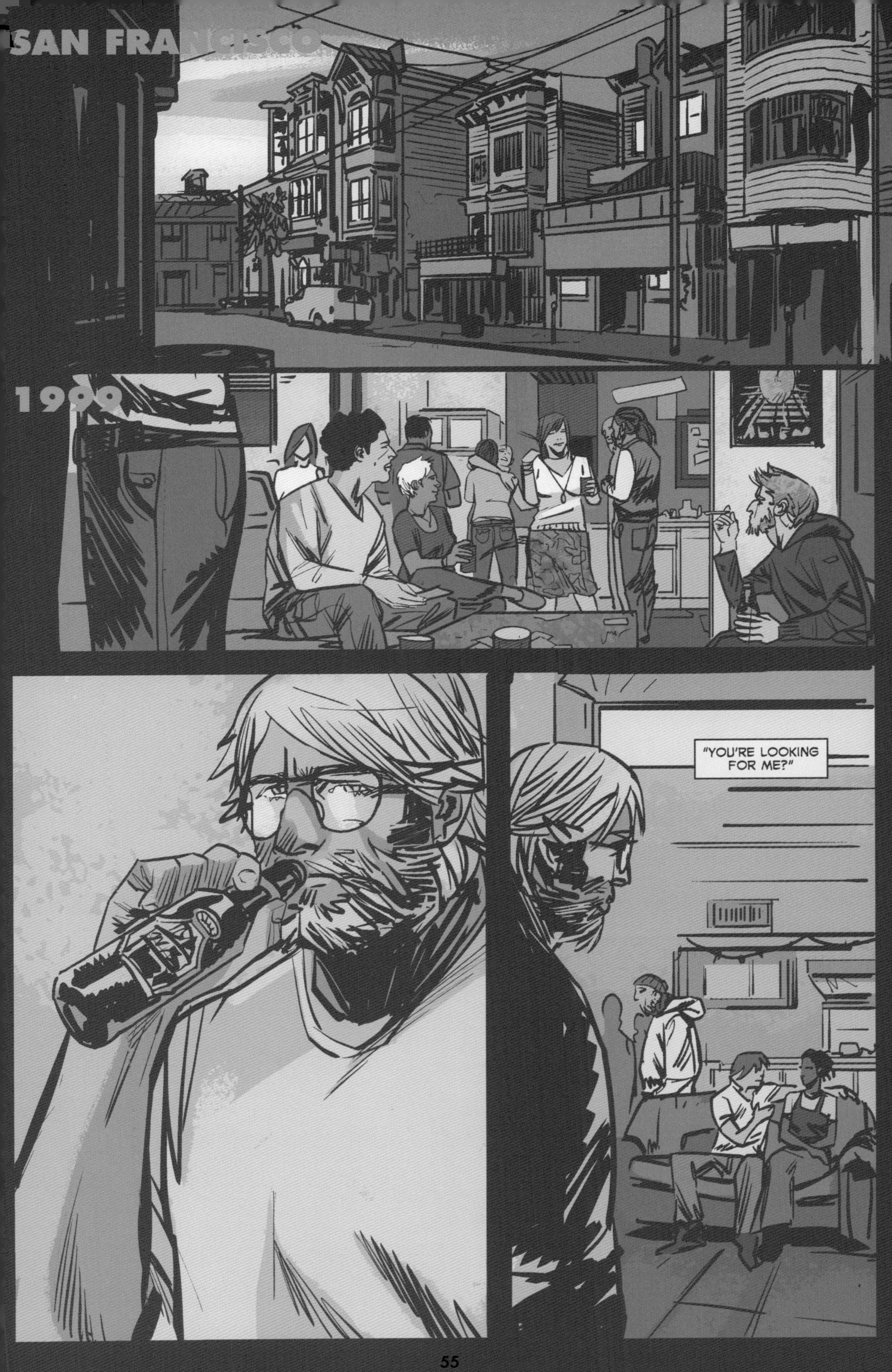
SAN FRANCISCO
1999
"YOU'RE LOOKING FOR ME?"

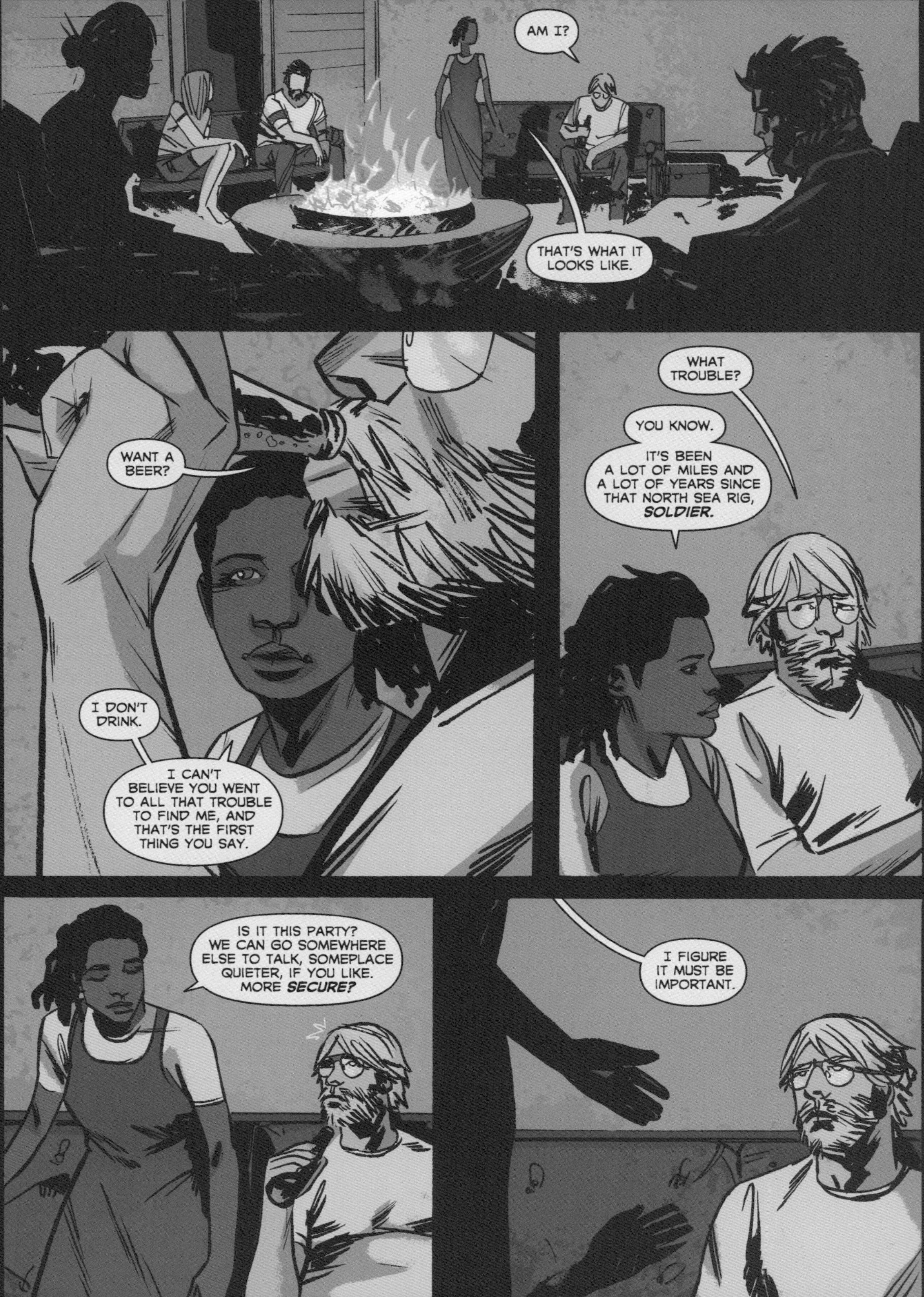
AM I?
THAT'S WHAT IT LOOKS LIKE.
WANT A BEER?
I DON'T DRINK.
I CAN'T BELIEVE YOU WENT TO ALL THAT TROUBLE TO FIND ME, AND THAT'S THE FIRST THING YOU SAY.
WHAT TROUBLE?
YOU KNOW.
IT'S BEEN A LOT OF MILES AND A LOT OF YEARS SINCE THAT NORTH SEA RIG, **SOLDIER.**
IS IT THIS PARTY? WE CAN GO SOMEWHERE ELSE TO TALK, SOMEPLACE QUIETER, IF YOU LIKE. MORE **SECURE?**
I FIGURE IT MUST BE IMPORTANT.

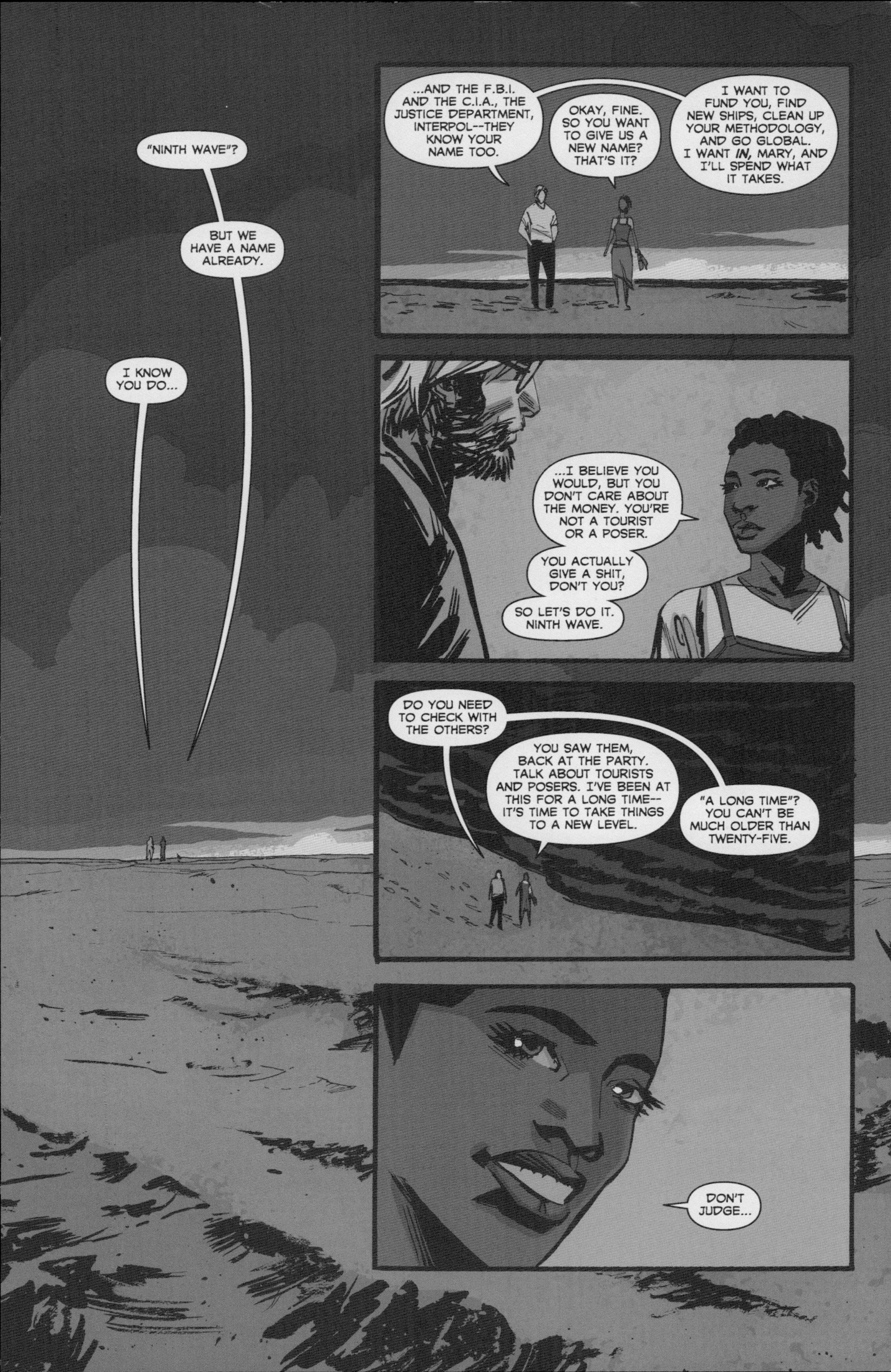
"NINTH WAVE"?
BUT WE HAVE A NAME ALREADY.
I KNOW YOU DO...
...AND THE F.B.I. AND THE C.I.A., THE JUSTICE DEPARTMENT, INTERPOL--THEY KNOW YOUR NAME TOO.
OKAY, FINE. SO YOU WANT TO GIVE US A NEW NAME? THAT'S IT?
I WANT TO FUND YOU, FIND NEW SHIPS, CLEAN UP YOUR METHODOLOGY, AND GO GLOBAL. I WANT *IN,* MARY, AND I'LL SPEND WHAT IT TAKES.
...I BELIEVE YOU WOULD, BUT YOU DON'T CARE ABOUT THE MONEY. YOU'RE NOT A TOURIST OR A POSER.
YOU ACTUALLY GIVE A SHIT, DON'T YOU?
SO LET'S DO IT. NINTH WAVE.
DO YOU NEED TO CHECK WITH THE OTHERS?
YOU SAW THEM, BACK AT THE PARTY. TALK ABOUT TOURISTS AND POSERS. I'VE BEEN AT THIS FOR A LONG TIME--IT'S TIME TO TAKE THINGS TO A NEW LEVEL.
"A LONG TIME"? YOU CAN'T BE MUCH OLDER THAN TWENTY-FIVE.
DON'T JUDGE...

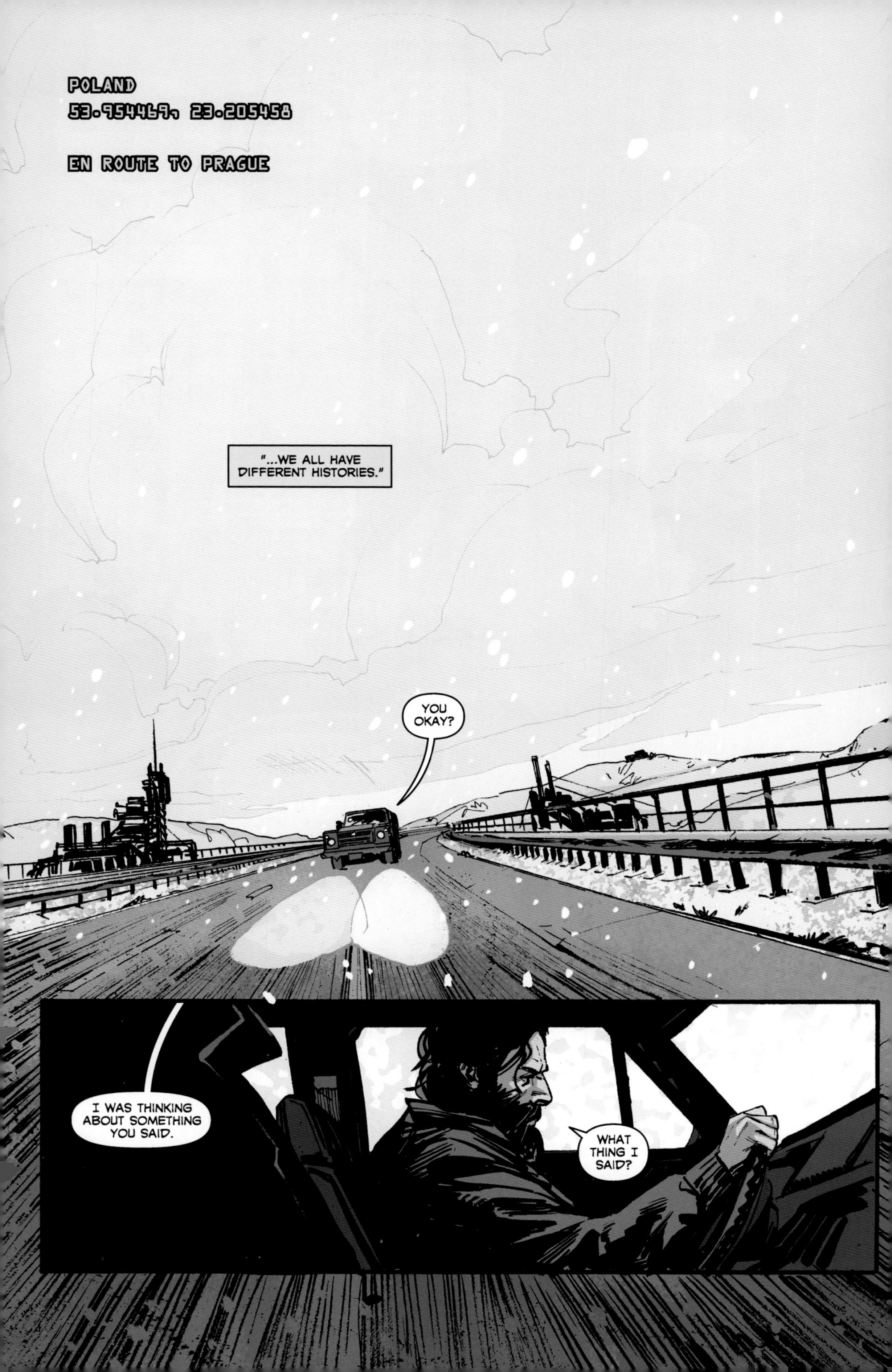
POLAND
53.954469, 23.205458
EN ROUTE TO PRAGUE
"...WE ALL HAVE DIFFERENT HISTORIES."
YOU OKAY?
I WAS THINKING ABOUT SOMETHING YOU SAID.
WHAT THING I SAID?

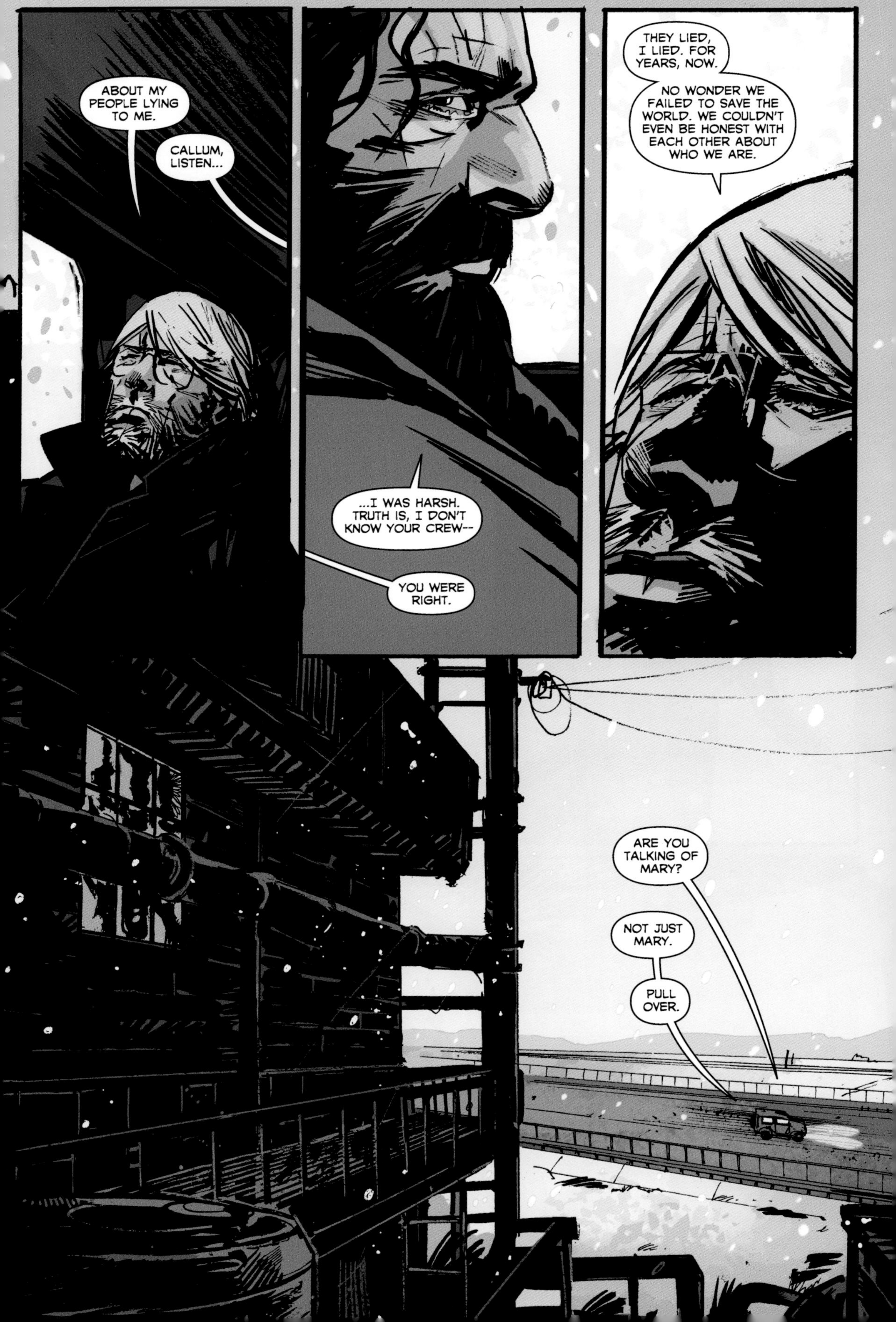
ABOUT MY PEOPLE LYING TO ME.
CALLUM, LISTEN...
...I WAS HARSH. TRUTH IS, I DON'T KNOW YOUR CREW--
YOU WERE RIGHT.
THEY LIED, I LIED. FOR YEARS, NOW.
NO WONDER WE FAILED TO SAVE THE WORLD. WE COULDN'T EVEN BE HONEST WITH EACH OTHER ABOUT WHO WE ARE.
ARE YOU TALKING OF MARY?
NOT JUST MARY.
PULL OVER.

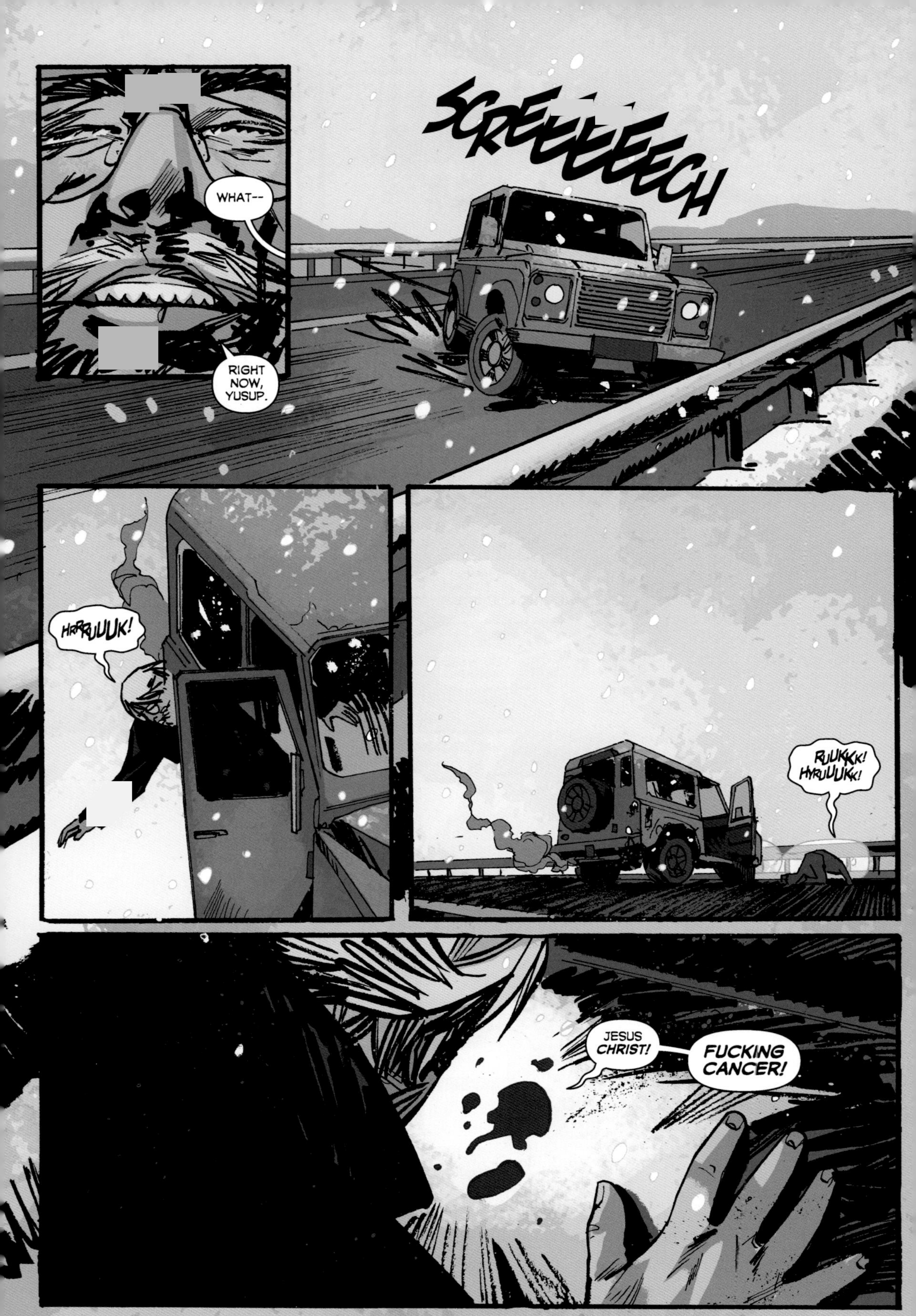
WHAT--
SCREEEEEECH
RIGHT NOW, YUSUP.
HRRRUUUK!
RUUKKK! HYRUUUKK!
JESUS CHRIST!
FUCKING CANCER!

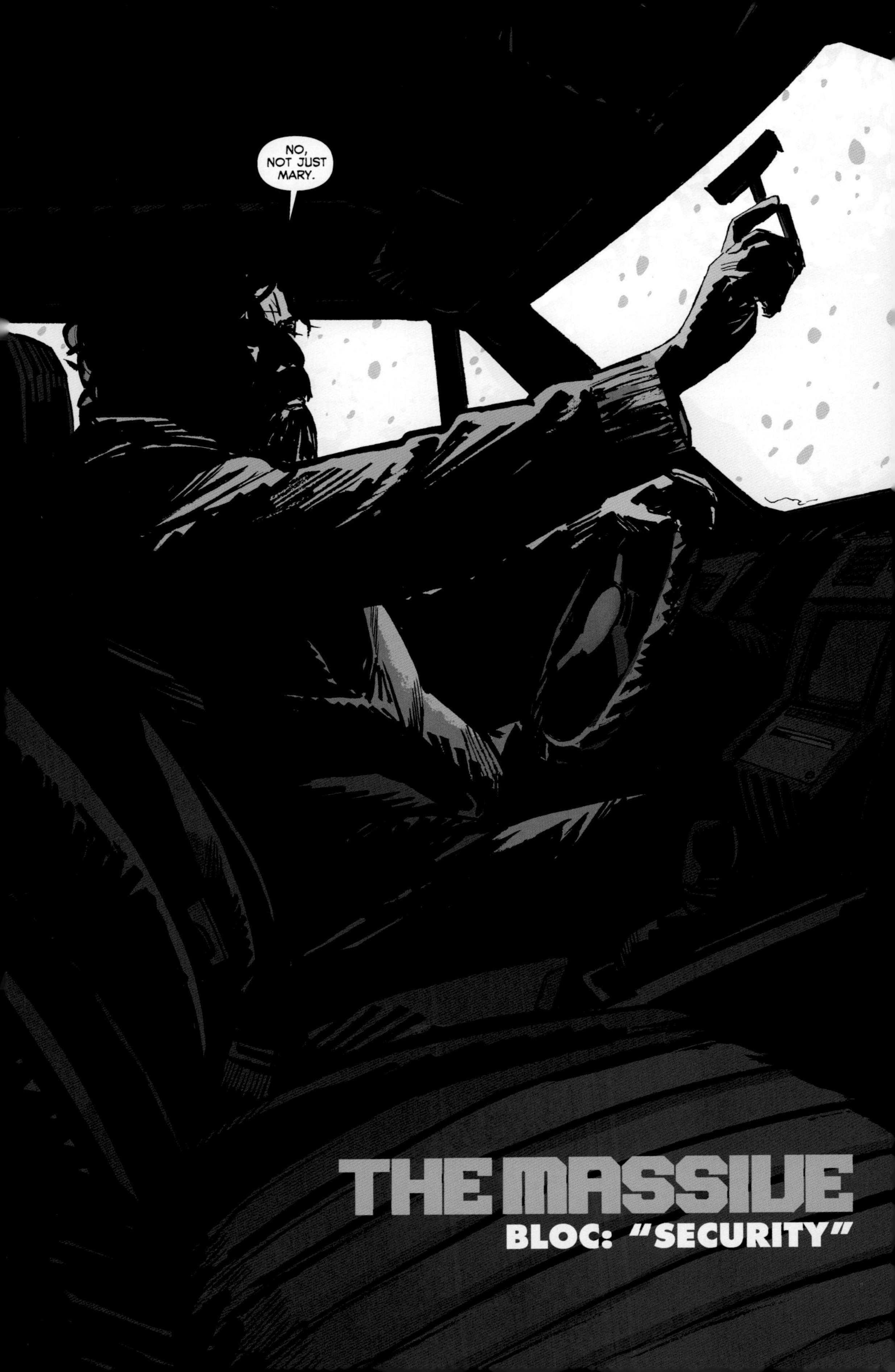
NO, NOT JUST MARY.
THE MASSIVE
BLOC: "SECURITY"

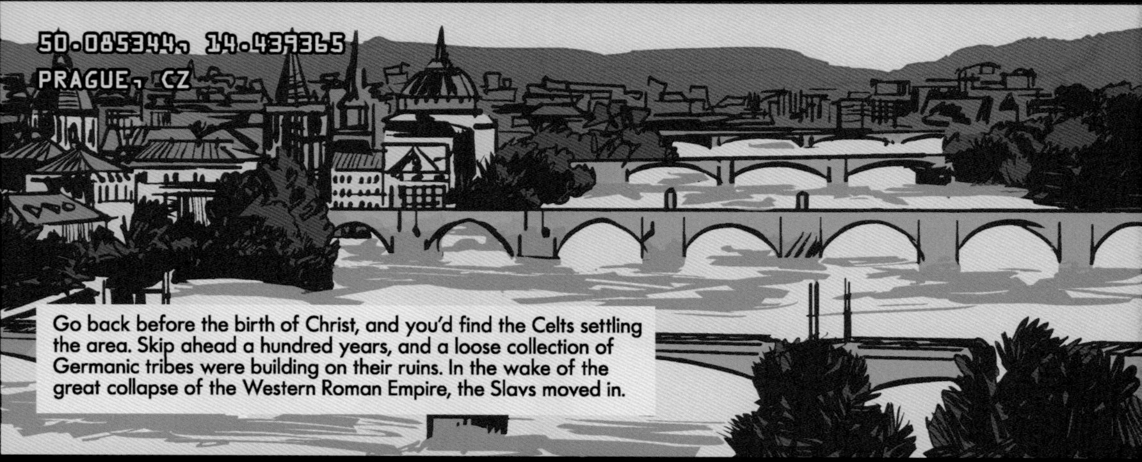
50.085344, 14.439365
PRAGUE, CZ
Go back before the birth of Christ, and you'd find the Celts settling the area. Skip ahead a hundred years, and a loose collection of Germanic tribes were building on their ruins. In the wake of the great collapse of the Western Roman Empire, the Slavs moved in.

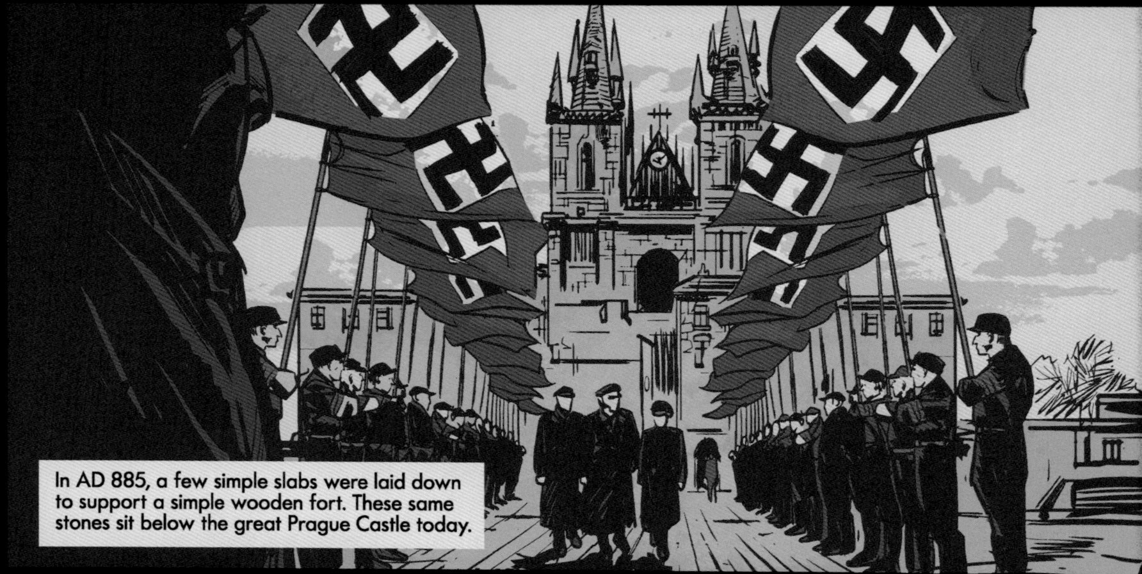
In AD 885, a few simple slabs were laid down to support a simple wooden fort. These same stones sit below the great Prague Castle today.

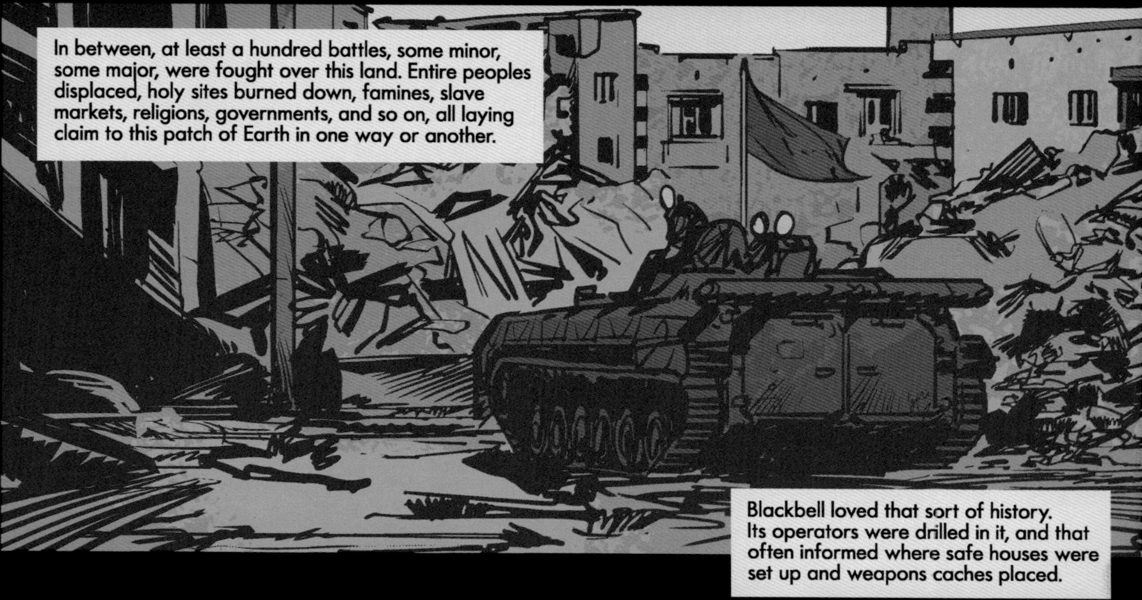
In between, at least a hundred battles, some minor, some major, were fought over this land. Entire peoples displaced, holy sites burned down, famines, slave markets, religions, governments, and so on, all laying claim to this patch of Earth in one way or another.
Blackbell loved that sort of history. Its operators were drilled in it, and that often informed where safe houses were set up and weapons caches placed.

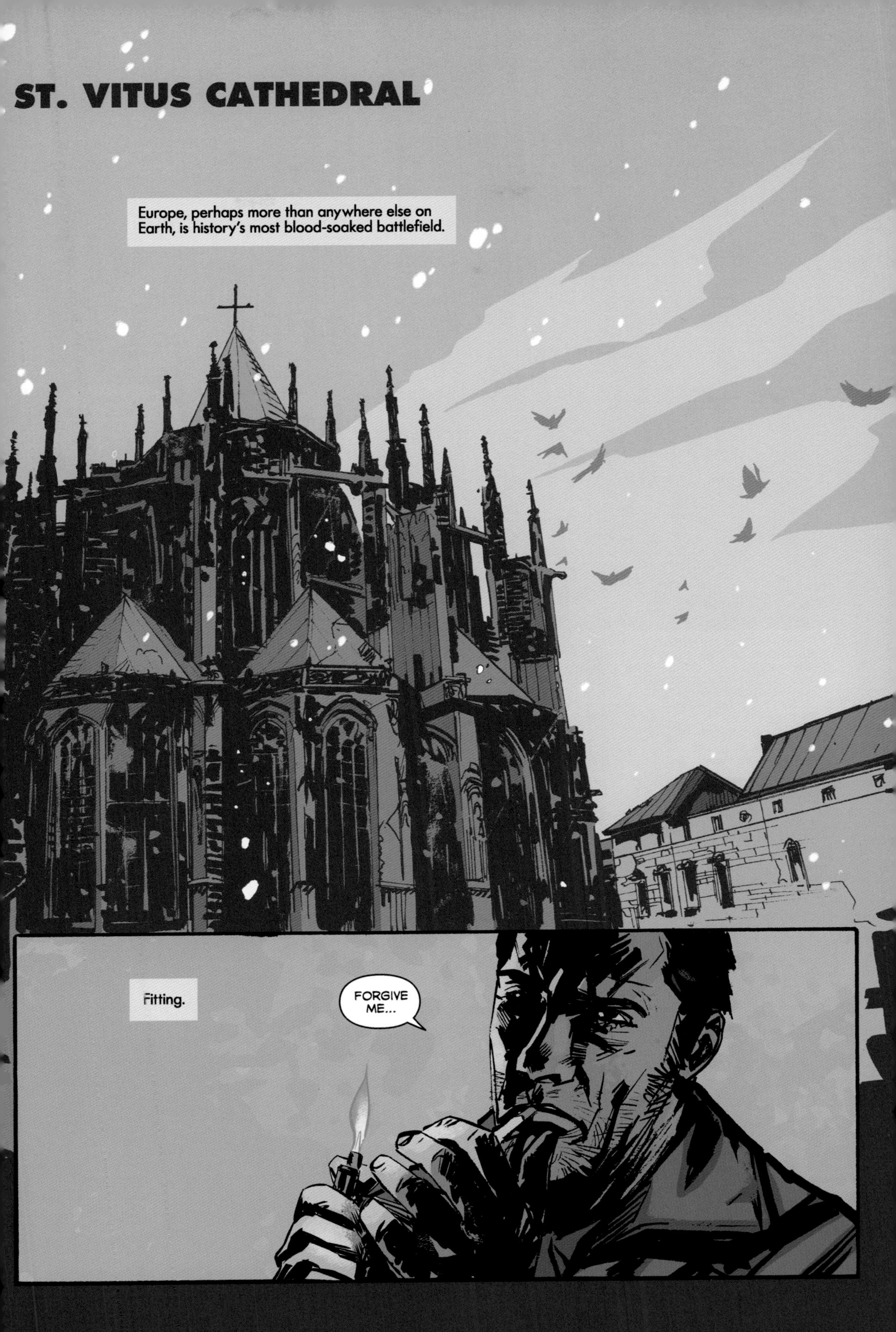
ST. VITUS CATHEDRAL
Europe, perhaps more than anywhere else on Earth, is history's most blood-soaked battlefield.
Fitting.
FORGIVE ME...

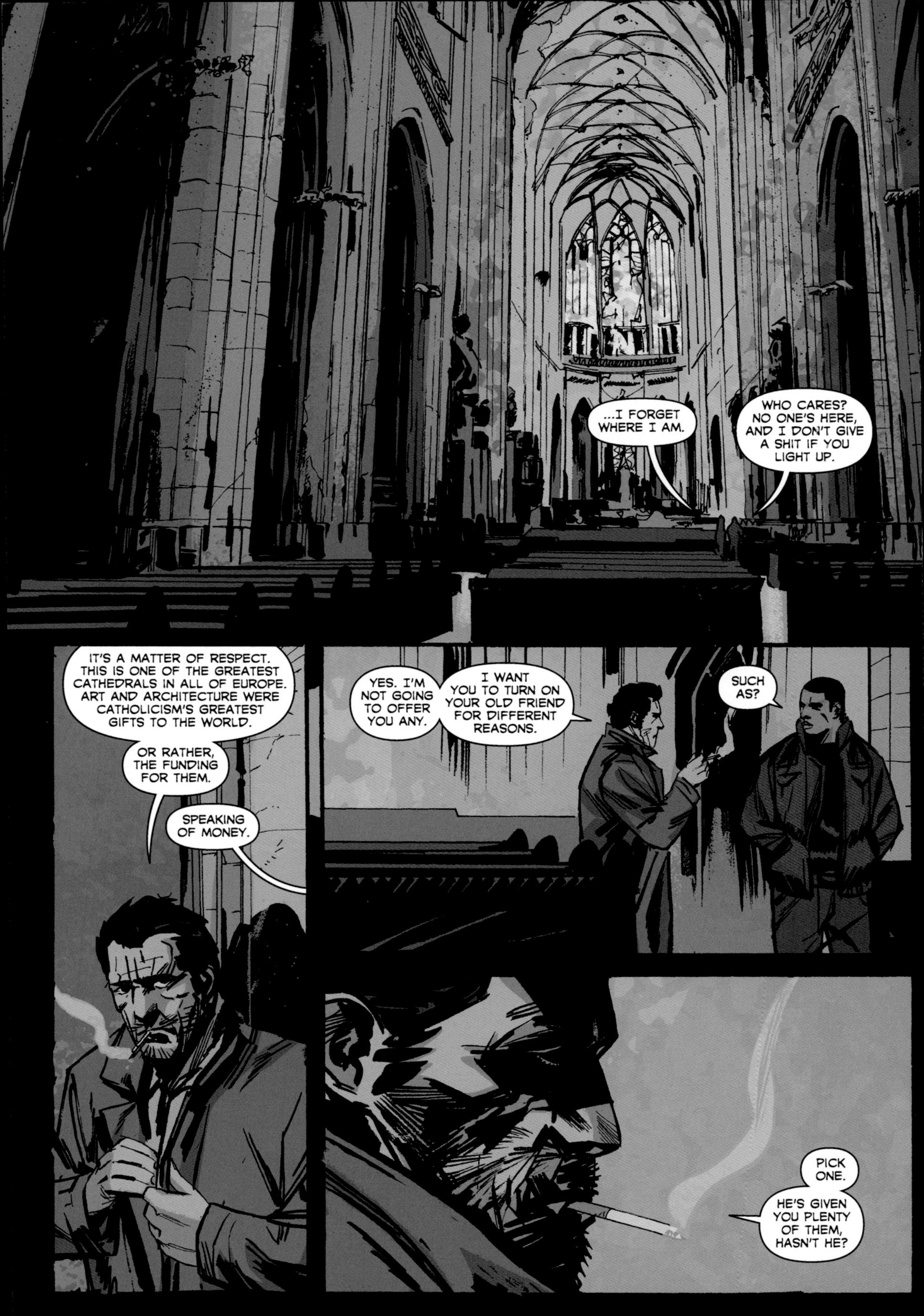
...I FORGET WHERE I AM.
WHO CARES? NO ONE'S HERE, AND I DON'T GIVE A SHIT IF YOU LIGHT UP.
IT'S A MATTER OF RESPECT. THIS IS ONE OF THE GREATEST CATHEDRALS IN ALL OF EUROPE. ART AND ARCHITECTURE WERE CATHOLICISM'S GREATEST GIFTS TO THE WORLD.
OR RATHER, THE FUNDING FOR THEM.
SPEAKING OF MONEY.
YES. I'M NOT GOING TO OFFER YOU ANY.
I WANT YOU TO TURN ON YOUR OLD FRIEND FOR DIFFERENT REASONS.
SUCH AS?
PICK ONE.
HE'S GIVEN YOU PLENTY OF THEM, HASN'T HE?

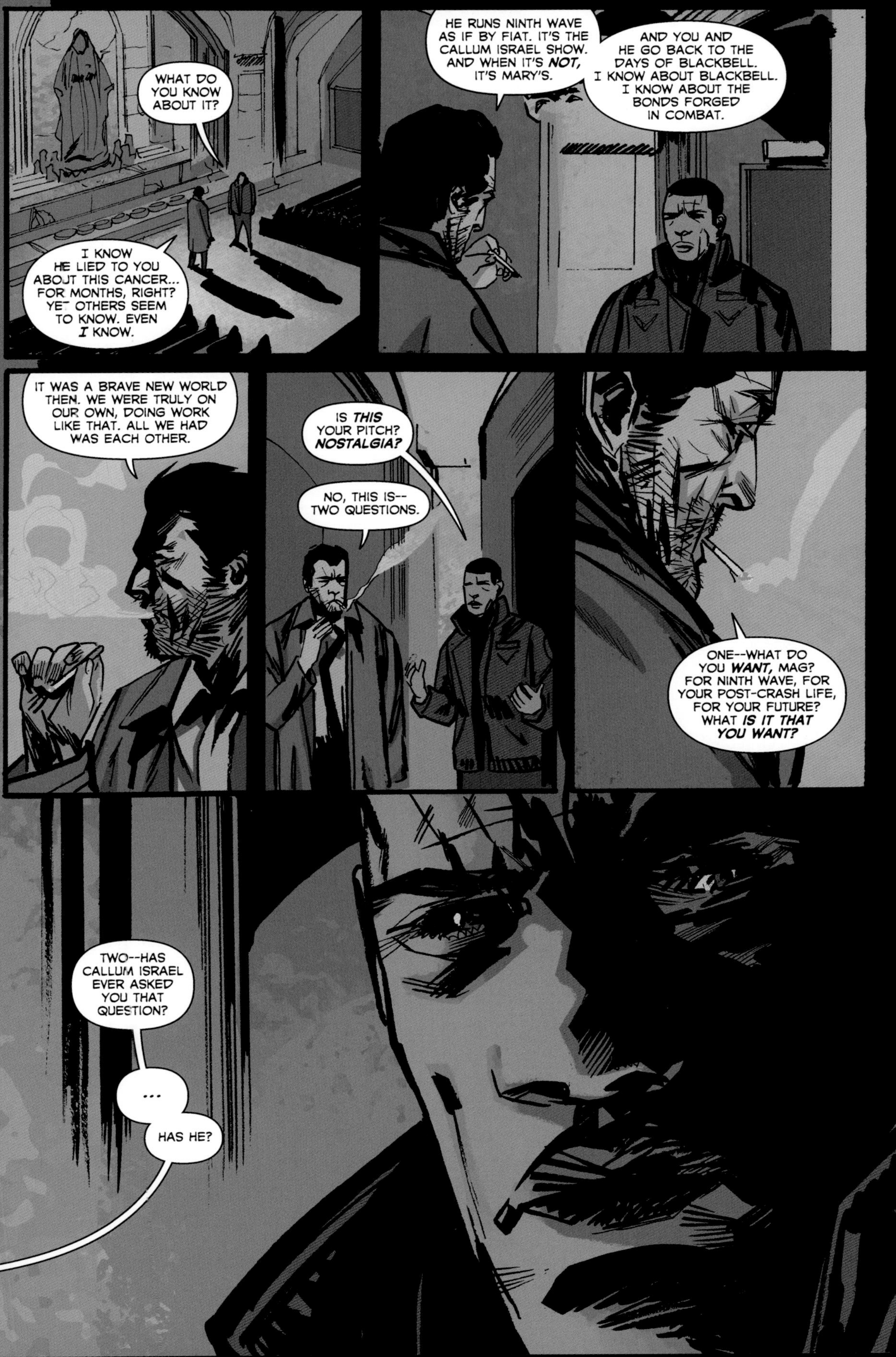
WHAT DO YOU KNOW ABOUT IT?
I KNOW HE LIED TO YOU ABOUT THIS CANCER... FOR MONTHS, RIGHT? YET OTHERS SEEM TO KNOW. EVEN *I* KNOW.
HE RUNS NINTH WAVE AS IF BY FIAT. IT'S THE CALLUM ISRAEL SHOW. AND WHEN IT'S *NOT,* IT'S MARY'S.
AND YOU AND HE GO BACK TO THE DAYS OF BLACKBELL. I KNOW ABOUT BLACKBELL. I KNOW ABOUT THE BONDS FORGED IN COMBAT.
IT WAS A BRAVE NEW WORLD THEN. WE WERE TRULY ON OUR OWN, DOING WORK LIKE THAT. ALL WE HAD WAS EACH OTHER.
IS *THIS* YOUR PITCH? *NOSTALGIA?*
NO, THIS IS-- TWO QUESTIONS.
ONE--WHAT DO YOU *WANT,* MAG? FOR NINTH WAVE, FOR YOUR POST-CRASH LIFE, FOR YOUR FUTURE? WHAT *IS IT THAT YOU WANT?*
TWO--HAS CALLUM ISRAEL EVER ASKED YOU THAT QUESTION?
...
HAS HE?

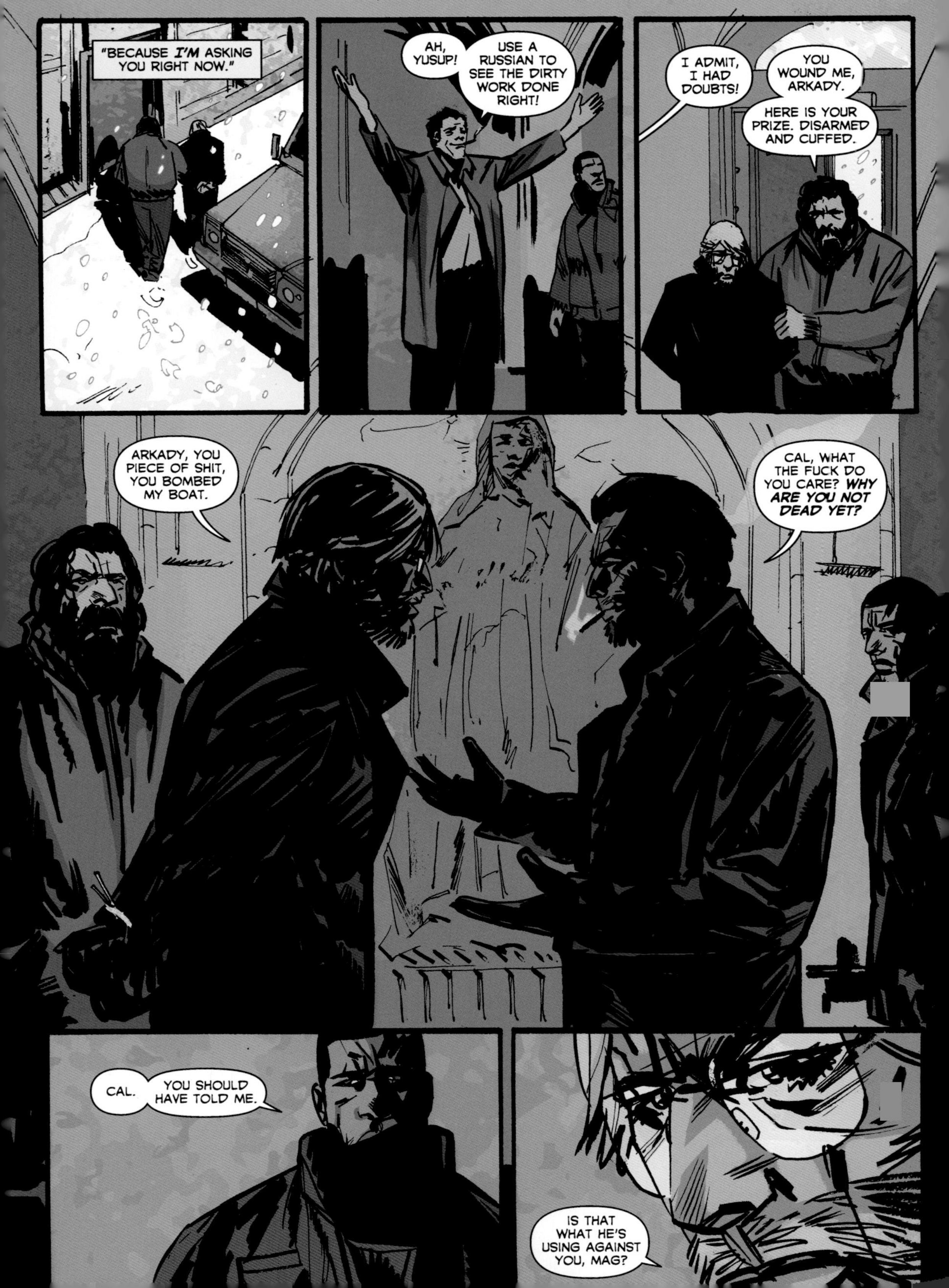
"BECAUSE *I'M* ASKING YOU RIGHT NOW."
AH, YUSUP!
USE A RUSSIAN TO SEE THE DIRTY WORK DONE RIGHT!
I ADMIT, I HAD DOUBTS!
YOU WOUND ME, ARKADY.
HERE IS YOUR PRIZE. DISARMED AND CUFFED.
ARKADY, YOU PIECE OF SHIT, YOU BOMBED MY BOAT.
CAL, WHAT THE FUCK DO YOU CARE? *WHY ARE YOU NOT DEAD YET?*
CAL.
YOU SHOULD HAVE TOLD ME.
IS THAT WHAT HE'S USING AGAINST YOU, MAG?

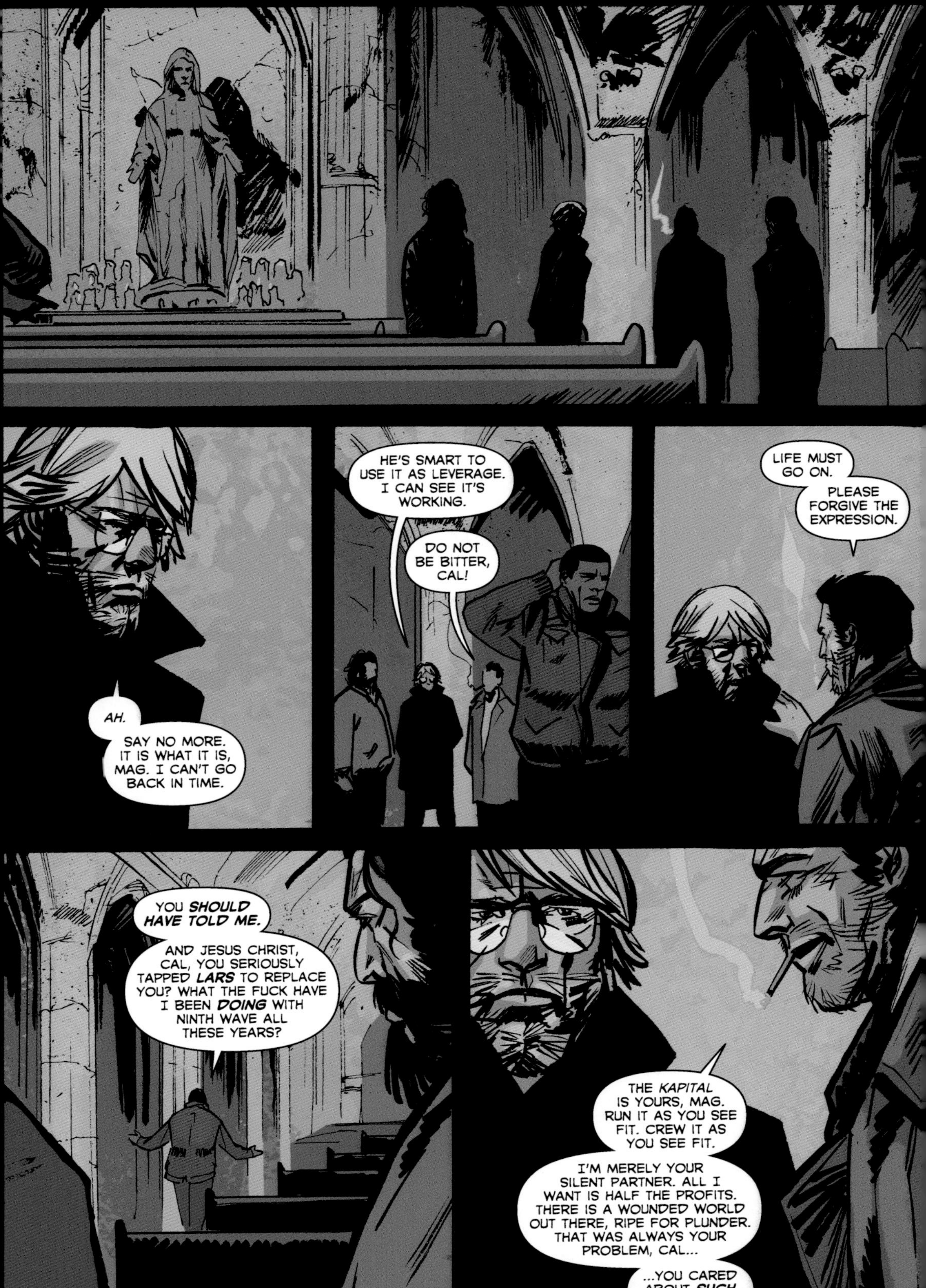
AH.
SAY NO MORE. IT IS WHAT IT IS, MAG. I CAN'T GO BACK IN TIME.
HE'S SMART TO USE IT AS LEVERAGE. I CAN SEE IT'S WORKING.
DO NOT BE BITTER, CAL!
LIFE MUST GO ON.
PLEASE FORGIVE THE EXPRESSION.
YOU SHOULD HAVE TOLD ME.
AND JESUS CHRIST, CAL, YOU SERIOUSLY TAPPED LARS TO REPLACE YOU? WHAT THE FUCK HAVE I BEEN DOING WITH NINTH WAVE ALL THESE YEARS?
THE KAPITAL IS YOURS, MAG. RUN IT AS YOU SEE FIT. CREW IT AS YOU SEE FIT.
I'M MERELY YOUR SILENT PARTNER. ALL I WANT IS HALF THE PROFITS. THERE IS A WOUNDED WORLD OUT THERE, RIPE FOR PLUNDER. THAT WAS ALWAYS YOUR PROBLEM, CAL...
...YOU CARED ABOUT SUCH STUPID SHIT.

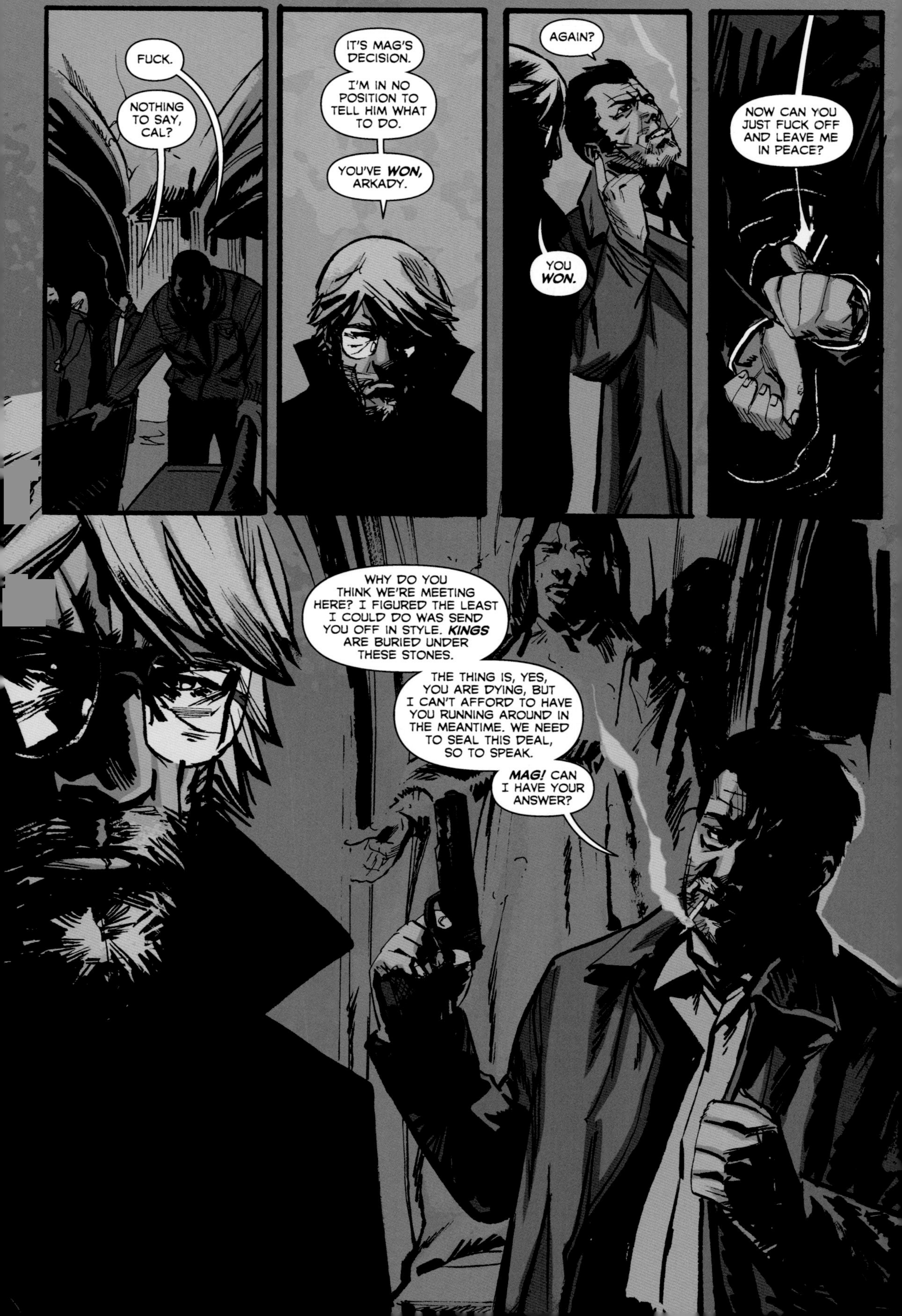
FUCK.
NOTHING TO SAY, CAL?
IT'S MAG'S DECISION.
I'M IN NO POSITION TO TELL HIM WHAT TO DO.
YOU'VE WON, ARKADY.
AGAIN?
YOU WON.
NOW CAN YOU JUST FUCK OFF AND LEAVE ME IN PEACE?
WHY DO YOU THINK WE'RE MEETING HERE? I FIGURED THE LEAST I COULD DO WAS SEND YOU OFF IN STYLE. KINGS ARE BURIED UNDER THESE STONES.
THE THING IS, YES, YOU ARE DYING, BUT I CAN'T AFFORD TO HAVE YOU RUNNING AROUND IN THE MEANTIME. WE NEED TO SEAL THIS DEAL, SO TO SPEAK.
MAG! CAN I HAVE YOUR ANSWER?

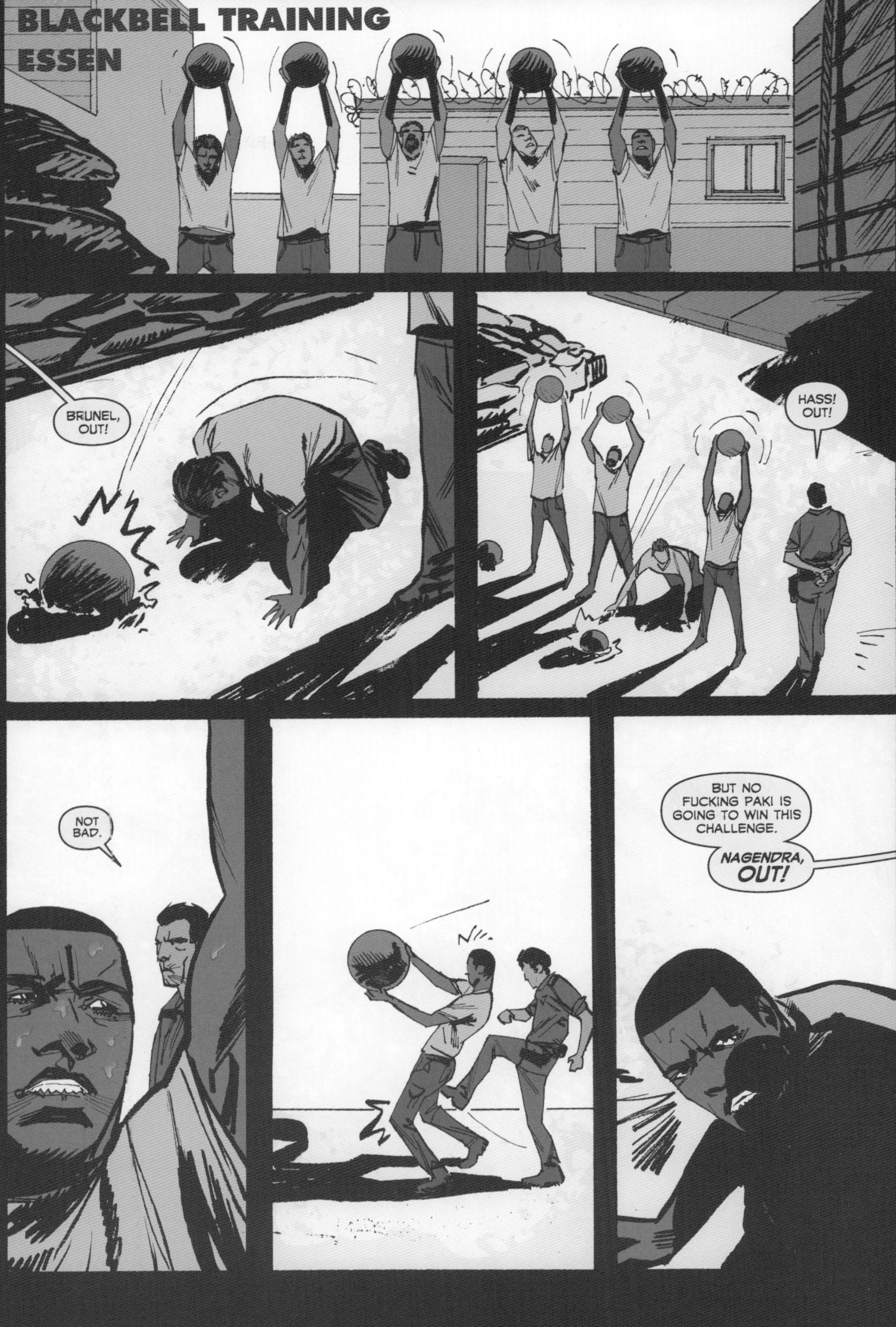
BLACKBELL TRAINING
ESSEN
BRUNEL, OUT!
HASS! OUT!
NOT BAD.
BUT NO FUCKING PAKI IS GOING TO WIN THIS CHALLENGE.
NAGENDRA, OUT!

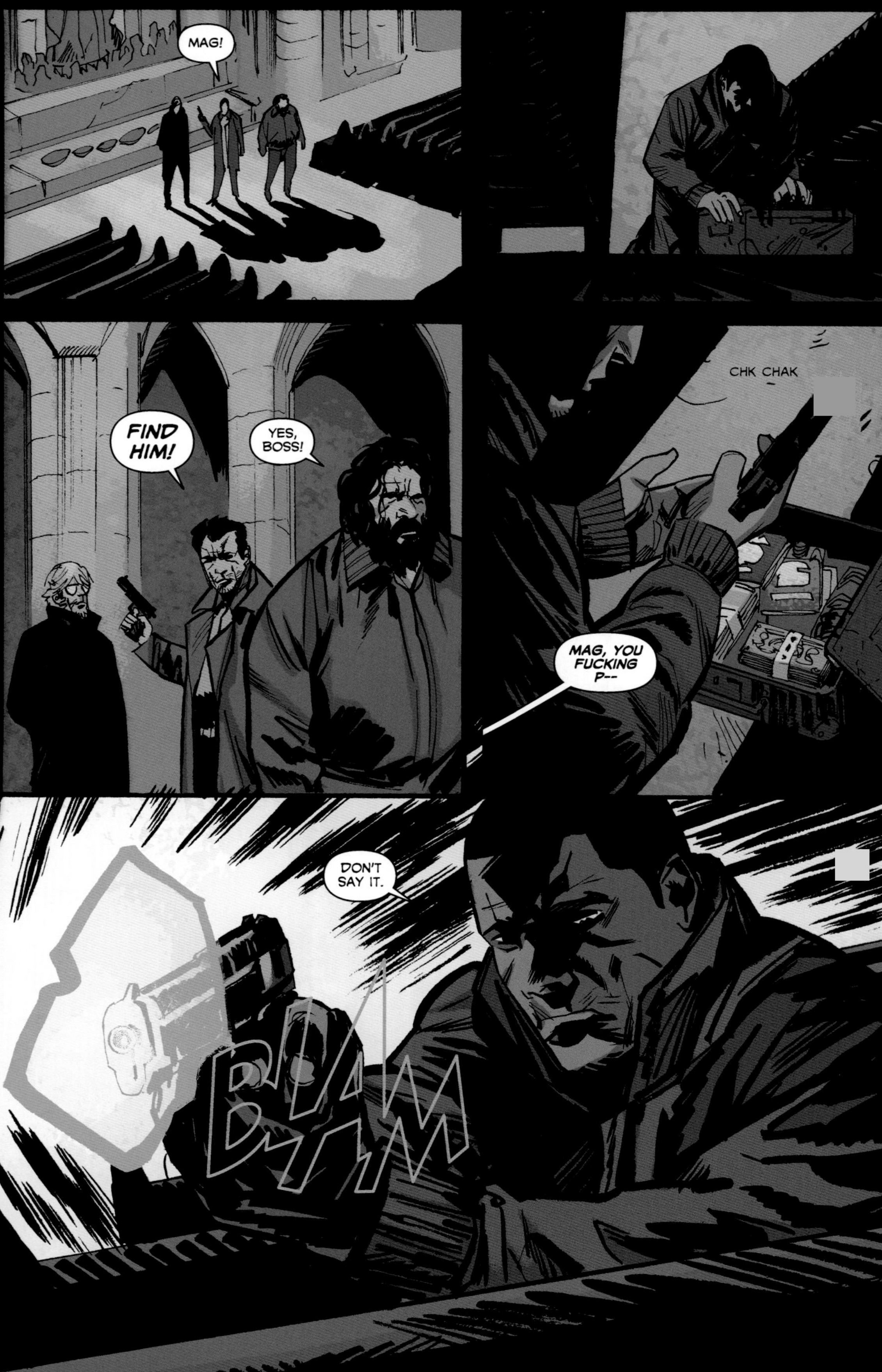
MAG!
FIND HIM!
YES, BOSS!
CHK CHAK
MAG, YOU FUCKING P--
DON'T SAY IT.
BLAM

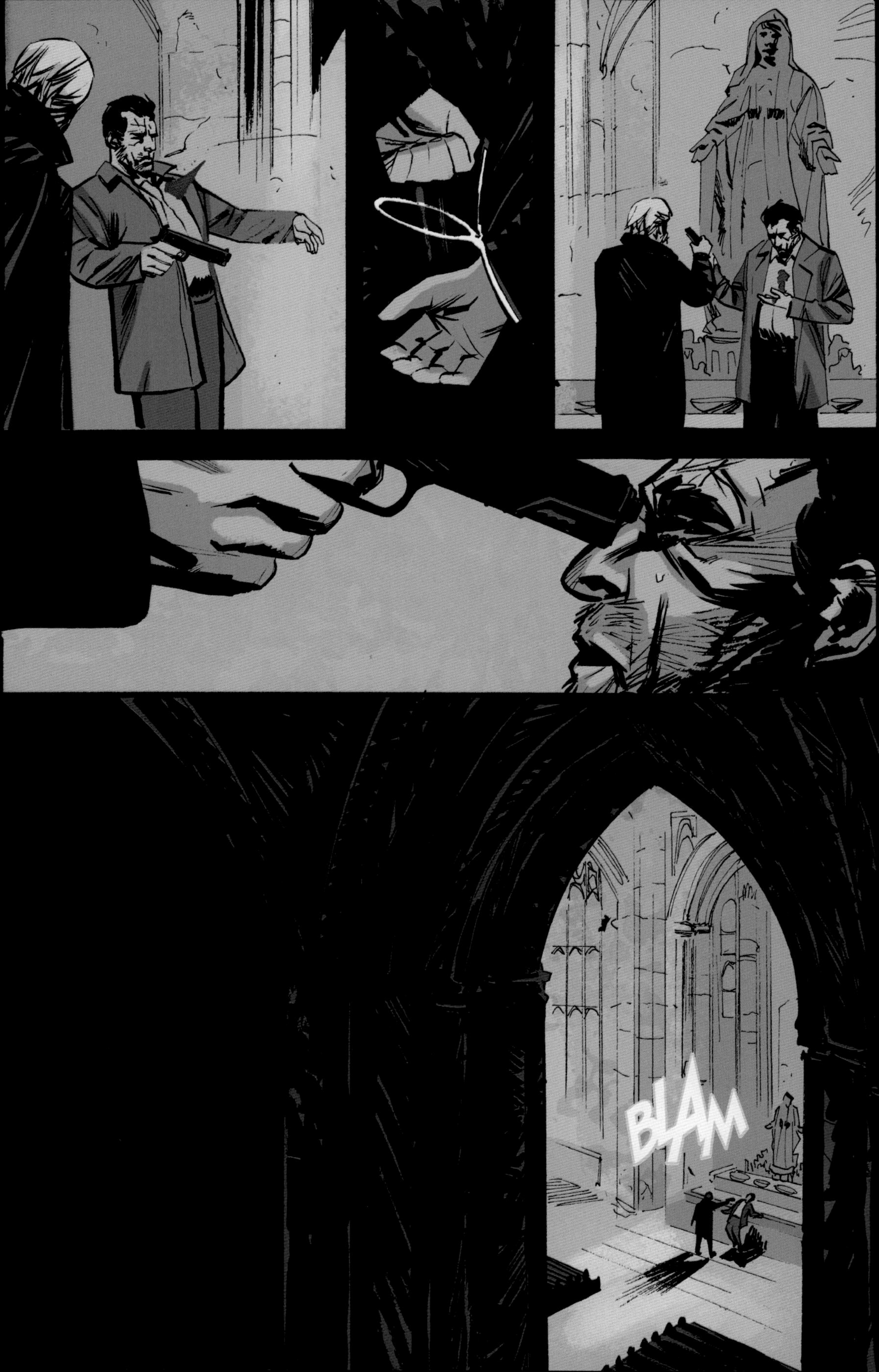
BLAM

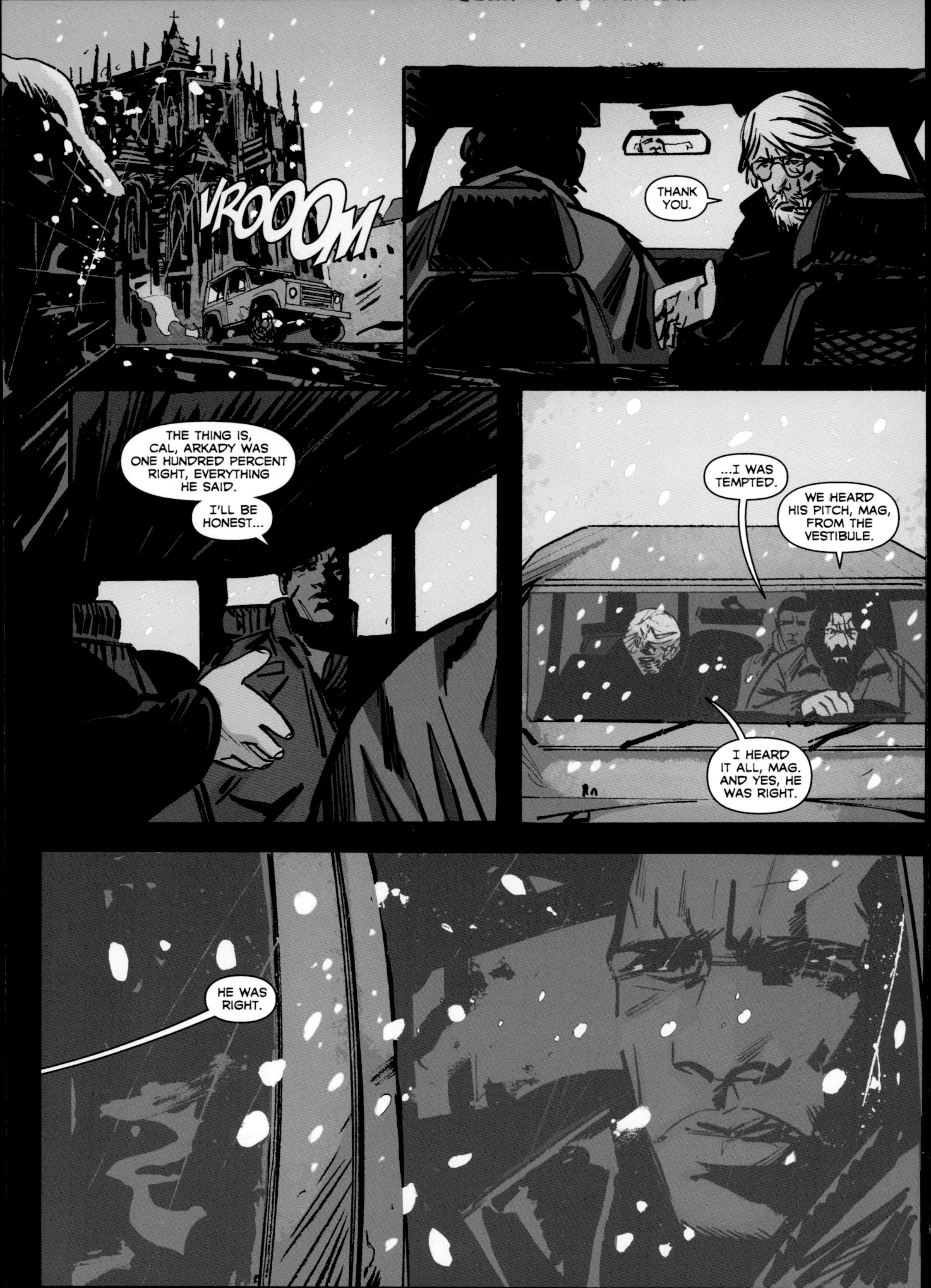
VROOOM
THANK YOU.
THE THING IS, CAL, ARKADY WAS ONE HUNDRED PERCENT RIGHT, EVERYTHING HE SAID.
I'LL BE HONEST...
...I WAS TEMPTED.
WE HEARD HIS PITCH, MAG, FROM THE VESTIBULE.
I HEARD IT ALL, MAG. AND YES, HE WAS RIGHT.
HE WAS RIGHT.

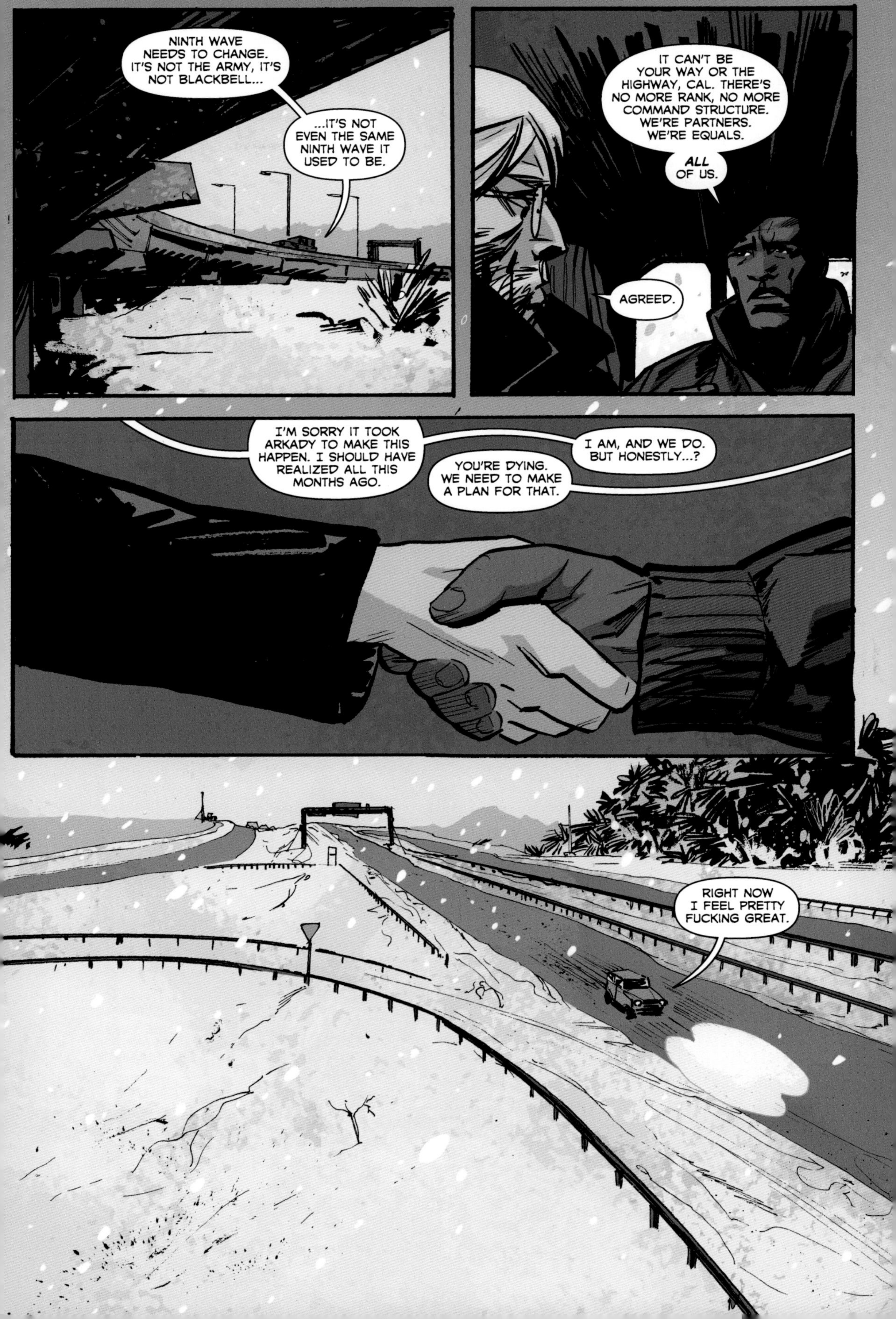
NINTH WAVE NEEDS TO CHANGE. IT'S NOT THE ARMY, IT'S NOT BLACKBELL...
...IT'S NOT EVEN THE SAME NINTH WAVE IT USED TO BE.
IT CAN'T BE YOUR WAY OR THE HIGHWAY, CAL. THERE'S NO MORE RANK, NO MORE COMMAND STRUCTURE. WE'RE PARTNERS. WE'RE EQUALS.
ALL OF US.
AGREED.
I'M SORRY IT TOOK ARKADY TO MAKE THIS HAPPEN. I SHOULD HAVE REALIZED ALL THIS MONTHS AGO.
I AM, AND WE DO. BUT HONESTLY...?
YOU'RE DYING. WE NEED TO MAKE A PLAN FOR THAT.
RIGHT NOW I FEEL PRETTY FUCKING GREAT.

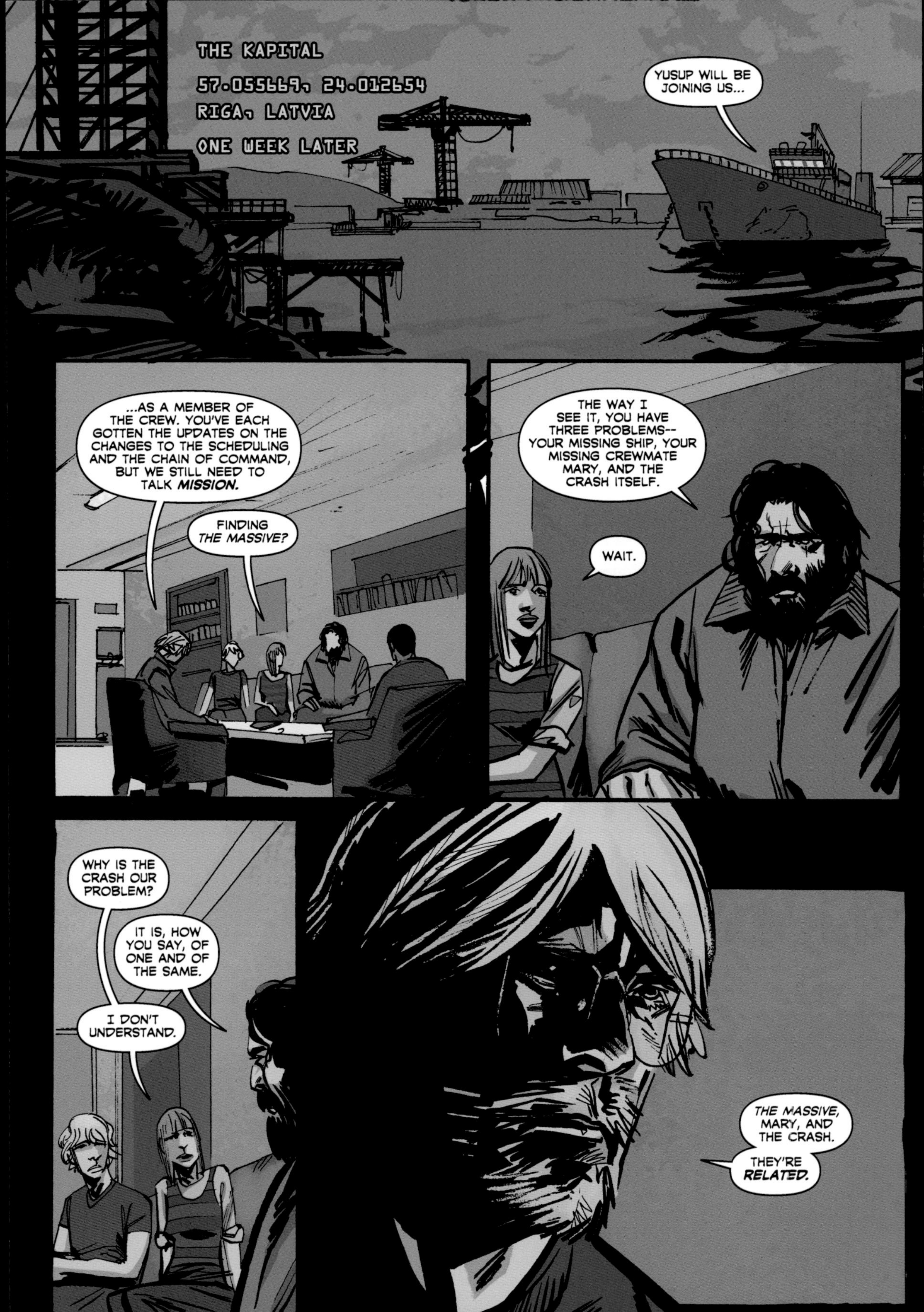
THE KAPITAL
57.055669, 24.012654
RIGA, LATVIA
ONE WEEK LATER
YUSUP WILL BE JOINING US...
...AS A MEMBER OF THE CREW. YOU'VE EACH GOTTEN THE UPDATES ON THE CHANGES TO THE SCHEDULING AND THE CHAIN OF COMMAND, BUT WE STILL NEED TO TALK MISSION.
FINDING THE MASSIVE?
THE WAY I SEE IT, YOU HAVE THREE PROBLEMS-- YOUR MISSING SHIP, YOUR MISSING CREWMATE MARY, AND THE CRASH ITSELF.
WAIT.
WHY IS THE CRASH OUR PROBLEM?
IT IS, HOW YOU SAY, OF ONE AND OF THE SAME.
I DON'T UNDERSTAND.
THE MASSIVE, MARY, AND THE CRASH.
THEY'RE RELATED.

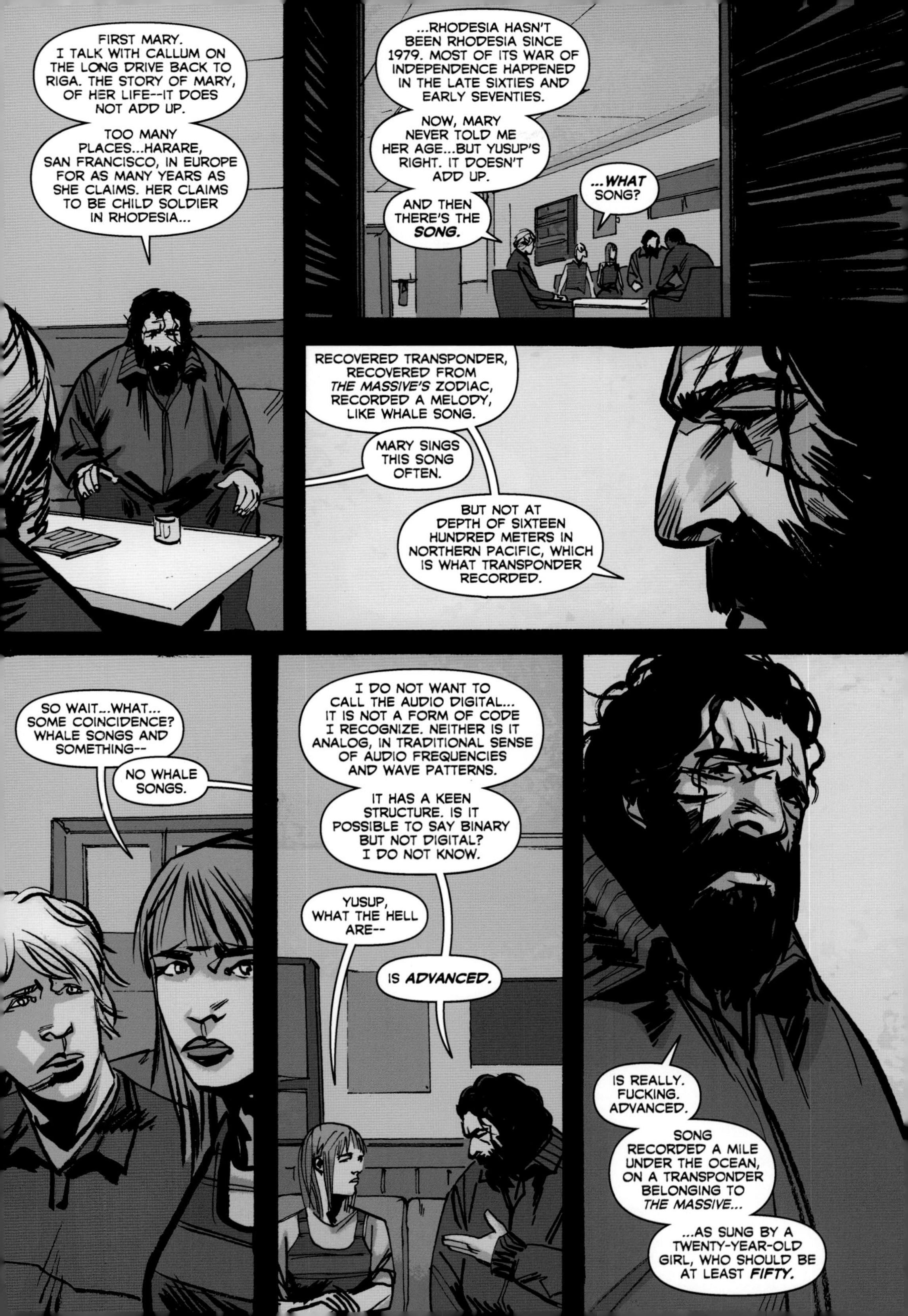
FIRST MARY. I TALK WITH CALLUM ON THE LONG DRIVE BACK TO RIGA. THE STORY OF MARY, OF HER LIFE--IT DOES NOT ADD UP.
TOO MANY PLACES...HARARE, SAN FRANCISCO, IN EUROPE FOR AS MANY YEARS AS SHE CLAIMS. HER CLAIMS TO BE CHILD SOLDIER IN RHODESIA...
...RHODESIA HASN'T BEEN RHODESIA SINCE 1979. MOST OF ITS WAR OF INDEPENDENCE HAPPENED IN THE LATE SIXTIES AND EARLY SEVENTIES.
NOW, MARY NEVER TOLD ME HER AGE...BUT YUSUP'S RIGHT. IT DOESN'T ADD UP.
AND THEN THERE'S THE *SONG.*
...WHAT SONG?
RECOVERED TRANSPONDER, RECOVERED FROM *THE MASSIVE'S* ZODIAC, RECORDED A MELODY, LIKE WHALE SONG.
MARY SINGS THIS SONG OFTEN.
BUT NOT AT DEPTH OF SIXTEEN HUNDRED METERS IN NORTHERN PACIFIC, WHICH IS WHAT TRANSPONDER RECORDED.
SO WAIT...WHAT... SOME COINCIDENCE? WHALE SONGS AND SOMETHING--
NO WHALE SONGS.
I DO NOT WANT TO CALL THE AUDIO DIGITAL... IT IS NOT A FORM OF CODE I RECOGNIZE. NEITHER IS IT ANALOG, IN TRADITIONAL SENSE OF AUDIO FREQUENCIES AND WAVE PATTERNS.
IT HAS A KEEN STRUCTURE. IS IT POSSIBLE TO SAY BINARY BUT NOT DIGITAL? I DO NOT KNOW.
YUSUP, WHAT THE HELL ARE--
IS *ADVANCED.*
IS REALLY. FUCKING. ADVANCED.
SONG RECORDED A MILE UNDER THE OCEAN, ON A TRANSPONDER BELONGING TO *THE MASSIVE...*
...AS SUNG BY A TWENTY-YEAR-OLD GIRL, WHO SHOULD BE AT LEAST *FIFTY.*

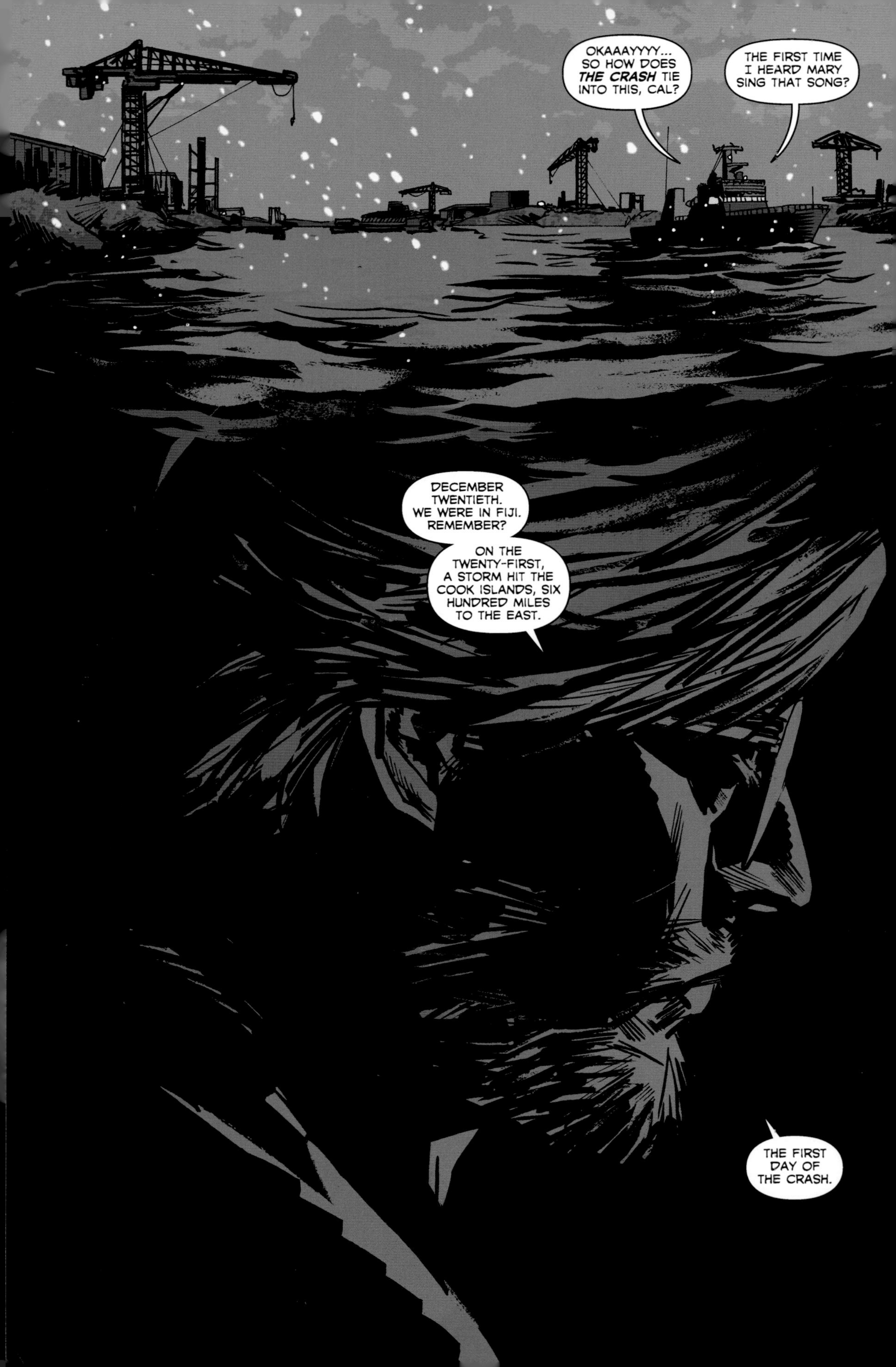
OKAAAYYYY... SO HOW DOES THE CRASH TIE INTO THIS, CAL?
THE FIRST TIME I HEARD MARY SING THAT SONG?
DECEMBER TWENTIETH. WE WERE IN FIJI. REMEMBER?
ON THE TWENTY-FIRST, A STORM HIT THE COOK ISLANDS, SIX HUNDRED MILES TO THE EAST.
THE FIRST DAY OF THE CRASH.

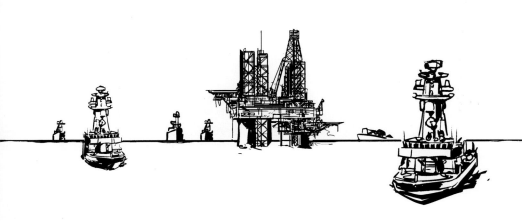

H2O
ण्याचे पाणी
JPL

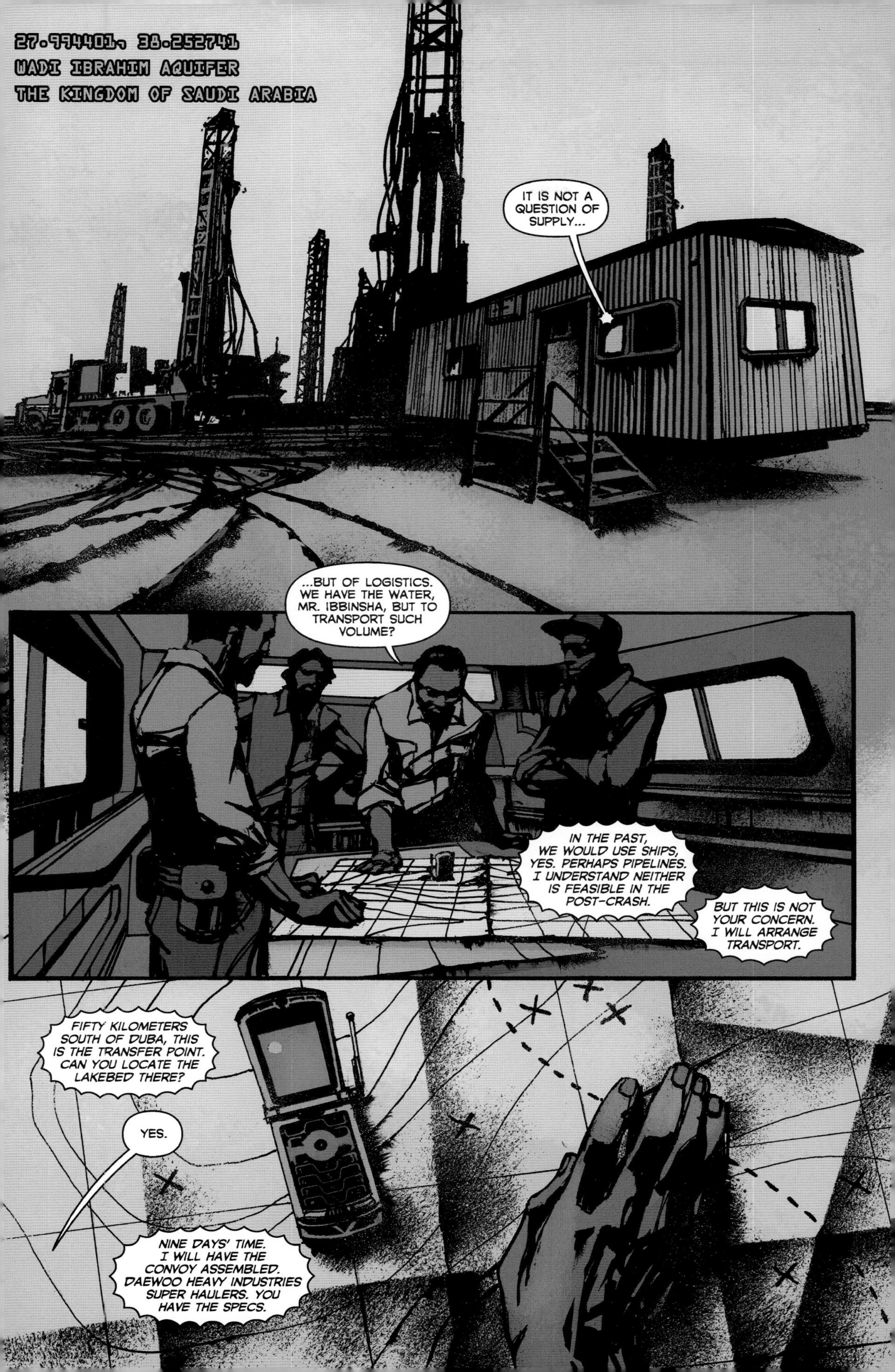
27.994401, 38.252741
WADI IBRAHIM AQUIFER
THE KINGDOM OF SAUDI ARABIA
IT IS NOT A QUESTION OF SUPPLY...
...BUT OF LOGISTICS. WE HAVE THE WATER, MR. IBBINSHA, BUT TO TRANSPORT SUCH VOLUME?
IN THE PAST, WE WOULD USE SHIPS, YES. PERHAPS PIPELINES. I UNDERSTAND NEITHER IS FEASIBLE IN THE POST-CRASH.
BUT THIS IS NOT YOUR CONCERN. I WILL ARRANGE TRANSPORT.
FIFTY KILOMETERS SOUTH OF DUBA, THIS IS THE TRANSFER POINT. CAN YOU LOCATE THE LAKEBED THERE?
YES.
NINE DAYS' TIME. I WILL HAVE THE CONVOY ASSEMBLED. DAEWOO HEAVY INDUSTRIES SUPER HAULERS. YOU HAVE THE SPECS.

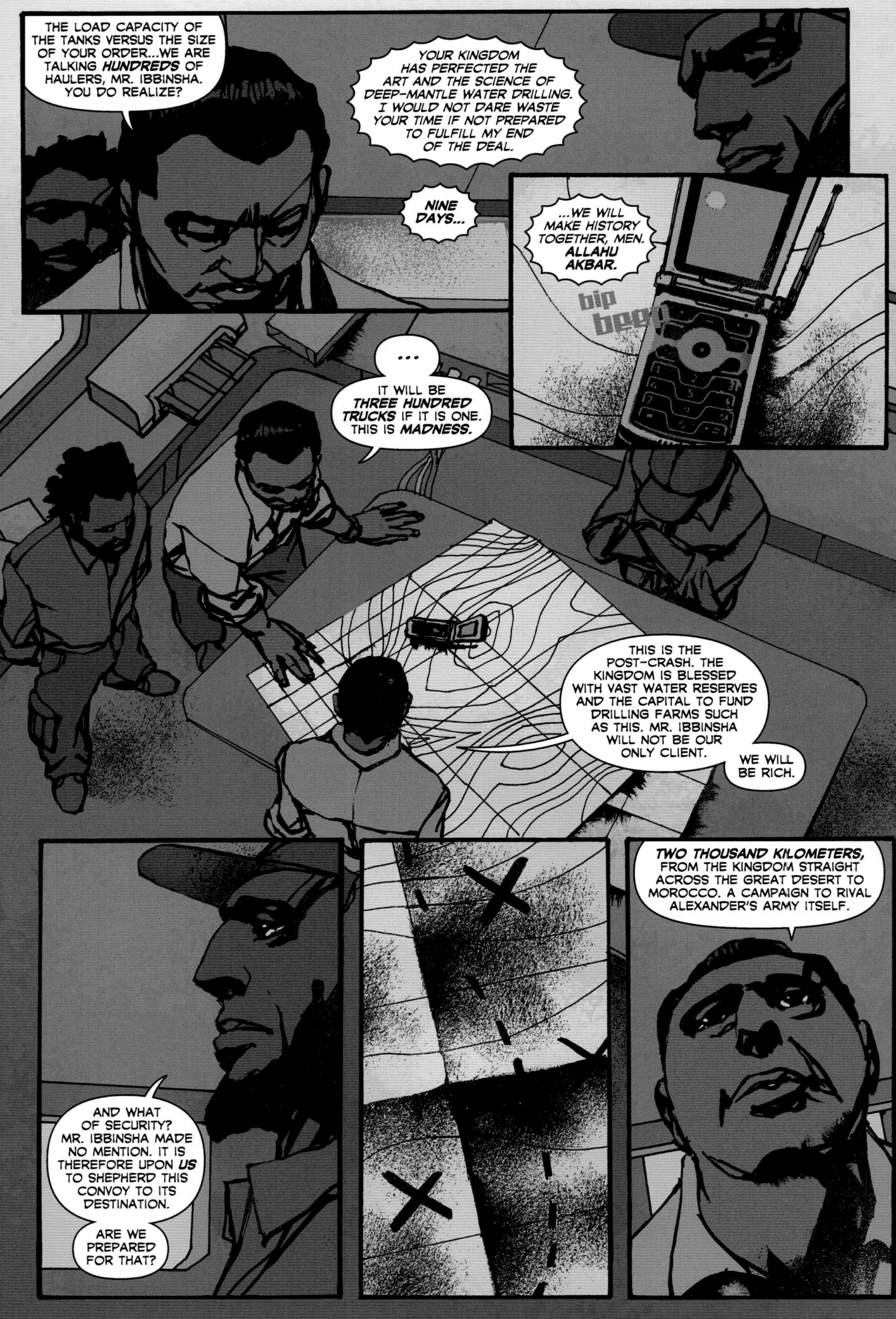
THE LOAD CAPACITY OF THE TANKS VERSUS THE SIZE OF YOUR ORDER...WE ARE TALKING ***HUNDREDS*** OF HAULERS, MR. IBBINSHA. YOU DO REALIZE?
YOUR KINGDOM HAS PERFECTED THE ART AND THE SCIENCE OF DEEP-MANTLE WATER DRILLING. I WOULD NOT DARE WASTE YOUR TIME IF NOT PREPARED TO FULFILL MY END OF THE DEAL.
NINE DAYS...
...WE WILL MAKE HISTORY TOGETHER, MEN. ***ALLAHU AKBAR.***
bip
...
IT WILL BE ***THREE HUNDRED TRUCKS*** IF IT IS ONE. THIS IS ***MADNESS.***
THIS IS THE POST-CRASH. THE KINGDOM IS BLESSED WITH VAST WATER RESERVES AND THE CAPITAL TO FUND DRILLING FARMS SUCH AS THIS. MR. IBBINSHA WILL NOT BE OUR ONLY CLIENT.
WE WILL BE RICH.
AND WHAT OF SECURITY? MR. IBBINSHA MADE NO MENTION. IT IS THEREFORE UPON ***US*** TO SHEPHERD THIS CONVOY TO ITS DESTINATION.
ARE WE PREPARED FOR THAT?
TWO THOUSAND KILOMETERS, FROM THE KINGDOM STRAIGHT ACROSS THE GREAT DESERT TO MOROCCO. A CAMPAIGN TO RIVAL ALEXANDER'S ARMY ITSELF.

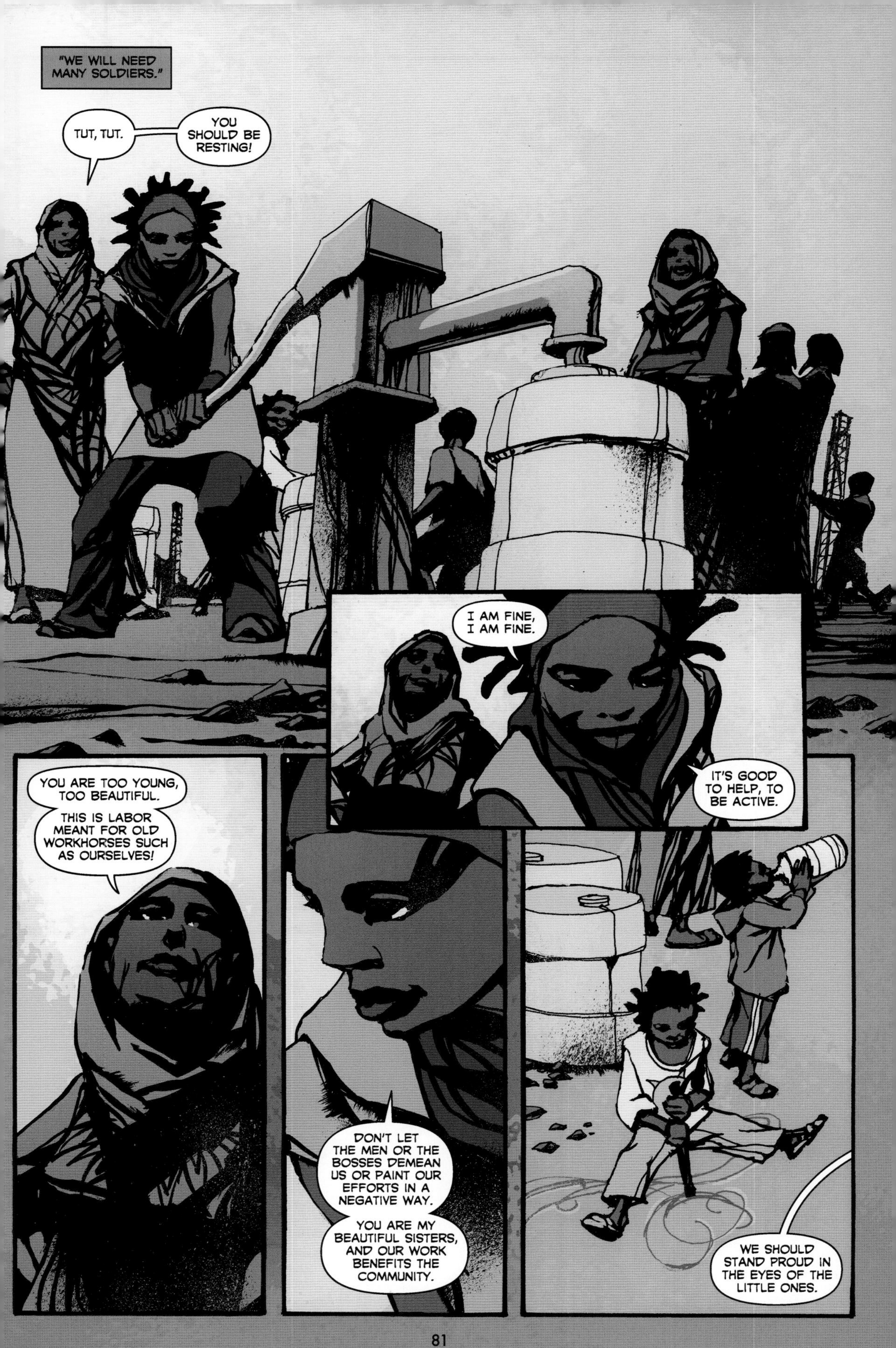
"WE WILL NEED MANY SOLDIERS."
TUT, TUT.
YOU SHOULD BE RESTING!
I AM FINE, I AM FINE.
IT'S GOOD TO HELP, TO BE ACTIVE.
YOU ARE TOO YOUNG, TOO BEAUTIFUL.
THIS IS LABOR MEANT FOR OLD WORKHORSES SUCH AS OURSELVES!
DON'T LET THE MEN OR THE BOSSES DEMEAN US OR PAINT OUR EFFORTS IN A NEGATIVE WAY.
YOU ARE MY BEAUTIFUL SISTERS, AND OUR WORK BENEFITS THE COMMUNITY.
WE SHOULD STAND PROUD IN THE EYES OF THE LITTLE ONES.

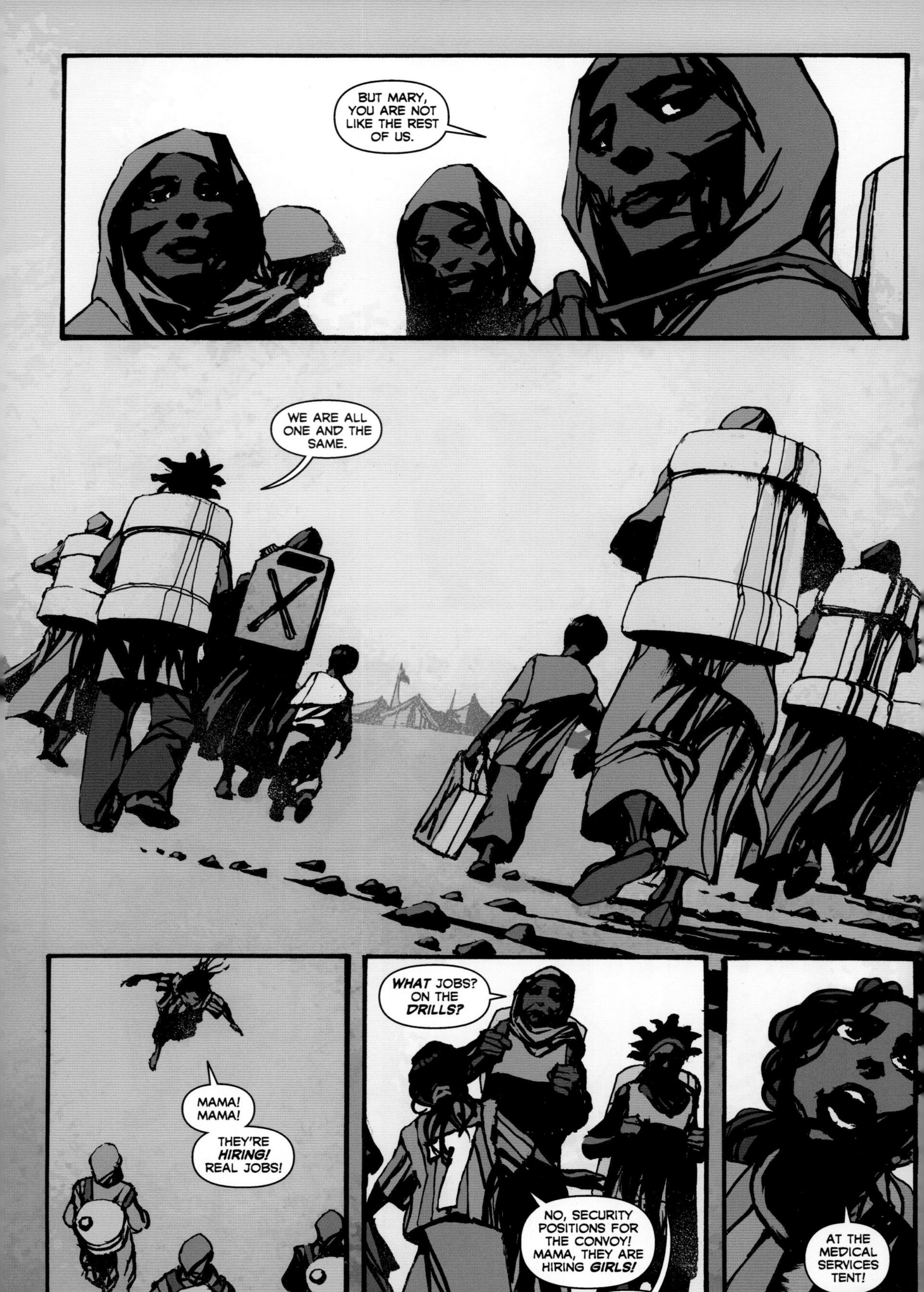
BUT MARY, YOU ARE NOT LIKE THE REST OF US.
WE ARE ALL ONE AND THE SAME.
MAMA! MAMA!
THEY'RE ***HIRING!*** REAL JOBS!
WHAT JOBS? ON THE ***DRILLS?***
NO, SECURITY POSITIONS FOR THE CONVOY! MAMA, THEY ARE HIRING ***GIRLS!***
WHERE, JAMEELAH?
AT THE MEDICAL SERVICES TENT!

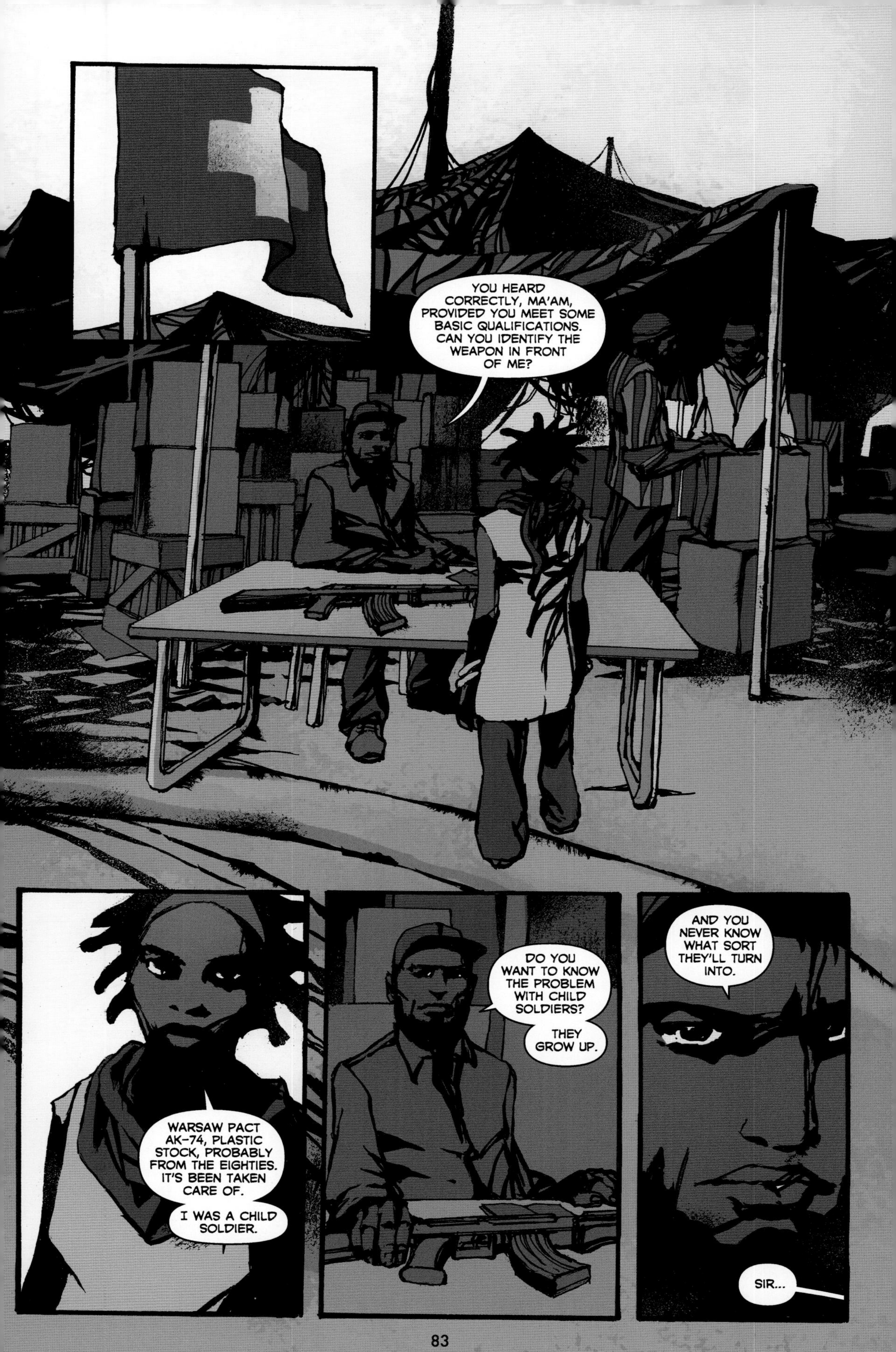
YOU HEARD CORRECTLY, MA'AM, PROVIDED YOU MEET SOME BASIC QUALIFICATIONS. CAN YOU IDENTIFY THE WEAPON IN FRONT OF ME?
WARSAW PACT AK-74, PLASTIC STOCK, PROBABLY FROM THE EIGHTIES. IT'S BEEN TAKEN CARE OF.
I WAS A CHILD SOLDIER.
DO YOU WANT TO KNOW THE PROBLEM WITH CHILD SOLDIERS?
THEY GROW UP.
AND YOU NEVER KNOW WHAT SORT THEY'LL TURN INTO.
SIR...

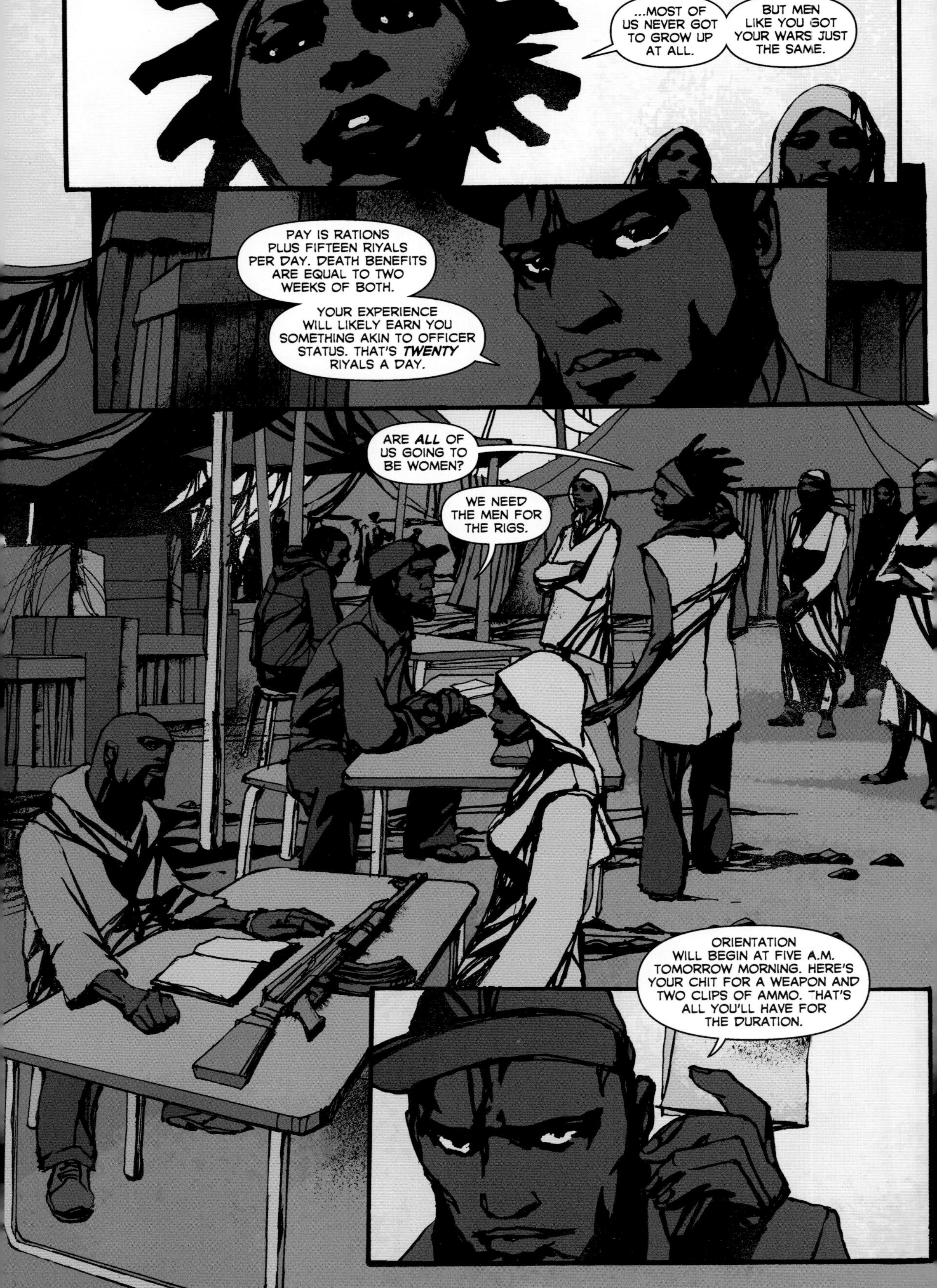
...MOST OF US NEVER GOT TO GROW UP AT ALL.
BUT MEN LIKE YOU GOT YOUR WARS JUST THE SAME.
PAY IS RATIONS PLUS FIFTEEN RIYALS PER DAY. DEATH BENEFITS ARE EQUAL TO TWO WEEKS OF BOTH.
YOUR EXPERIENCE WILL LIKELY EARN YOU SOMETHING AKIN TO OFFICER STATUS. THAT'S *TWENTY* RIYALS A DAY.
ARE *ALL* OF US GOING TO BE WOMEN?
WE NEED THE MEN FOR THE RIGS.
ORIENTATION WILL BEGIN AT FIVE A.M. TOMORROW MORNING. HERE'S YOUR CHIT FOR A WEAPON AND TWO CLIPS OF AMMO. THAT'S ALL YOU'LL HAVE FOR THE DURATION.

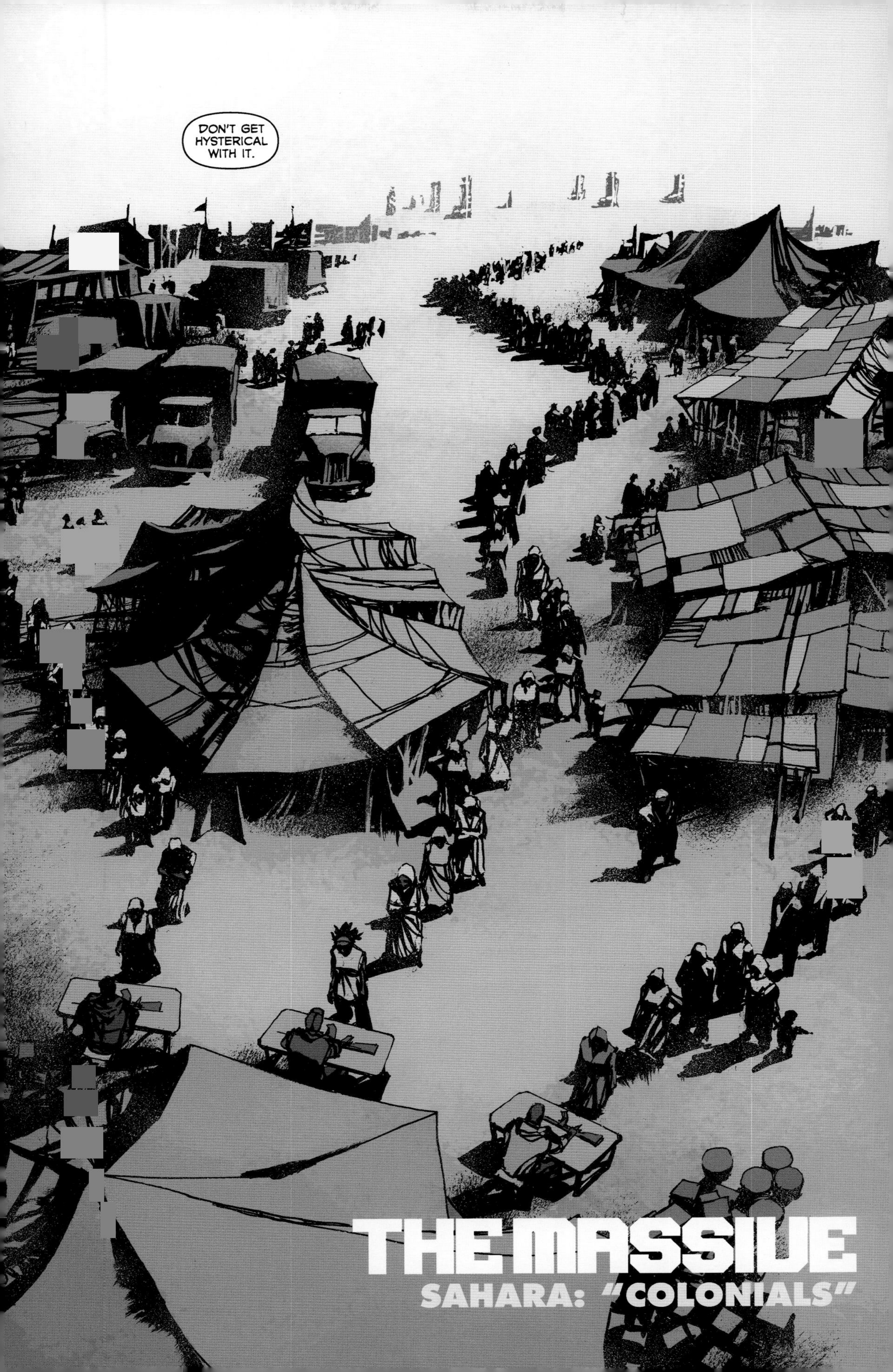
DON'T GET HYSTERICAL WITH IT.
THE MASSIVE
SAHARA: "COLONIALS"

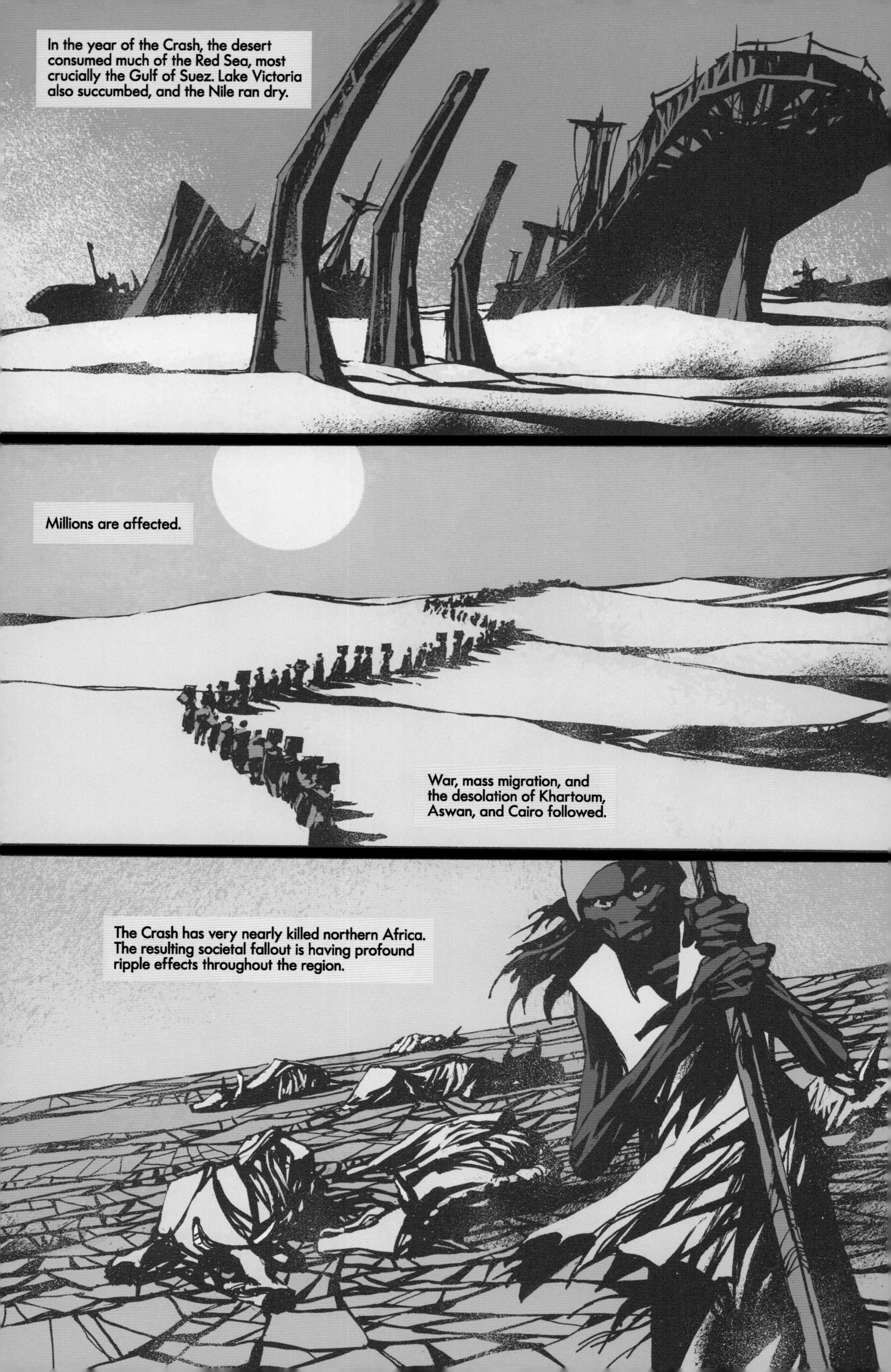
In the year of the Crash, the desert consumed much of the Red Sea, most crucially the Gulf of Suez. Lake Victoria also succumbed, and the Nile ran dry.
Millions are affected.
War, mass migration, and the desolation of Khartoum, Aswan, and Cairo followed.
The Crash has very nearly killed northern Africa. The resulting societal fallout is having profound ripple effects throughout the region.

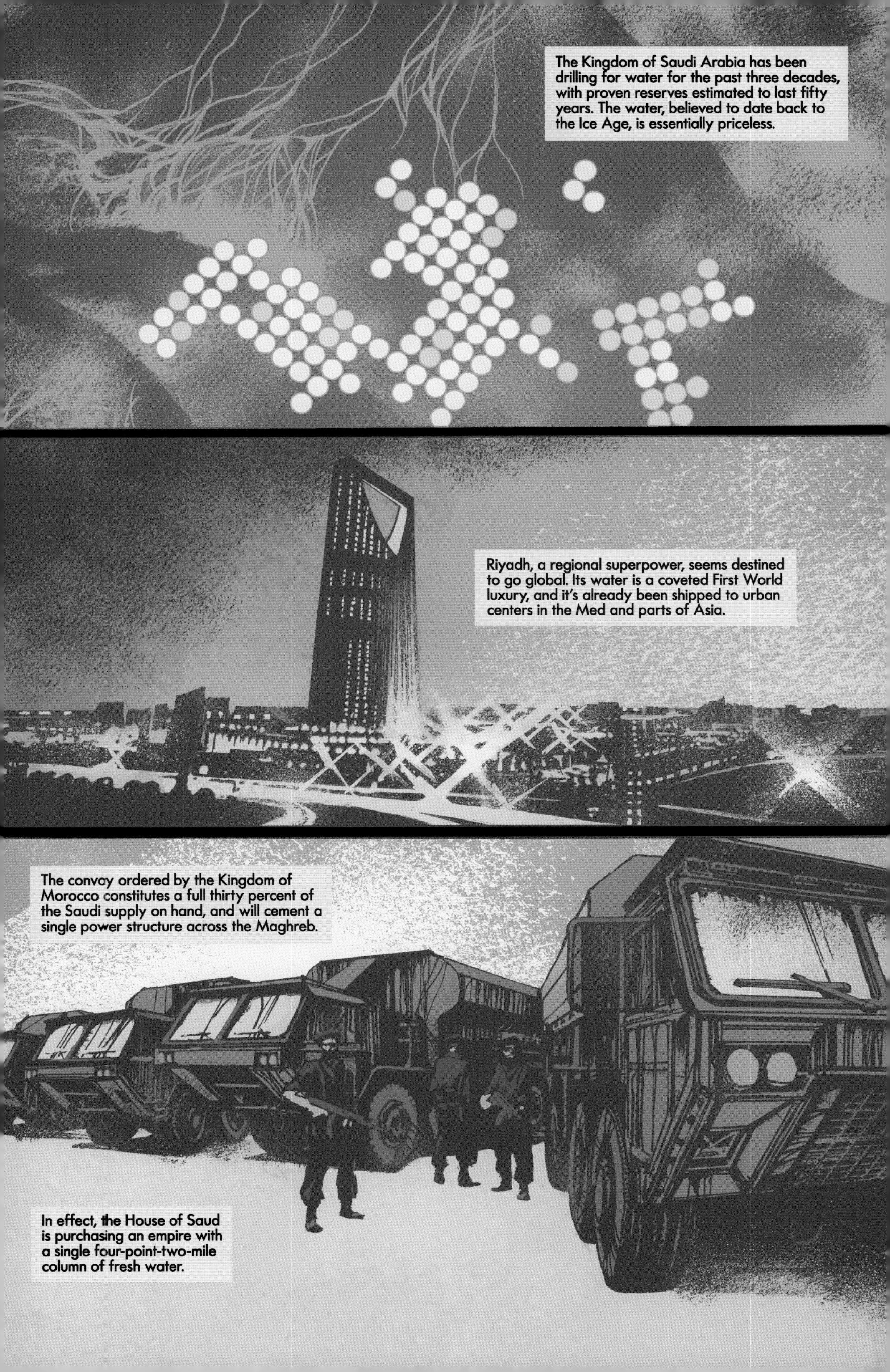
The Kingdom of Saudi Arabia has been drilling for water for the past three decades, with proven reserves estimated to last fifty years. The water, believed to date back to the Ice Age, is essentially priceless.
Riyadh, a regional superpower, seems destined to go global. Its water is a coveted First World luxury, and it's already been shipped to urban centers in the Med and parts of Asia.
The convoy ordered by the Kingdom of Morocco constitutes a full thirty percent of the Saudi supply on hand, and will cement a single power structure across the Maghreb.
In effect, the House of Saud is purchasing an empire with a single four-point-two-mile column of fresh water.

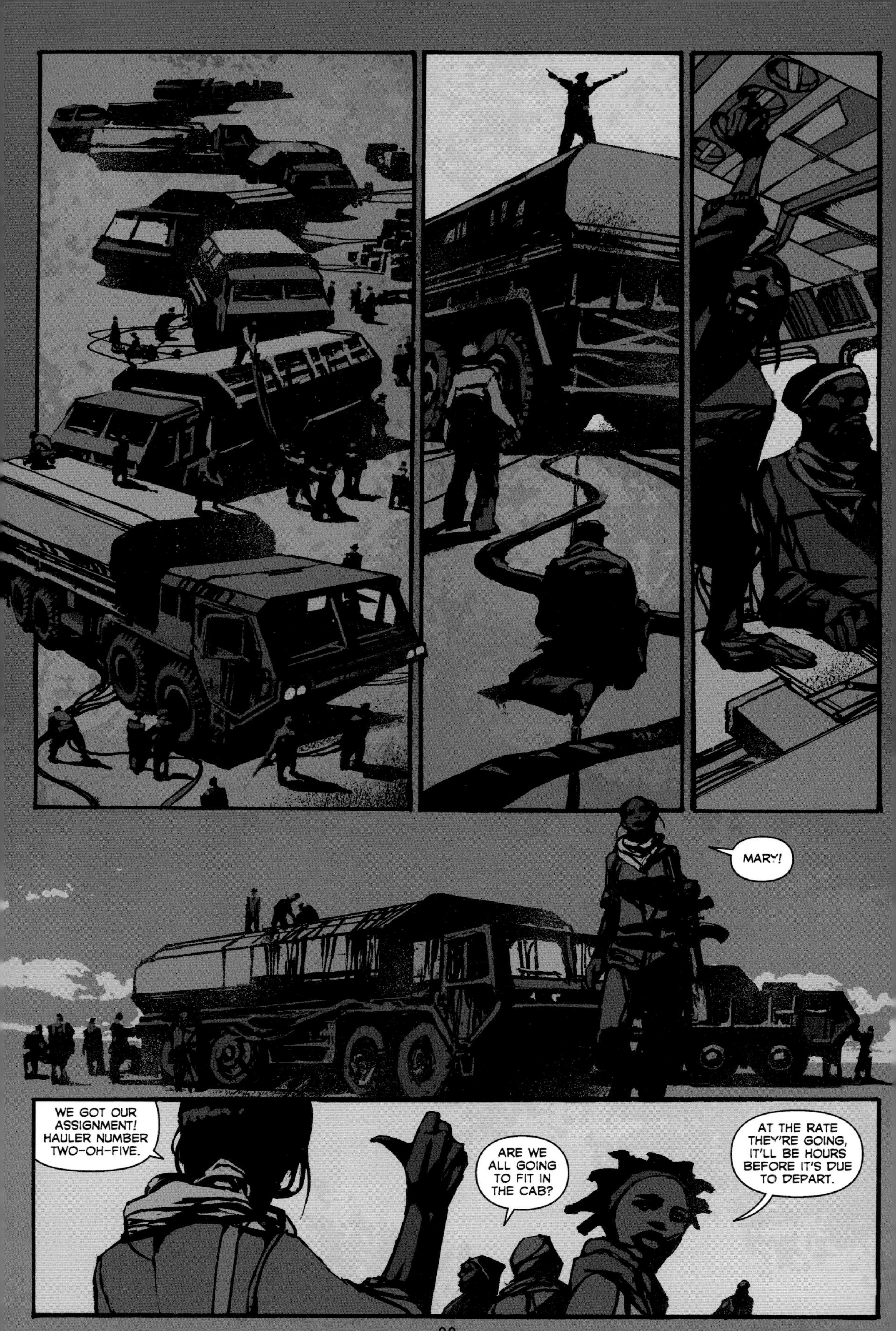
MARY!
WE GOT OUR ASSIGNMENT! HAULER NUMBER TWO-OH-FIVE.
ARE WE ALL GOING TO FIT IN THE CAB?
AT THE RATE THEY'RE GOING, IT'LL BE HOURS BEFORE IT'S DUE TO DEPART.

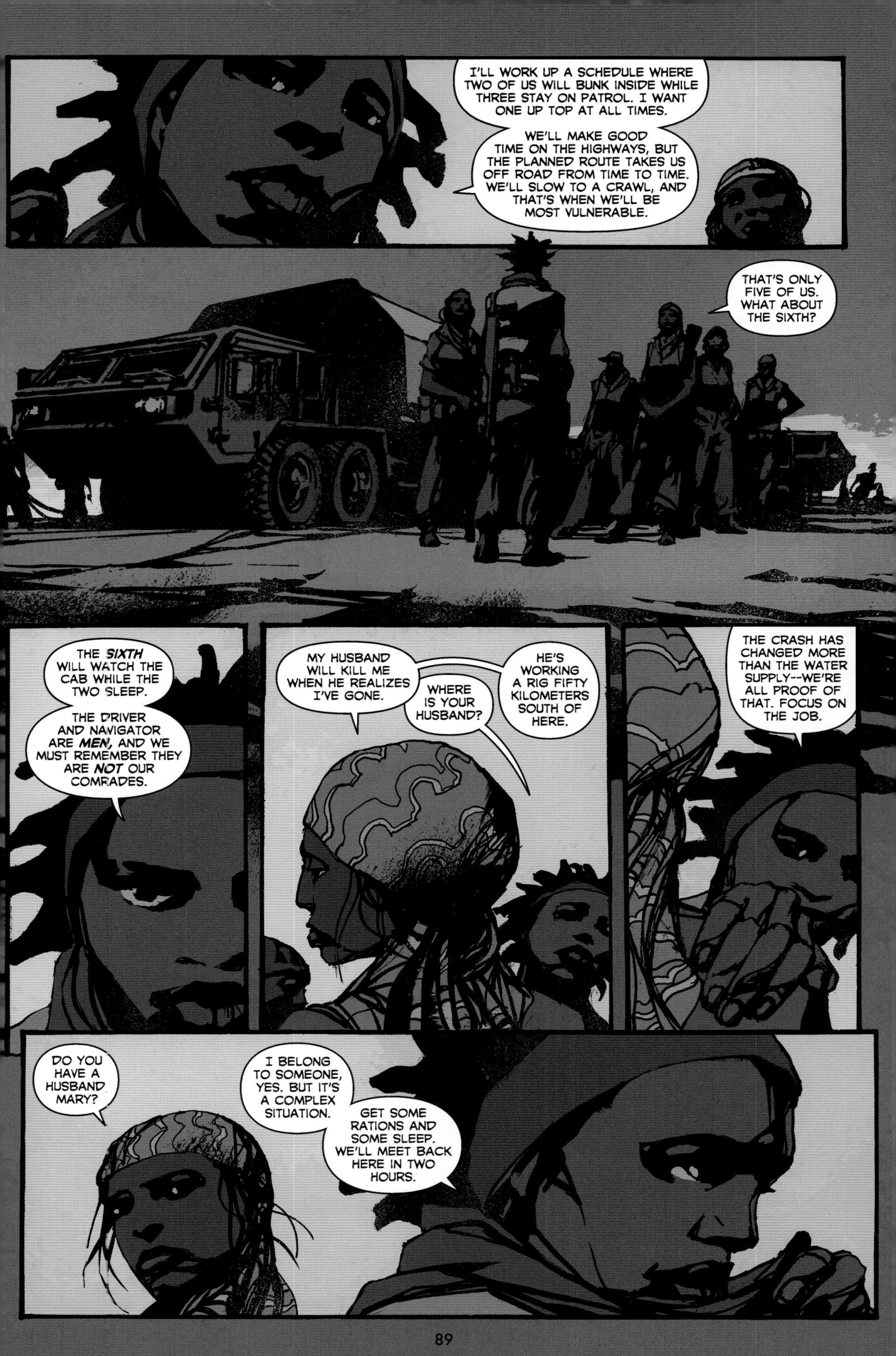
I'LL WORK UP A SCHEDULE WHERE TWO OF US WILL BUNK INSIDE WHILE THREE STAY ON PATROL. I WANT ONE UP TOP AT ALL TIMES.
WE'LL MAKE GOOD TIME ON THE HIGHWAYS, BUT THE PLANNED ROUTE TAKES US OFF ROAD FROM TIME TO TIME. WE'LL SLOW TO A CRAWL, AND THAT'S WHEN WE'LL BE MOST VULNERABLE.
THAT'S ONLY FIVE OF US. WHAT ABOUT THE SIXTH?
THE *SIXTH* WILL WATCH THE CAB WHILE THE TWO SLEEP.
THE DRIVER AND NAVIGATOR ARE *MEN*, AND WE MUST REMEMBER THEY ARE *NOT* OUR COMRADES.
MY HUSBAND WILL KILL ME WHEN HE REALIZES I'VE GONE.
WHERE IS YOUR HUSBAND?
HE'S WORKING A RIG FIFTY KILOMETERS SOUTH OF HERE.
THE CRASH HAS CHANGED MORE THAN THE WATER SUPPLY--WE'RE ALL PROOF OF THAT. FOCUS ON THE JOB.
DO YOU HAVE A HUSBAND MARY?
I BELONG TO SOMEONE, YES. BUT IT'S A COMPLEX SITUATION.
GET SOME RATIONS AND SOME SLEEP. WE'LL MEET BACK HERE IN TWO HOURS.

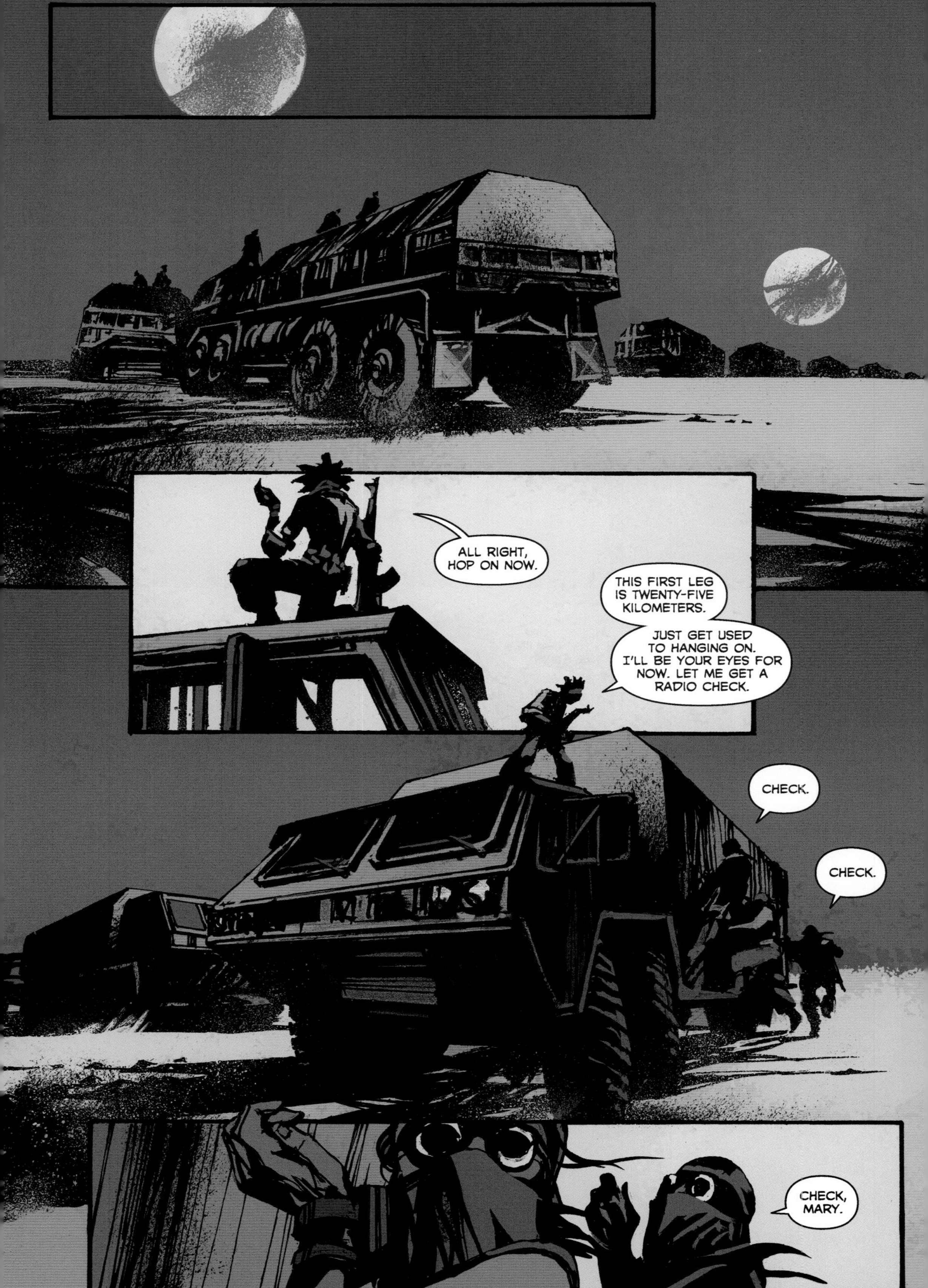
ALL RIGHT, HOP ON NOW.
THIS FIRST LEG IS TWENTY-FIVE KILOMETERS.
JUST GET USED TO HANGING ON. I'LL BE YOUR EYES FOR NOW. LET ME GET A RADIO CHECK.
CHECK.
CHECK.
CHECK, MARY.

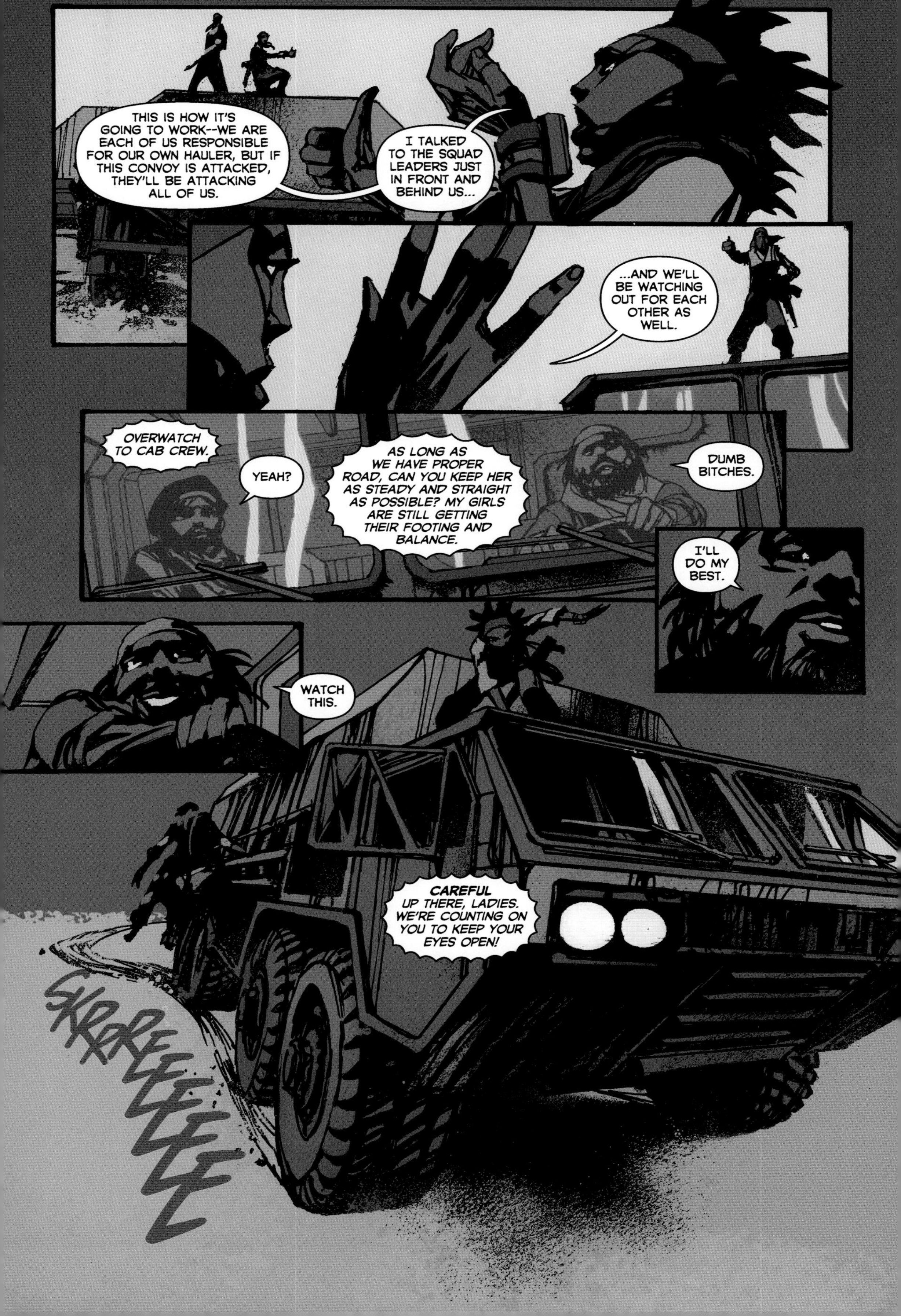
THIS IS HOW IT'S GOING TO WORK--WE ARE EACH OF US RESPONSIBLE FOR OUR OWN HAULER, BUT IF THIS CONVOY IS ATTACKED, THEY'LL BE ATTACKING ALL OF US.
I TALKED TO THE SQUAD LEADERS JUST IN FRONT AND BEHIND US...
...AND WE'LL BE WATCHING OUT FOR EACH OTHER AS WELL.
OVERWATCH TO CAB CREW.
YEAH?
AS LONG AS WE HAVE PROPER ROAD, CAN YOU KEEP HER AS STEADY AND STRAIGHT AS POSSIBLE? MY GIRLS ARE STILL GETTING THEIR FOOTING AND BALANCE.
DUMB BITCHES.
I'LL DO MY BEST.
WATCH THIS.
CAREFUL UP THERE, LADIES. WE'RE COUNTING ON YOU TO KEEP YOUR EYES OPEN!
SKREEEEEE

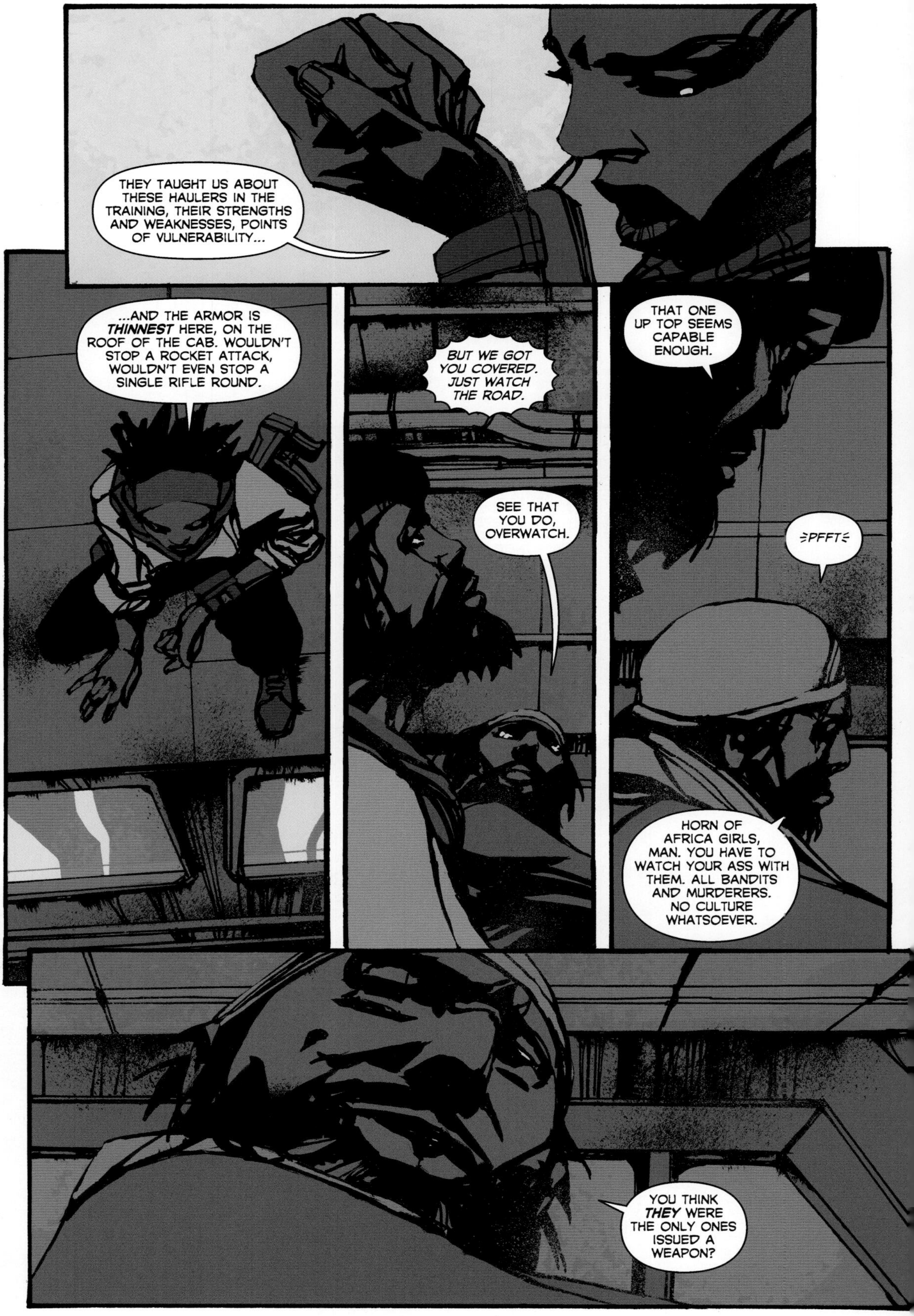
THEY TAUGHT US ABOUT THESE HAULERS IN THE TRAINING, THEIR STRENGTHS AND WEAKNESSES, POINTS OF VULNERABILITY...
...AND THE ARMOR IS *THINNEST* HERE, ON THE ROOF OF THE CAB. WOULDN'T STOP A ROCKET ATTACK, WOULDN'T EVEN STOP A SINGLE RIFLE ROUND.
BUT WE GOT YOU COVERED. JUST WATCH THE ROAD.
SEE THAT YOU DO, OVERWATCH.
THAT ONE UP TOP SEEMS CAPABLE ENOUGH.
PFFT
HORN OF AFRICA GIRLS, MAN. YOU HAVE TO WATCH YOUR ASS WITH THEM. ALL BANDITS AND MURDERERS. NO CULTURE WHATSOEVER.
YOU THINK *THEY* WERE THE ONLY ONES ISSUED A WEAPON?

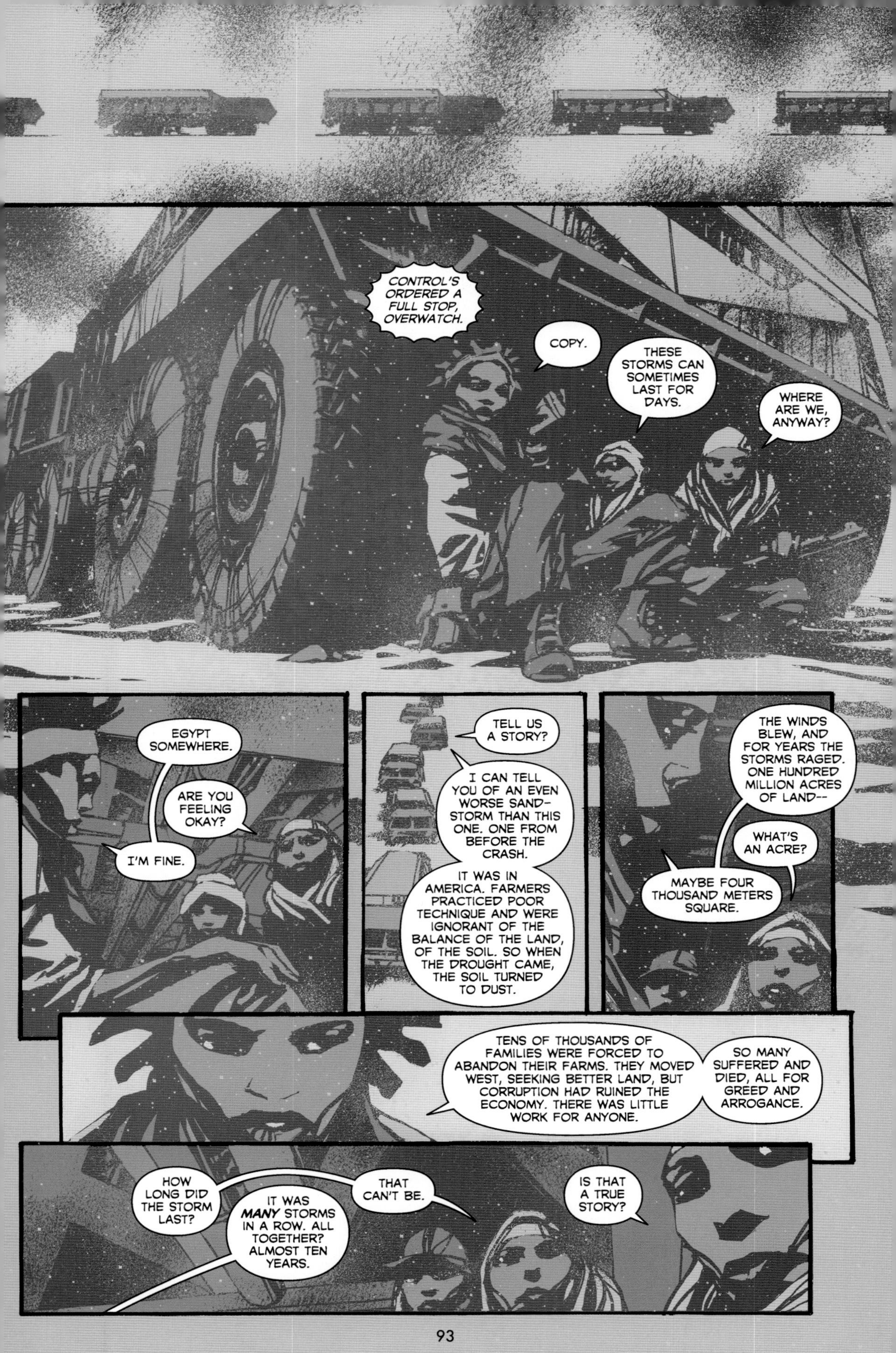
CONTROL'S ORDERED A FULL STOP, OVERWATCH.
COPY.
THESE STORMS CAN SOMETIMES LAST FOR DAYS.
WHERE ARE WE, ANYWAY?
EGYPT SOMEWHERE.
ARE YOU FEELING OKAY?
I'M FINE.
TELL US A STORY?
I CAN TELL YOU OF AN EVEN WORSE SAND-STORM THAN THIS ONE. ONE FROM BEFORE THE CRASH.
IT WAS IN AMERICA. FARMERS PRACTICED POOR TECHNIQUE AND WERE IGNORANT OF THE BALANCE OF THE LAND, OF THE SOIL. SO WHEN THE DROUGHT CAME, THE SOIL TURNED TO DUST.
THE WINDS BLEW, AND FOR YEARS THE STORMS RAGED. ONE HUNDRED MILLION ACRES OF LAND--
WHAT'S AN ACRE?
MAYBE FOUR THOUSAND METERS SQUARE.
TENS OF THOUSANDS OF FAMILIES WERE FORCED TO ABANDON THEIR FARMS. THEY MOVED WEST, SEEKING BETTER LAND, BUT CORRUPTION HAD RUINED THE ECONOMY. THERE WAS LITTLE WORK FOR ANYONE.
SO MANY SUFFERED AND DIED, ALL FOR GREED AND ARROGANCE.
HOW LONG DID THE STORM LAST?
IT WAS MANY STORMS IN A ROW. ALL TOGETHER? ALMOST TEN YEARS.
THAT CAN'T BE.
IS THAT A TRUE STORY?

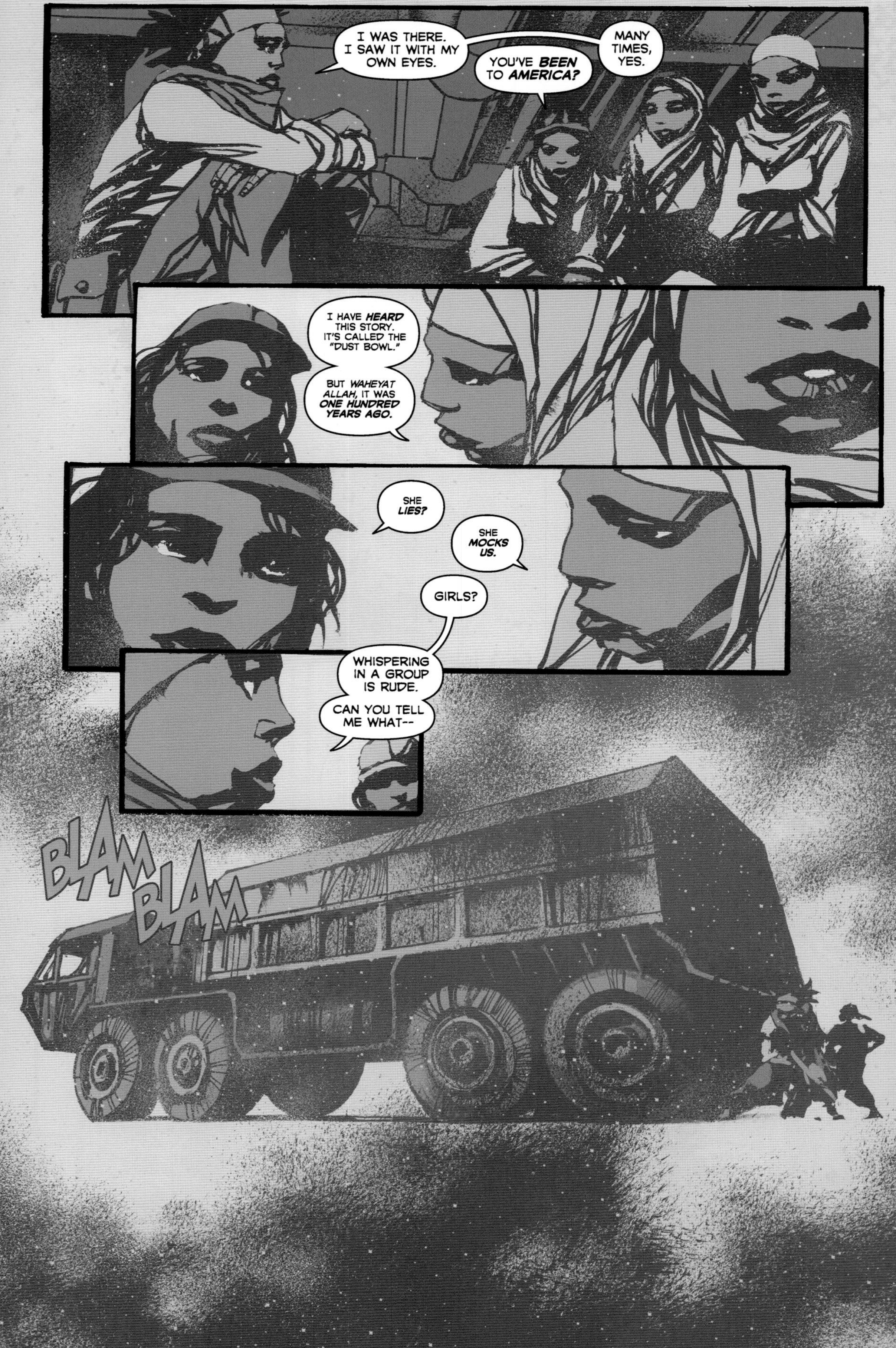

I WAS THERE. I SAW IT WITH MY OWN EYES.
YOU'VE BEEN TO AMERICA?
MANY TIMES, YES.
I HAVE HEARD THIS STORY. IT'S CALLED THE "DUST BOWL."
BUT WAHEYAT ALLAH, IT WAS ONE HUNDRED YEARS AGO.
SHE LIES?
SHE MOCKS US.
GIRLS?
WHISPERING IN A GROUP IS RUDE.
CAN YOU TELL ME WHAT--
BLAM BLAM

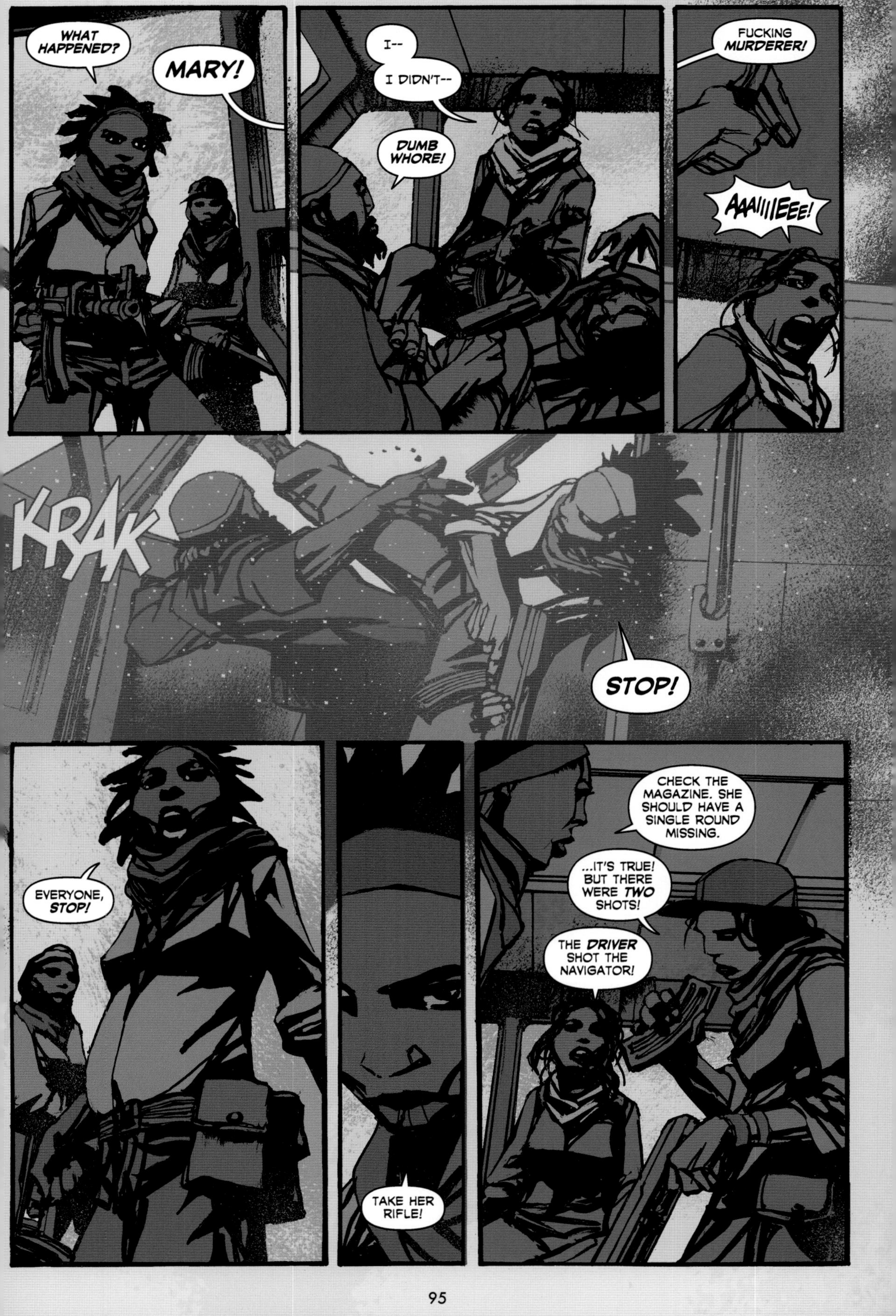
WHAT HAPPENED?
MARY!
I--
I DIDN'T--
DUMB WHORE!
FUCKING MURDERER!
AAAIIIIEEE!
KRAK
STOP!
EVERYONE, STOP!
TAKE HER RIFLE!
CHECK THE MAGAZINE. SHE SHOULD HAVE A SINGLE ROUND MISSING.
...IT'S TRUE! BUT THERE WERE TWO SHOTS!
THE DRIVER SHOT THE NAVIGATOR!

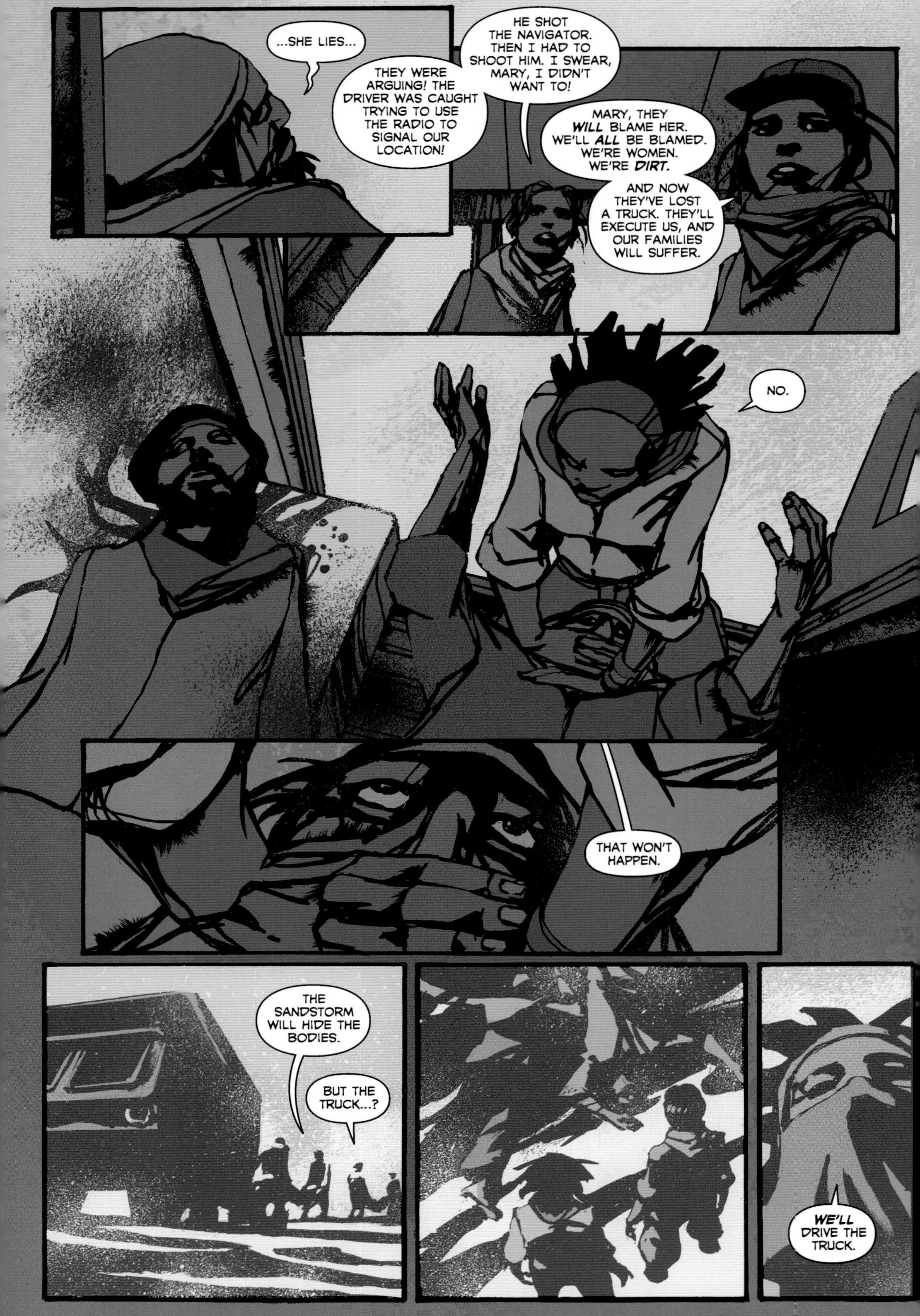
...SHE LIES...
THEY WERE ARGUING! THE DRIVER WAS CAUGHT TRYING TO USE THE RADIO TO SIGNAL OUR LOCATION!
HE SHOT THE NAVIGATOR. THEN I HAD TO SHOOT HIM. I SWEAR, MARY, I DIDN'T WANT TO!
MARY, THEY WILL BLAME HER. WE'LL ALL BE BLAMED. WE'RE WOMEN. WE'RE DIRT.
AND NOW THEY'VE LOST A TRUCK. THEY'LL EXECUTE US, AND OUR FAMILIES WILL SUFFER.
NO.
THAT WON'T HAPPEN.
THE SANDSTORM WILL HIDE THE BODIES.
BUT THE TRUCK...?
WE'LL DRIVE THE TRUCK.

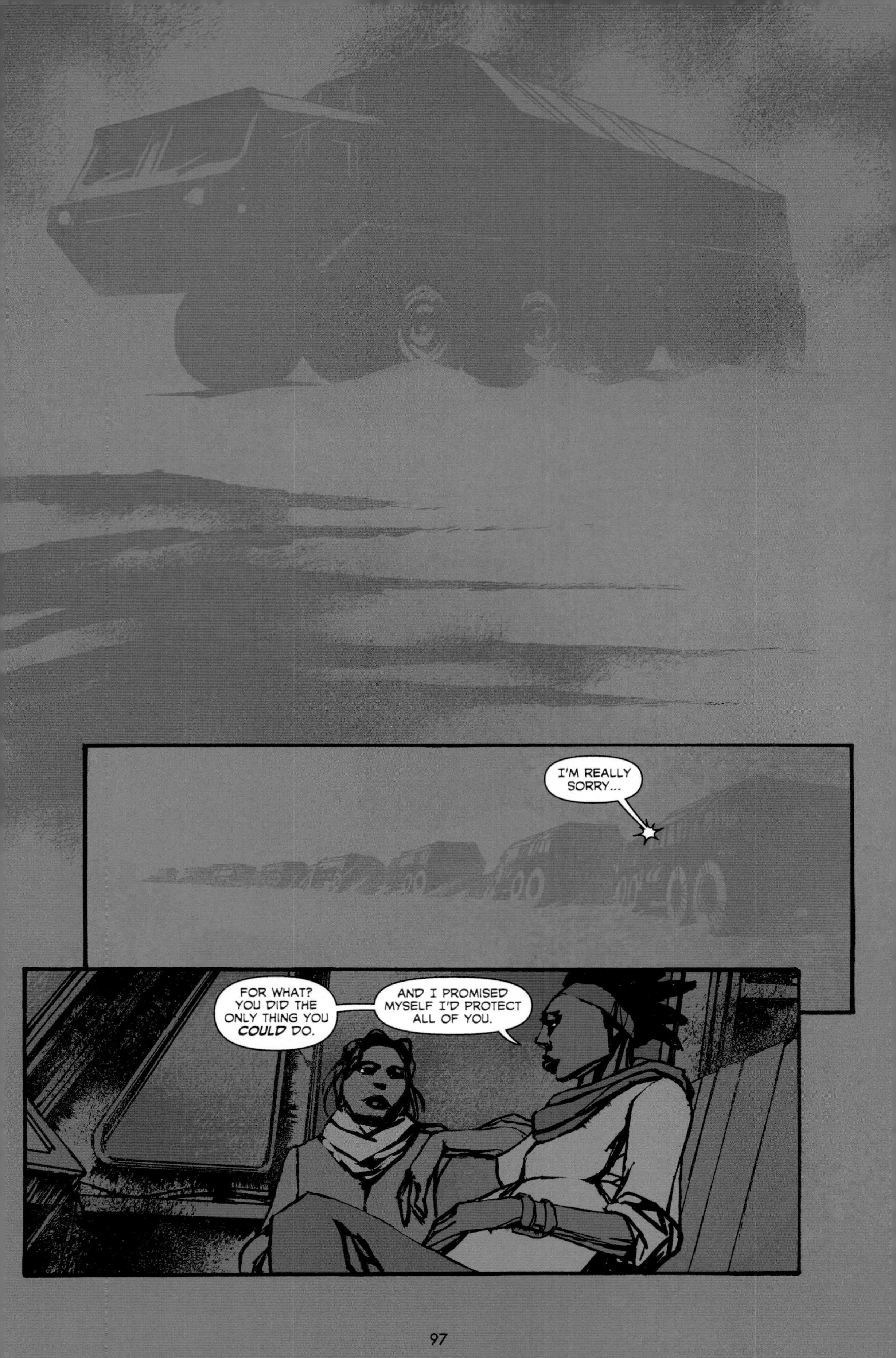
I'M REALLY SORRY...
FOR WHAT? YOU DID THE ONLY THING YOU COULD DO.
AND I PROMISED MYSELF I'D PROTECT ALL OF YOU.

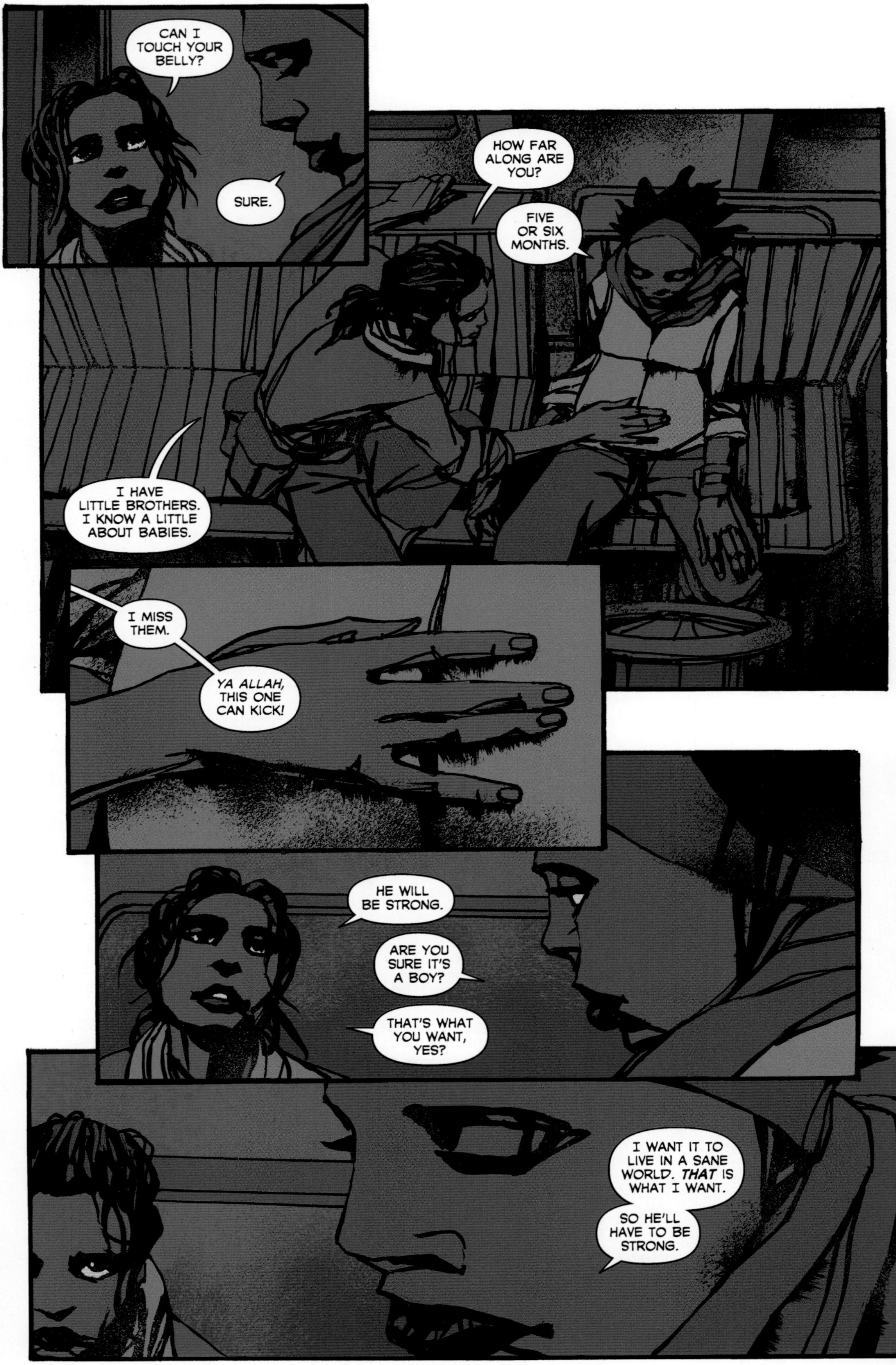
CAN I TOUCH YOUR BELLY?
SURE.
HOW FAR ALONG ARE YOU?
FIVE OR SIX MONTHS.
I HAVE LITTLE BROTHERS. I KNOW A LITTLE ABOUT BABIES.
I MISS THEM.
YA ALLAH, THIS ONE CAN KICK!
HE WILL BE STRONG.
ARE YOU SURE IT'S A BOY?
THAT'S WHAT YOU WANT, YES?
I WANT IT TO LIVE IN A SANE WORLD. ***THAT*** IS WHAT I WANT.
SO HE'LL HAVE TO BE STRONG.

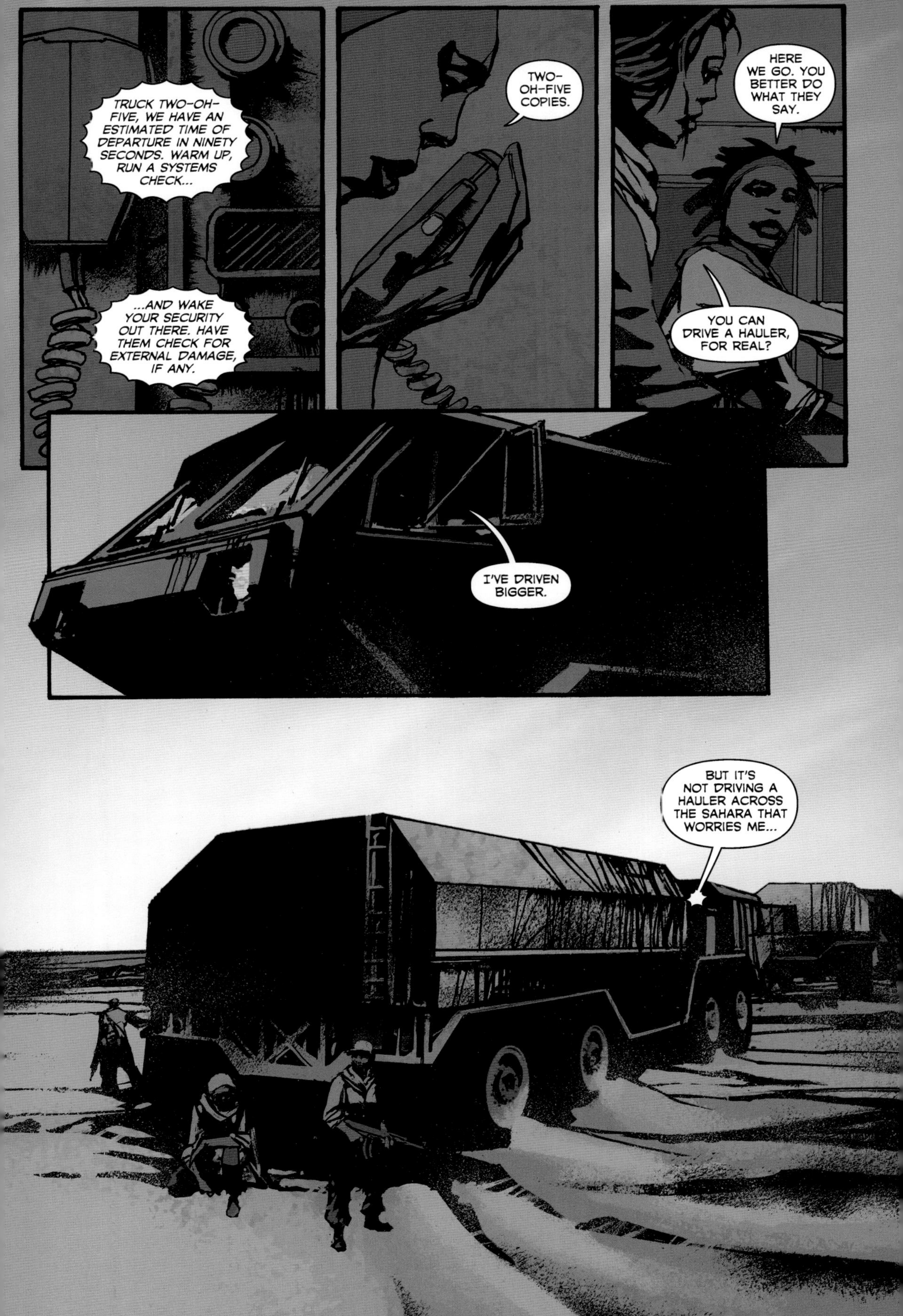
TRUCK TWO-OH-FIVE, WE HAVE AN ESTIMATED TIME OF DEPARTURE IN NINETY SECONDS. WARM UP, RUN A SYSTEMS CHECK...
...AND WAKE YOUR SECURITY OUT THERE. HAVE THEM CHECK FOR EXTERNAL DAMAGE, IF ANY.
TWO-OH-FIVE COPIES.
HERE WE GO. YOU BETTER DO WHAT THEY SAY.
YOU CAN DRIVE A HAULER, FOR REAL?
I'VE DRIVEN BIGGER.
BUT IT'S NOT DRIVING A HAULER ACROSS THE SAHARA THAT WORRIES ME...

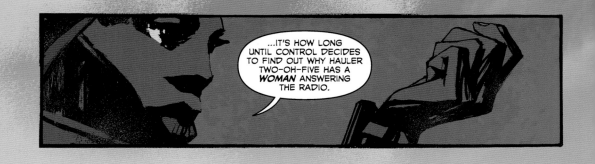

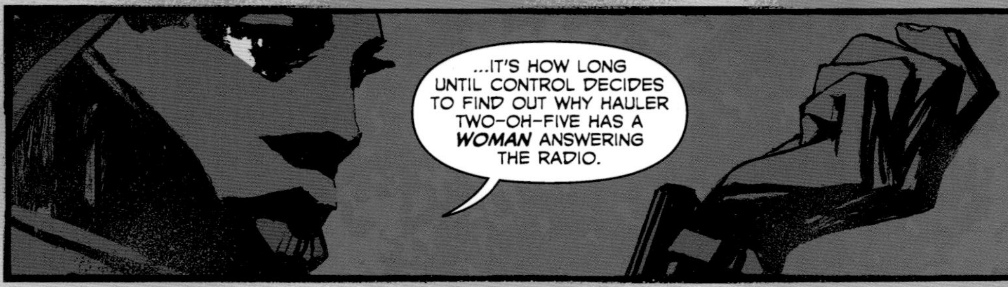
...IT'S HOW LONG UNTIL CONTROL DECIDES TO FIND OUT WHY HAULER TWO-OH-FIVE HAS A WOMAN ANSWERING THE RADIO.

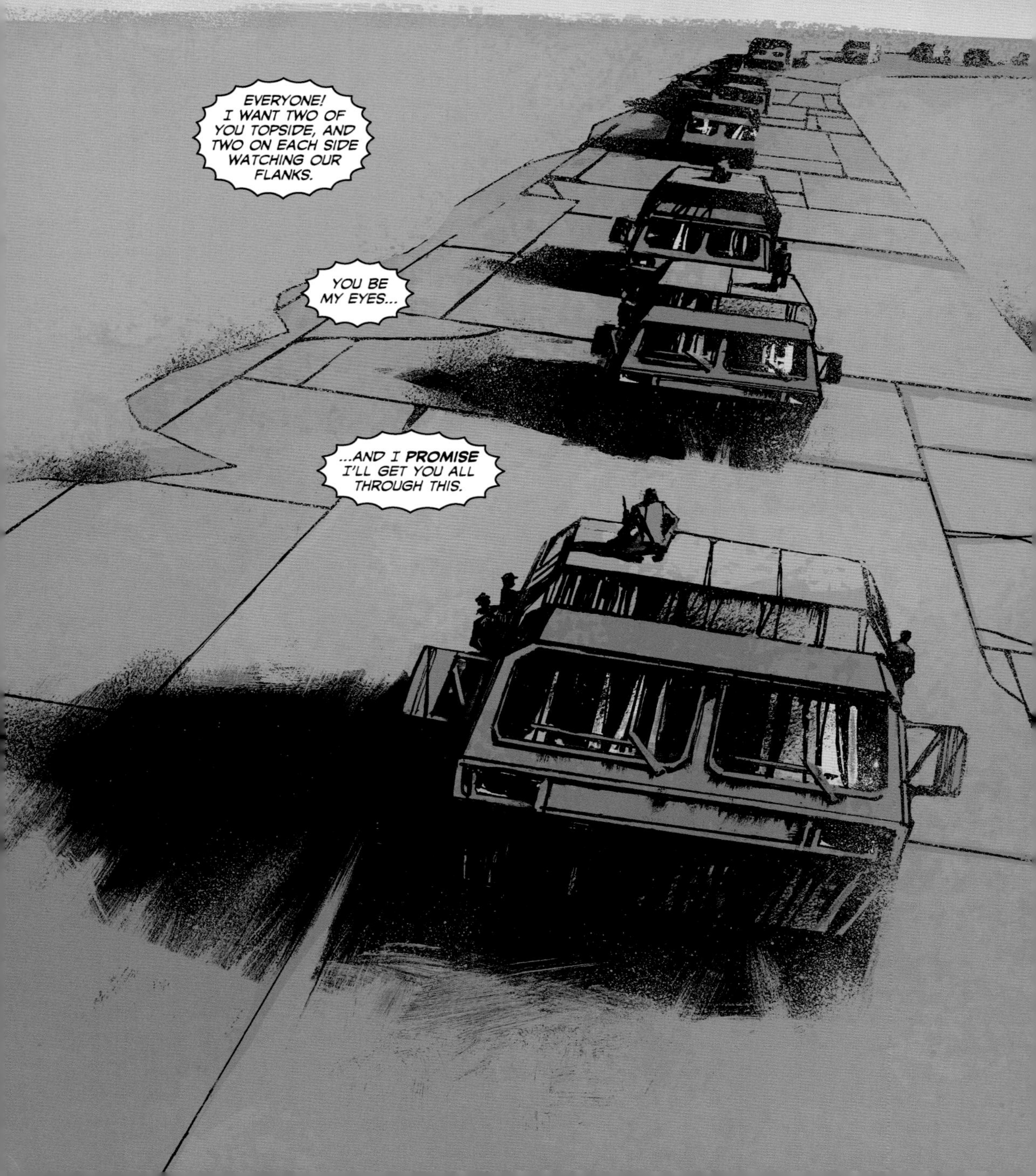
EVERYONE! I WANT TWO OF YOU TOPSIDE, AND TWO ON EACH SIDE WATCHING OUR FLANKS.
YOU BE MY EYES...
...AND I PROMISE I'LL GET YOU ALL THROUGH THIS.

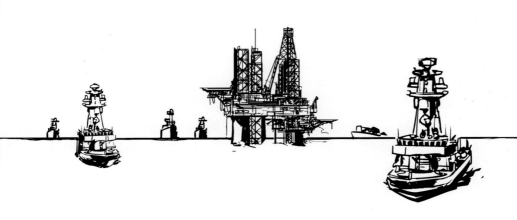

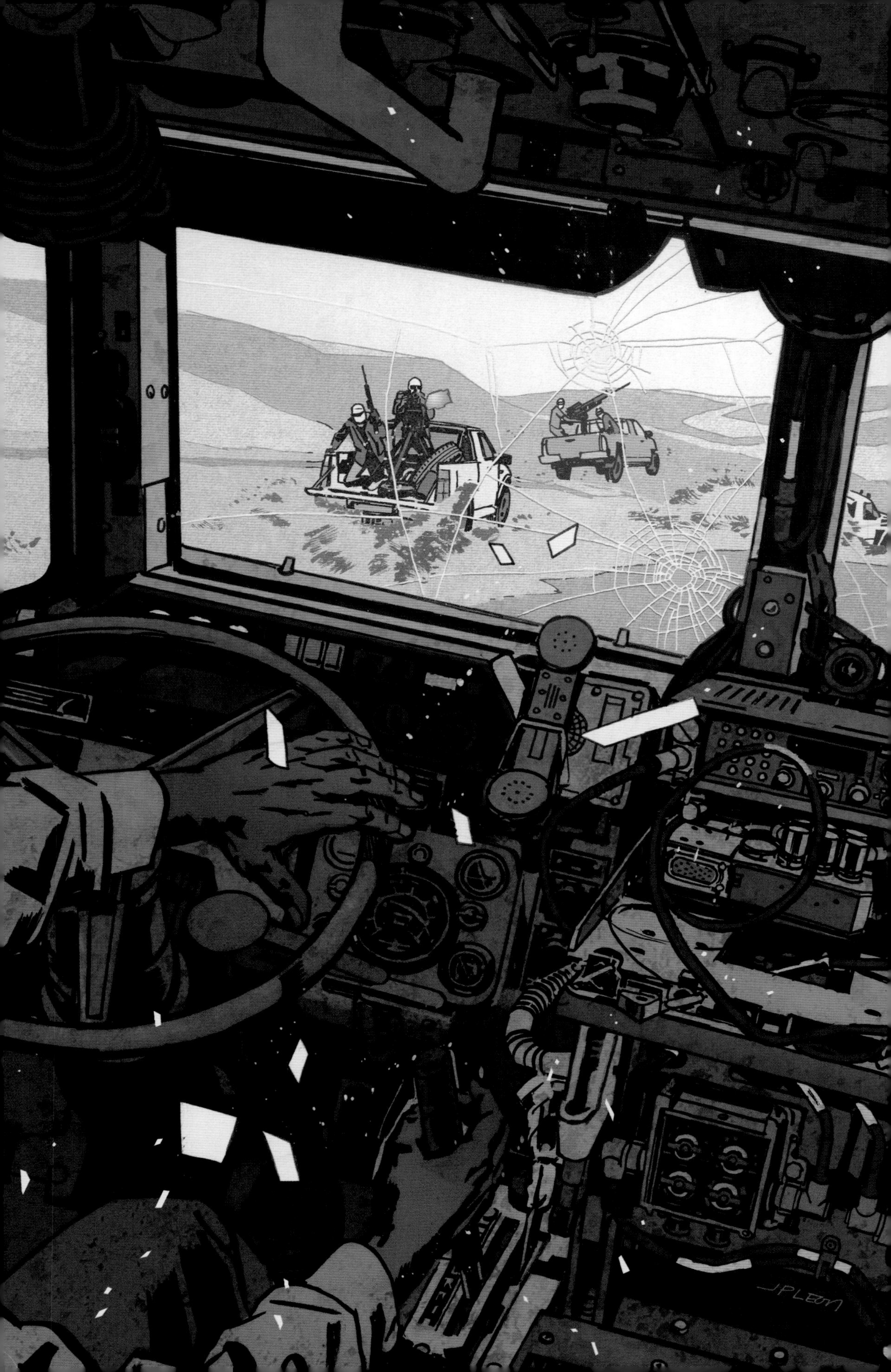
JPLEON

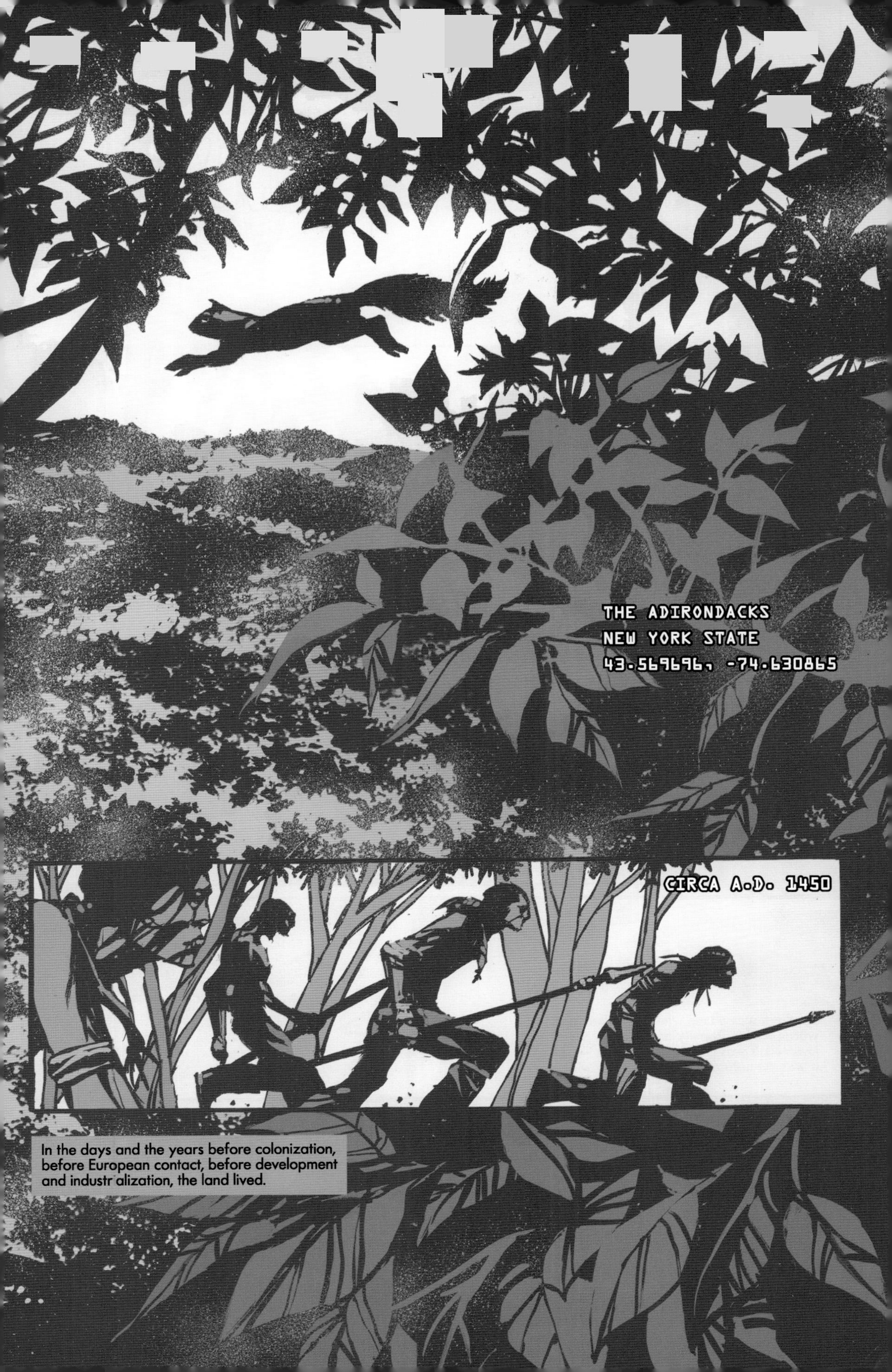
THE ADIRONDACKS
NEW YORK STATE
43.569696, -74.630865
CIRCA A.D. 1450
In the days and the years before colonization, before European contact, before development and industrialization, the land lived.

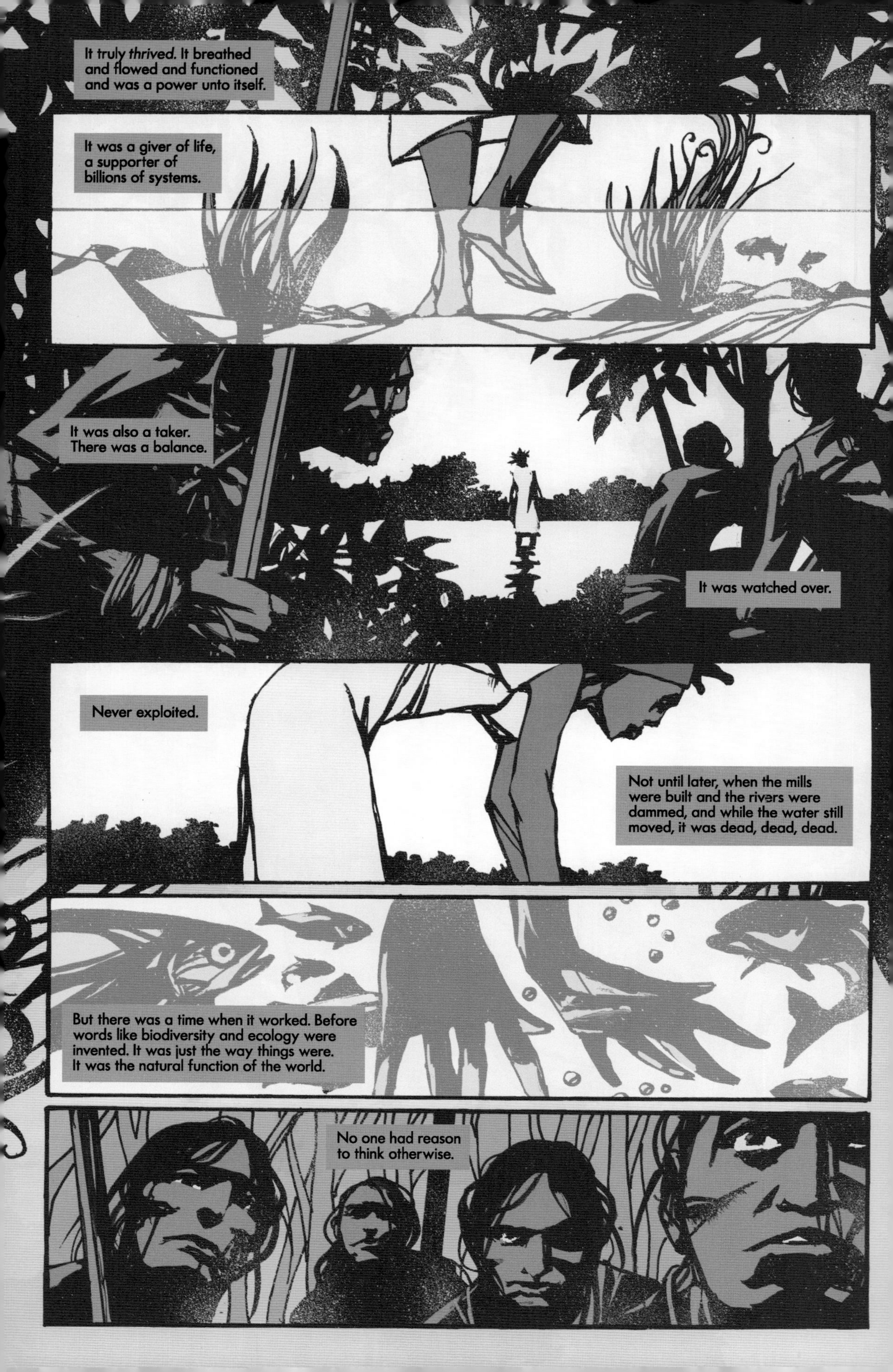
It truly *thrived.* It breathed and flowed and functioned and was a power unto itself.
It was a giver of life, a supporter of billions of systems.
It was also a taker. There was a balance.
It was watched over.
Never exploited.
Not until later, when the mills were built and the rivers were dammed, and while the water still moved, it was dead, dead, dead.
But there was a time when it worked. Before words like biodiversity and ecology were invented. It was just the way things were. It was the natural function of the world.
No one had reason to think otherwise.

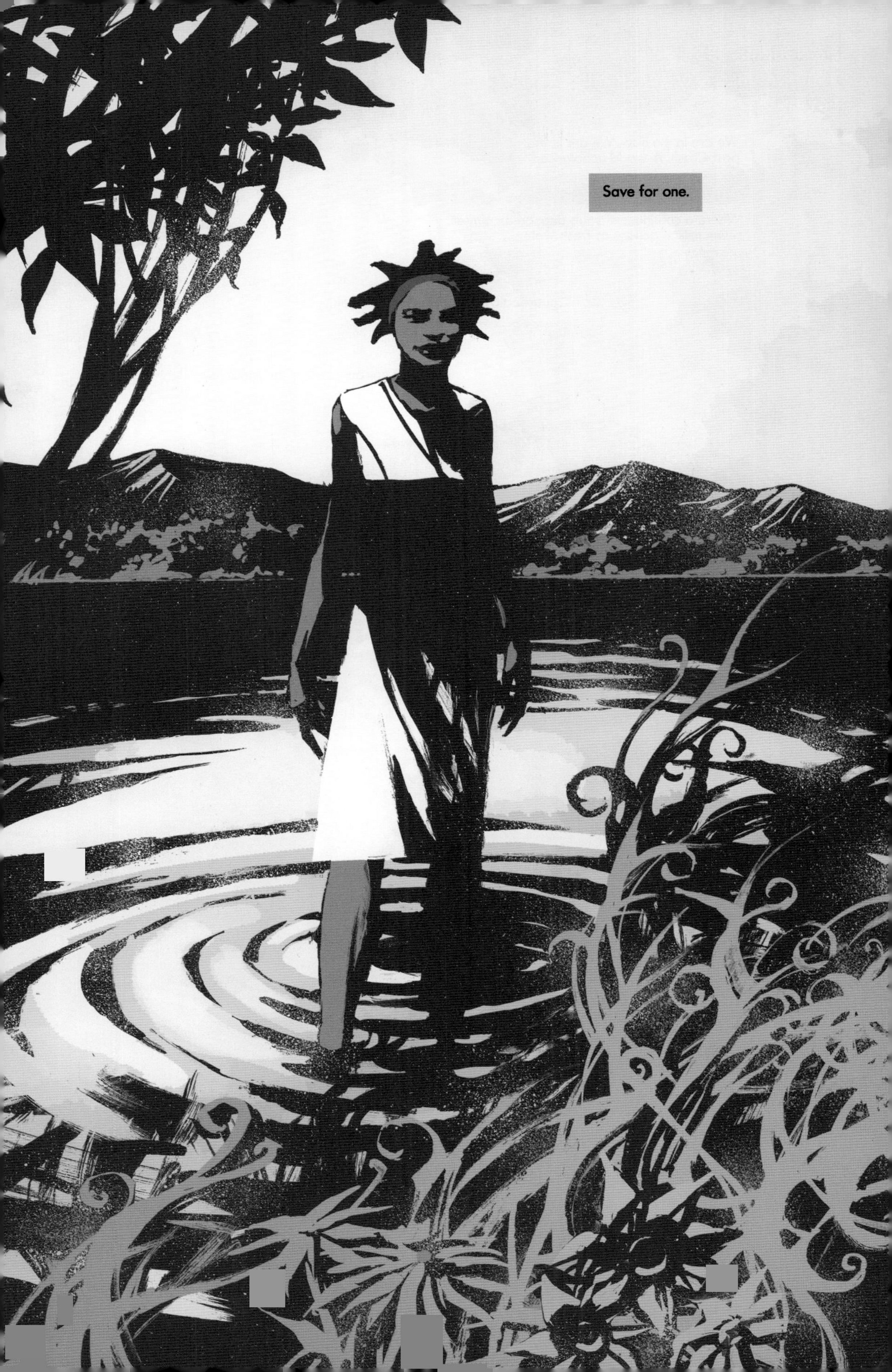
Save for one.

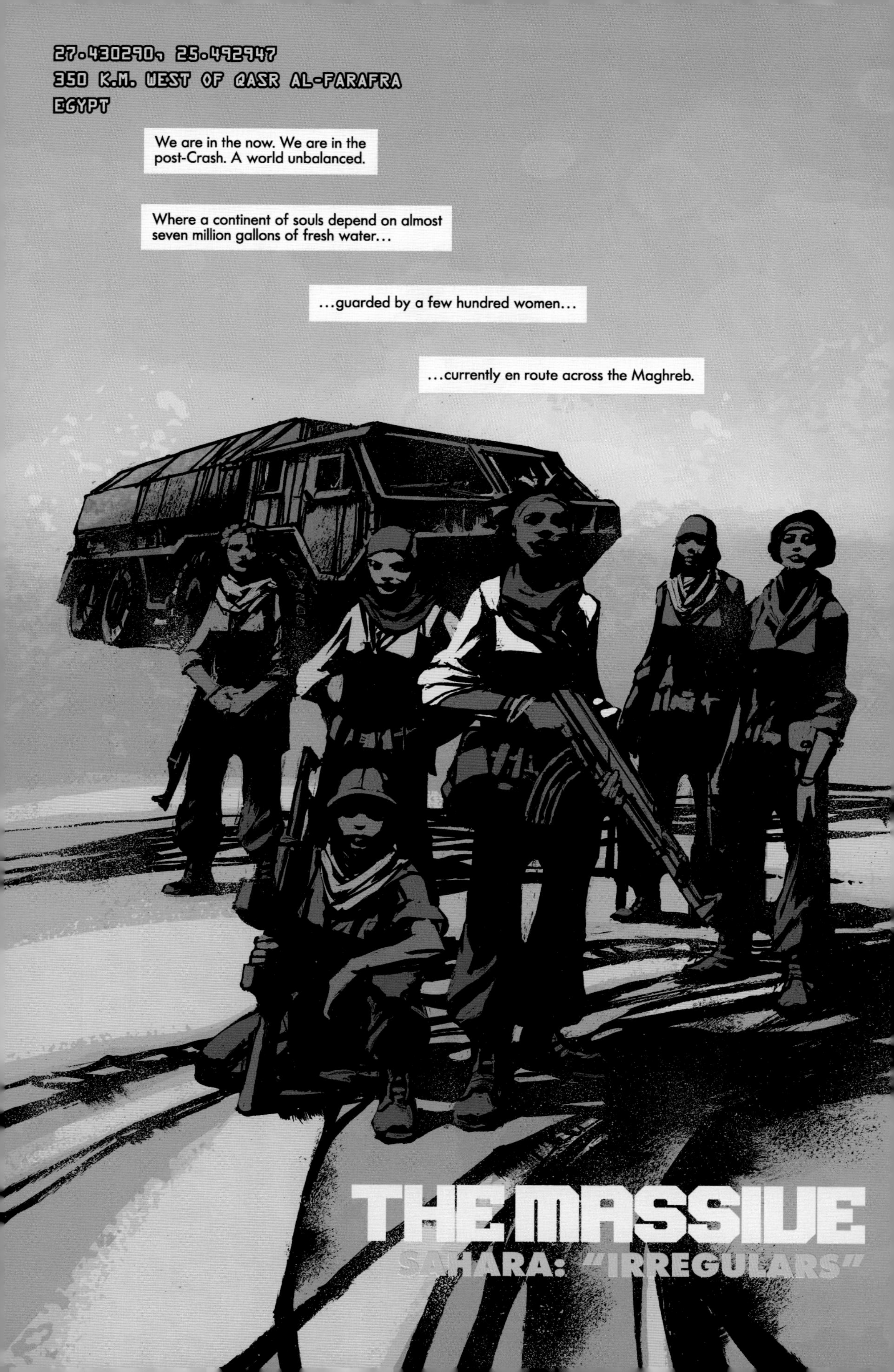
27.430290, 25.492947
350 K.M. WEST OF QASR AL-FARAFRA
EGYPT
We are in the now. We are in the post-Crash. A world unbalanced.
Where a continent of souls depend on almost seven million gallons of fresh water...
...guarded by a few hundred women...
...currently en route across the Maghreb.
THE MASSIVE
SAHARA: "IRREGULARS"

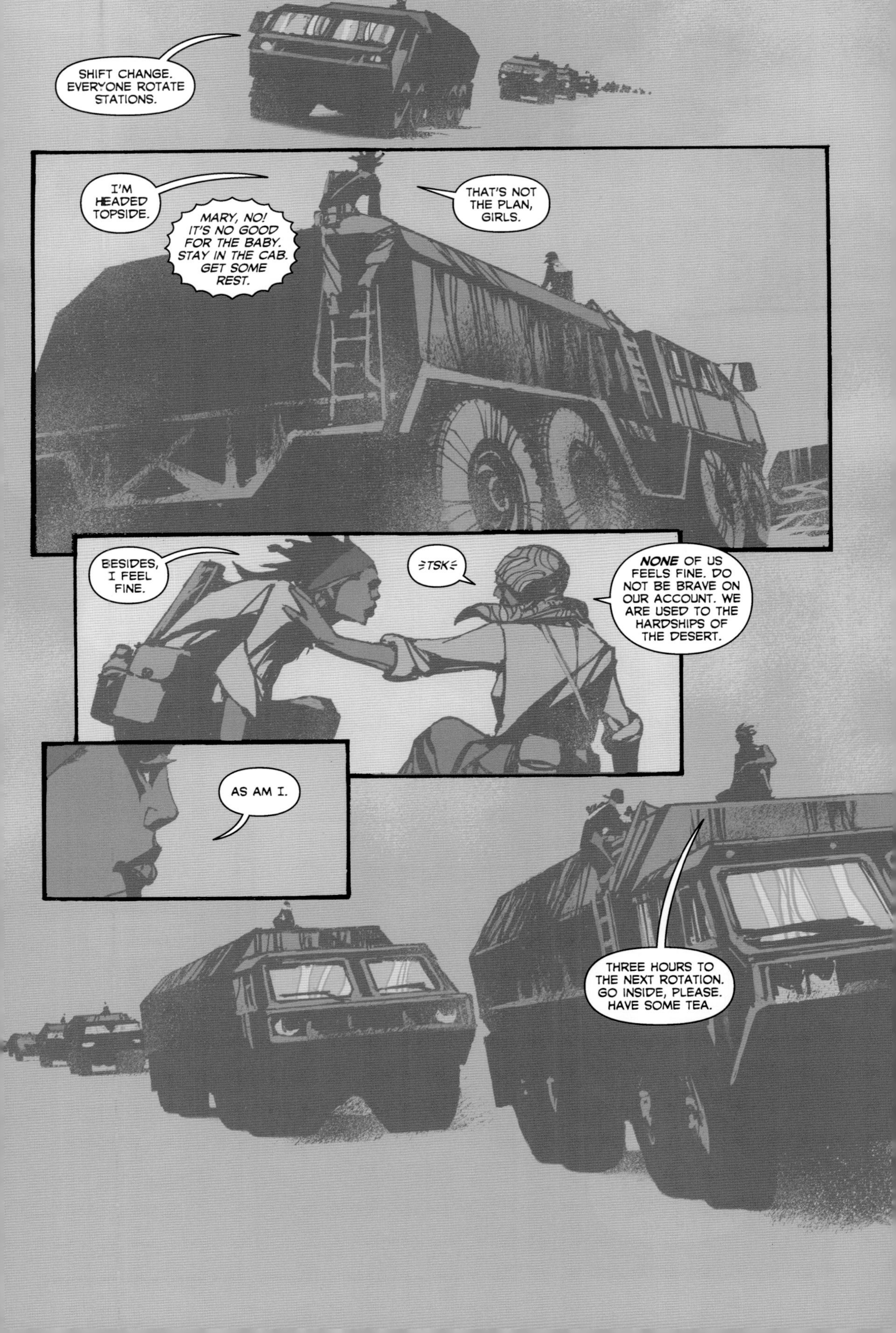
SHIFT CHANGE. EVERYONE ROTATE STATIONS.
I'M HEADED TOPSIDE.
MARY, NO! IT'S NO GOOD FOR THE BABY. STAY IN THE CAB. GET SOME REST.
THAT'S NOT THE PLAN, GIRLS.
BESIDES, I FEEL FINE.
TSK
NONE OF US FEELS FINE. DO NOT BE BRAVE ON OUR ACCOUNT. WE ARE USED TO THE HARDSHIPS OF THE DESERT.
AS AM I.
THREE HOURS TO THE NEXT ROTATION. GO INSIDE, PLEASE. HAVE SOME TEA.

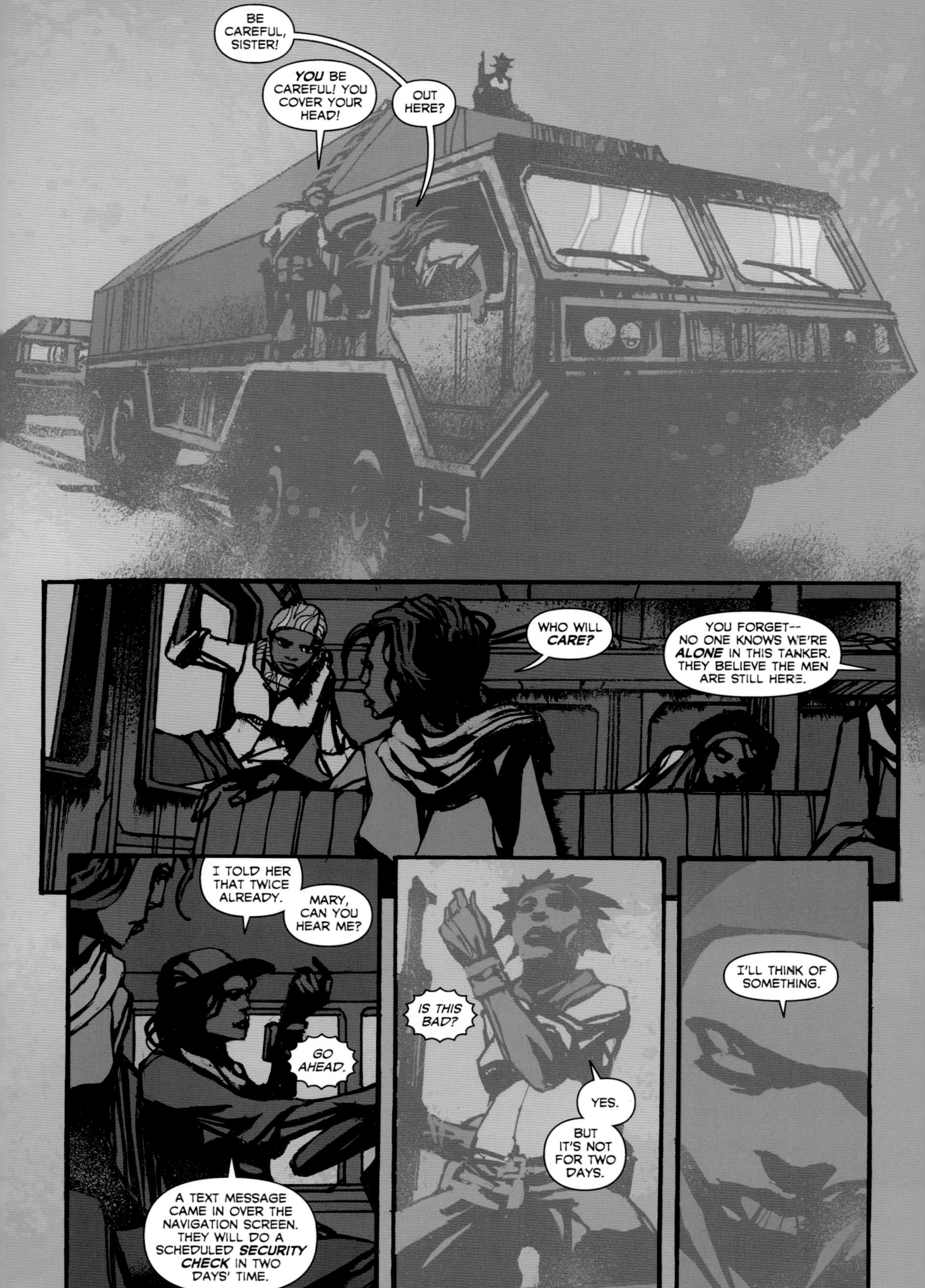
BE CAREFUL, SISTER!
OUT HERE?
YOU BE CAREFUL! YOU COVER YOUR HEAD!
WHO WILL *CARE?*
YOU FORGET-- NO ONE KNOWS WE'RE *ALONE* IN THIS TANKER. THEY BELIEVE THE MEN ARE STILL HERE.
I TOLD HER THAT TWICE ALREADY.
MARY, CAN YOU HEAR ME?
GO AHEAD.
A TEXT MESSAGE CAME IN OVER THE NAVIGATION SCREEN. THEY WILL DO A SCHEDULED *SECURITY CHECK* IN TWO DAYS' TIME.
IS THIS BAD?
YES.
BUT IT'S NOT FOR TWO DAYS.
I'LL THINK OF SOMETHING.

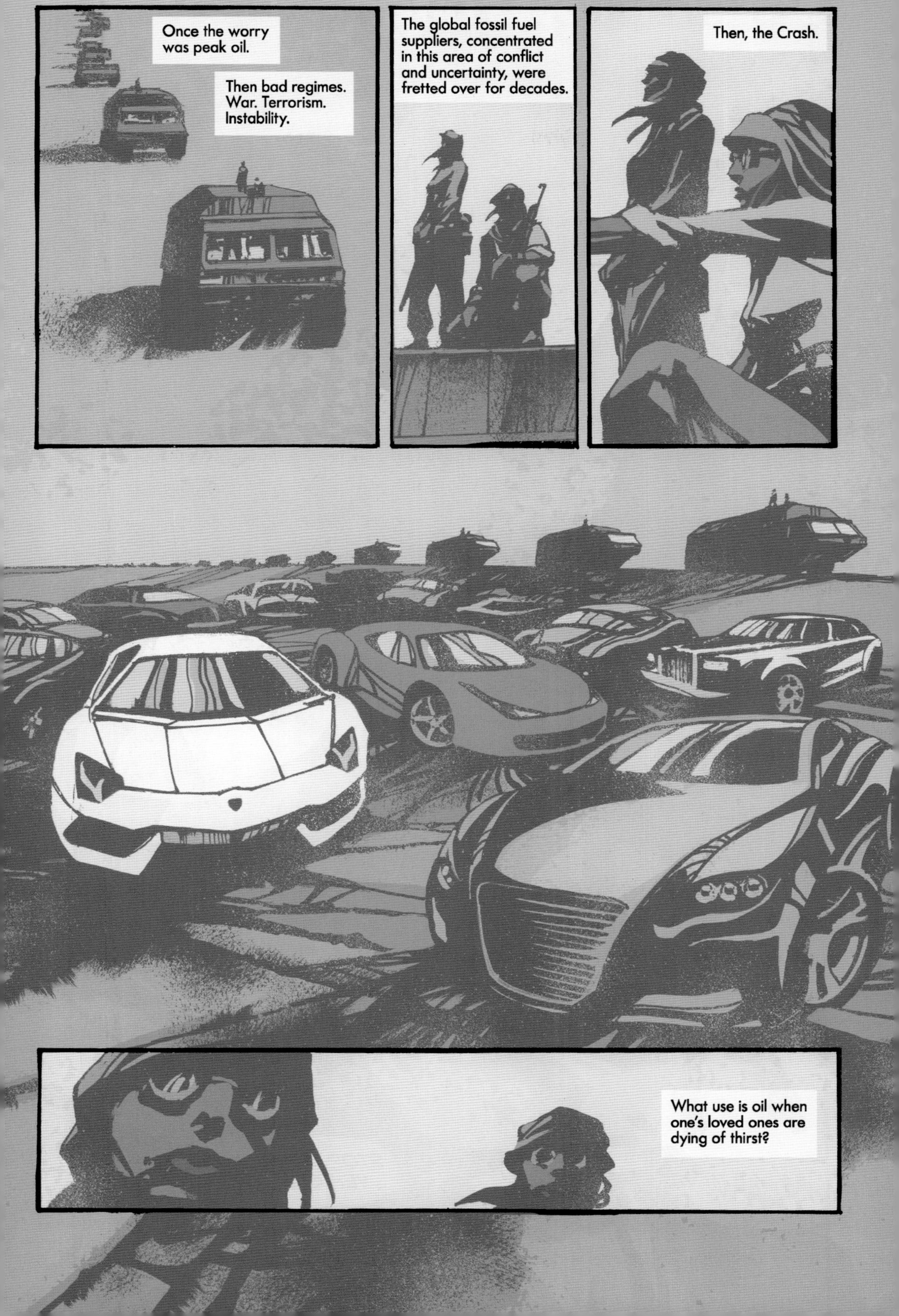
Once the worry was peak oil.
Then bad regimes. War. Terrorism. Instability.
The global fossil fuel suppliers, concentrated in this area of conflict and uncertainty, were fretted over for decades.
Then, the Crash.
What use is oil when one's loved ones are dying of thirst?

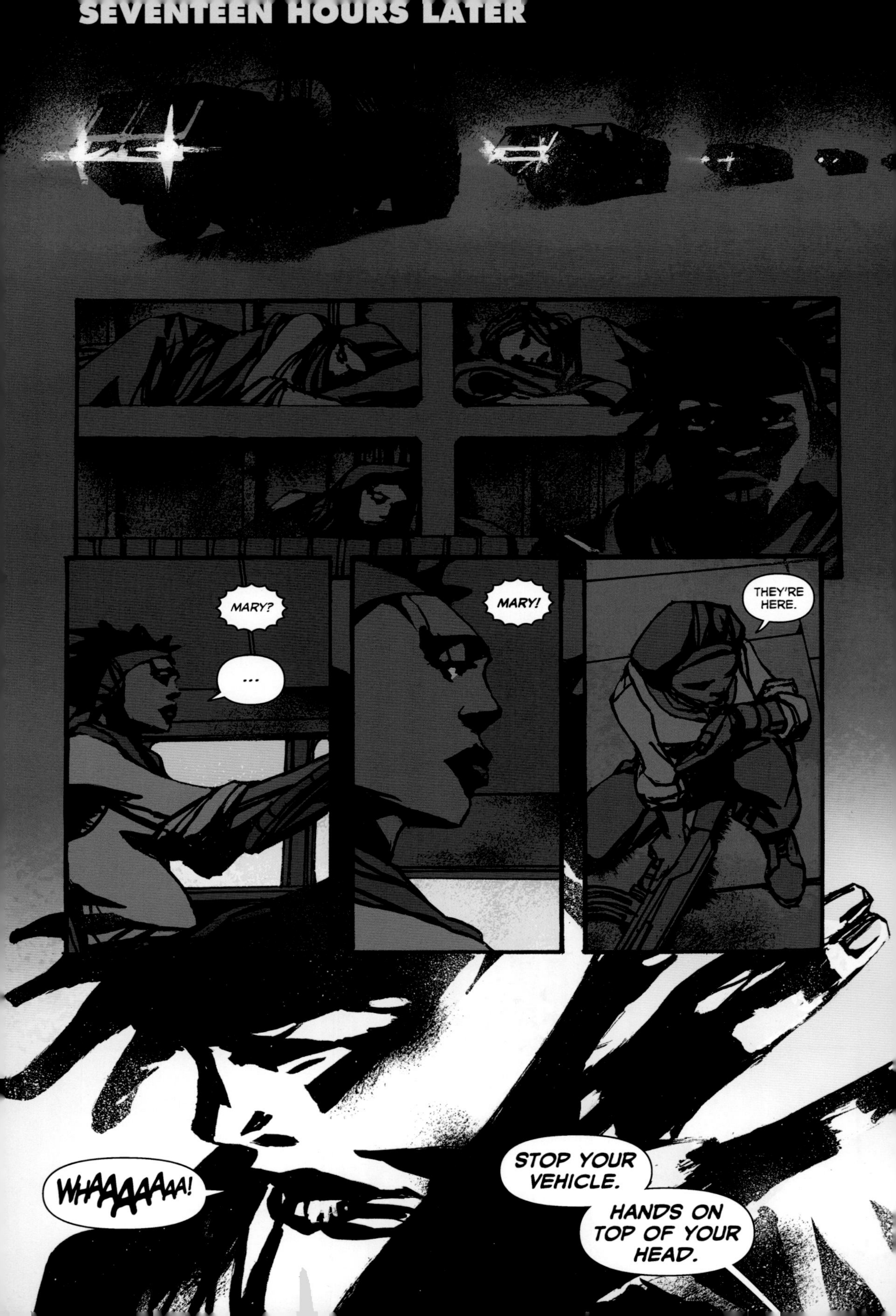
SEVENTEEN HOURS LATER
MARY?
...
MARY!
THEY'RE HERE.
WHAAAAAAA!
STOP YOUR VEHICLE.
HANDS ON TOP OF YOUR HEAD.

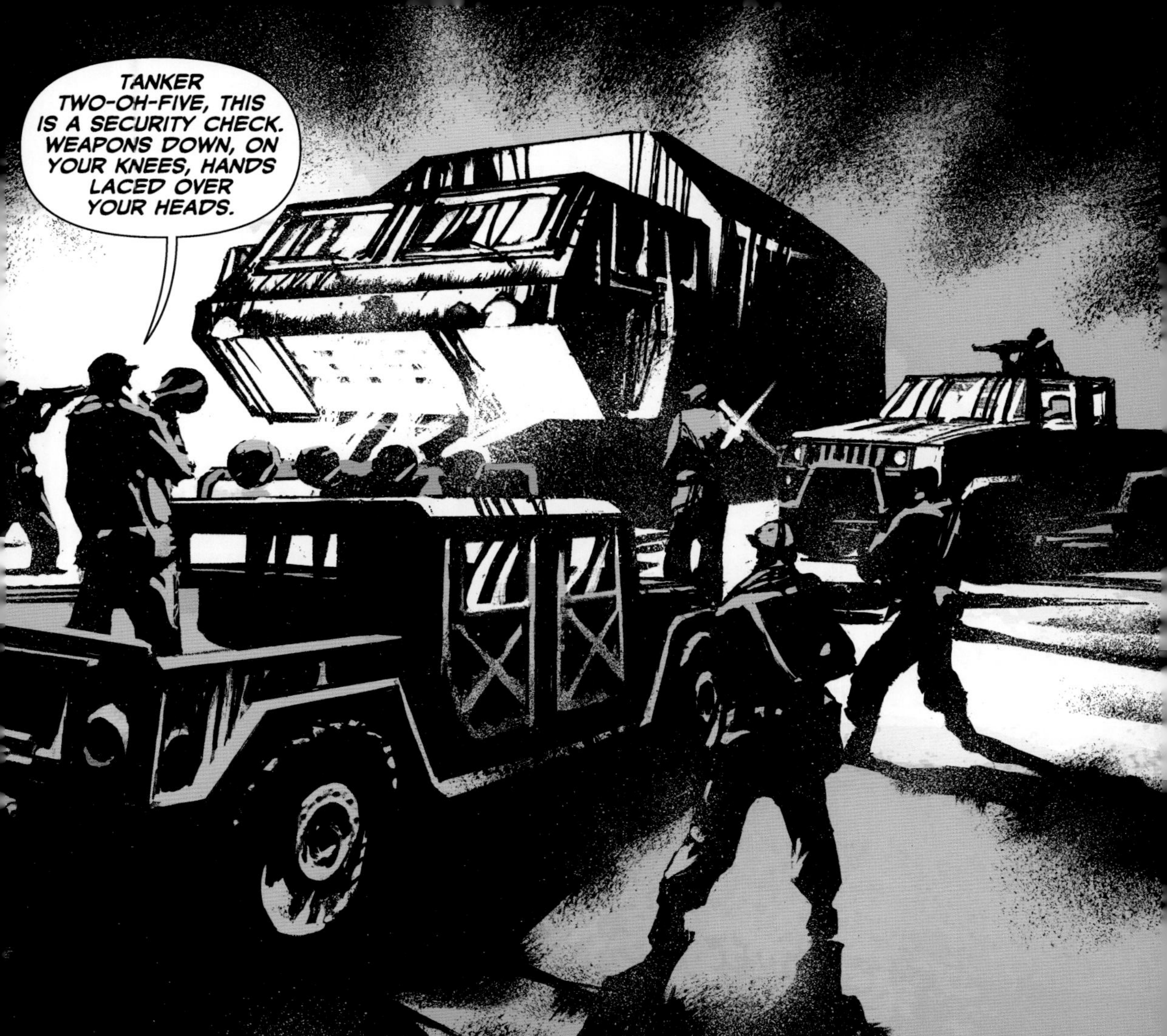
TANKER TWO-OH-FIVE, THIS IS A SECURITY CHECK. WEAPONS DOWN, ON YOUR KNEES, HANDS LACED OVER YOUR HEADS.

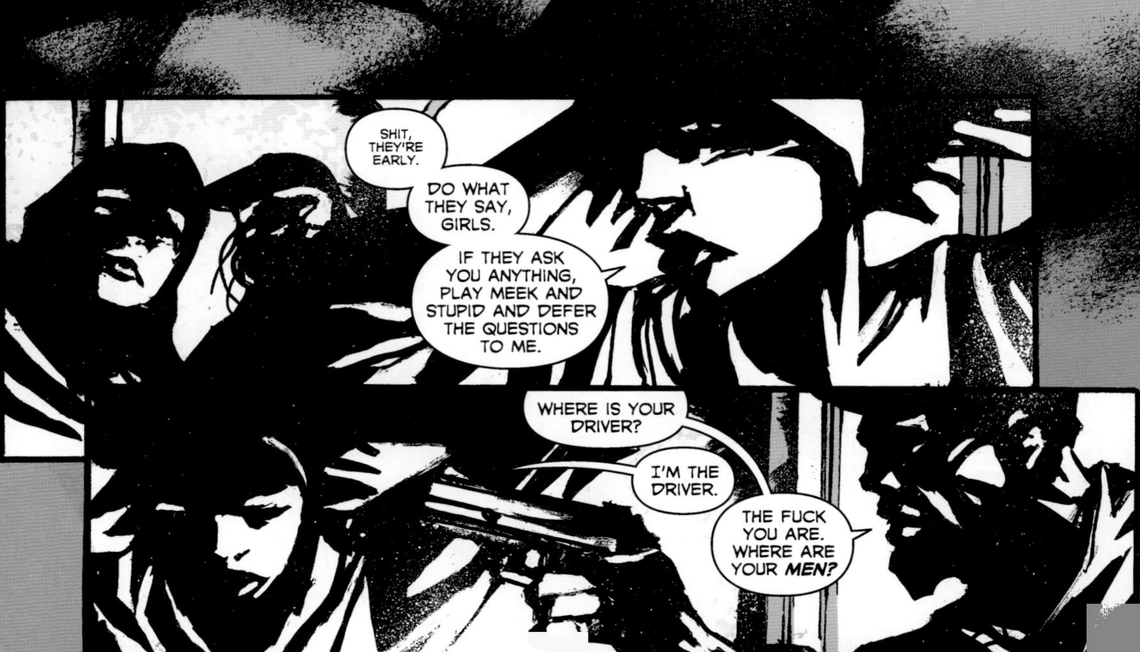
SHIT, THEY'RE EARLY.
DO WHAT THEY SAY, GIRLS.
IF THEY ASK YOU ANYTHING, PLAY MEEK AND STUPID AND DEFER THE QUESTIONS TO ME.
WHERE IS YOUR DRIVER?
I'M THE DRIVER.
THE FUCK YOU ARE. WHERE ARE YOUR *MEN?*

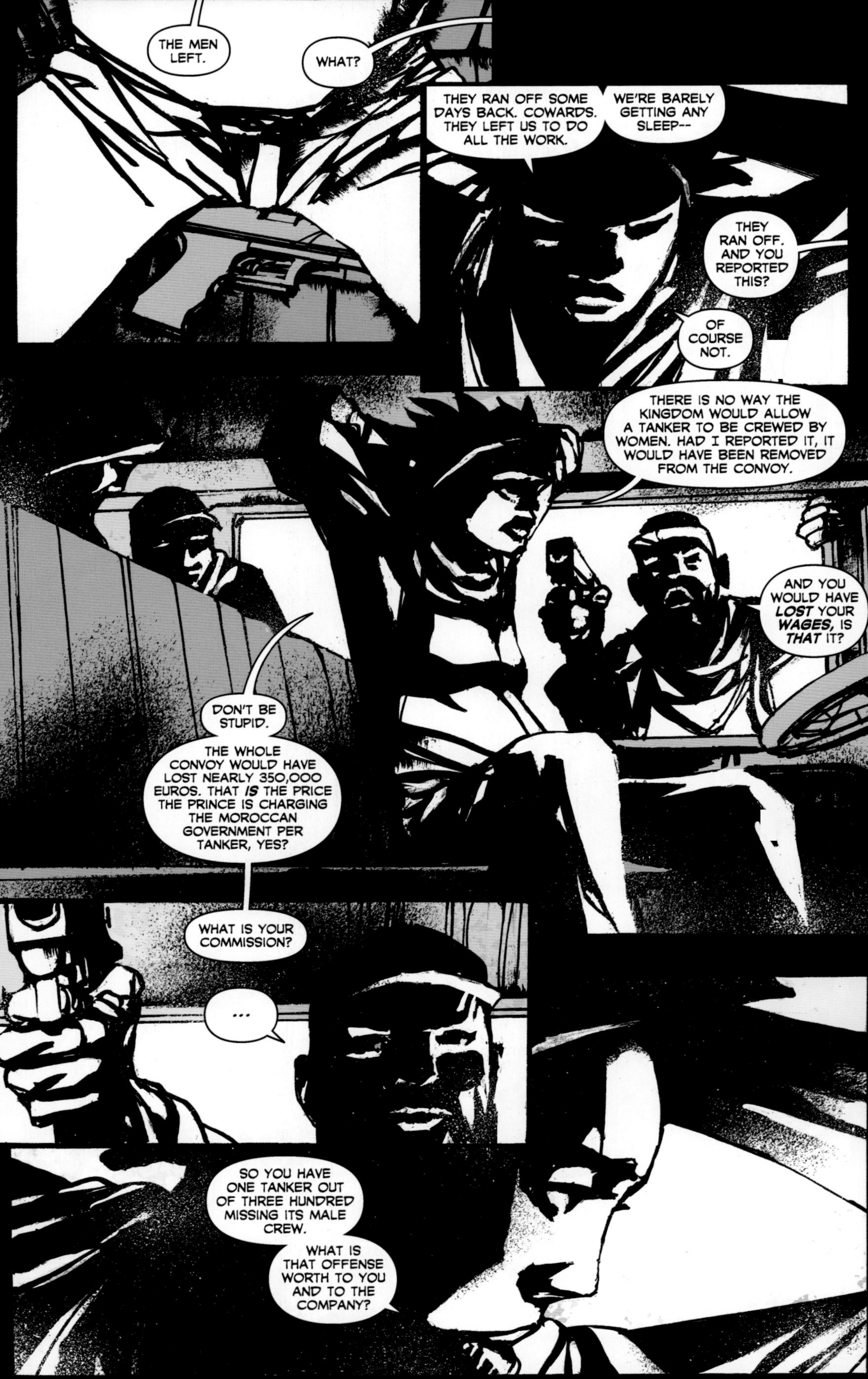
THE MEN LEFT.
WHAT?
THEY RAN OFF SOME DAYS BACK. COWARDS. THEY LEFT US TO DO ALL THE WORK.
WE'RE BARELY GETTING ANY SLEEP--
THEY RAN OFF. AND YOU REPORTED THIS?
OF COURSE NOT.
THERE IS NO WAY THE KINGDOM WOULD ALLOW A TANKER TO BE CREWED BY WOMEN. HAD I REPORTED IT, IT WOULD HAVE BEEN REMOVED FROM THE CONVOY.
AND YOU WOULD HAVE LOST YOUR WAGES, IS THAT IT?
DON'T BE STUPID.
THE WHOLE CONVOY WOULD HAVE LOST NEARLY 350,000 EUROS. THAT IS THE PRICE THE PRINCE IS CHARGING THE MOROCCAN GOVERNMENT PER TANKER, YES?
WHAT IS YOUR COMMISSION?
...
SO YOU HAVE ONE TANKER OUT OF THREE HUNDRED MISSING ITS MALE CREW.
WHAT IS THAT OFFENSE WORTH TO YOU AND TO THE COMPANY?

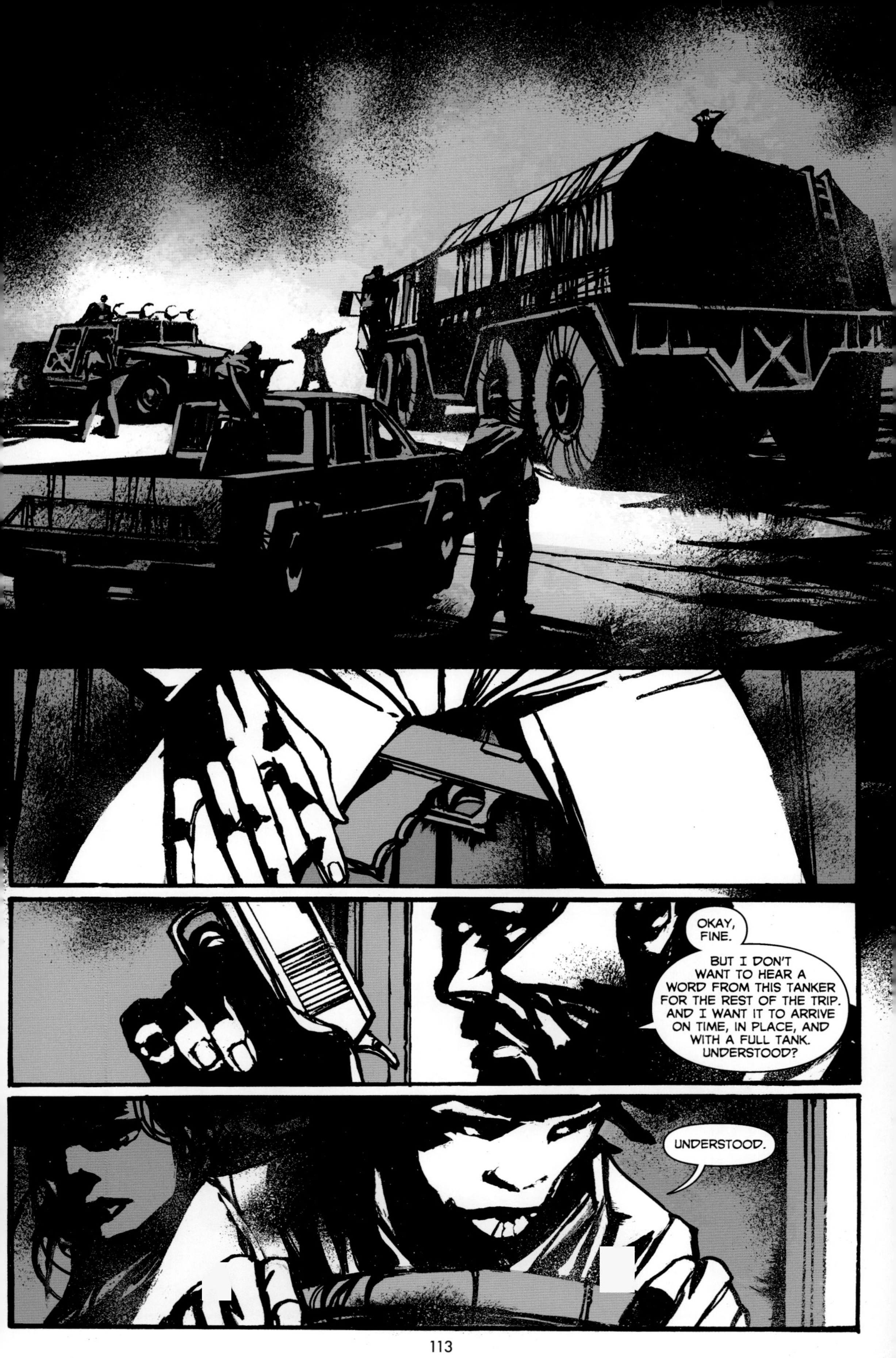
OKAY, FINE.
BUT I DON'T WANT TO HEAR A WORD FROM THIS TANKER FOR THE REST OF THE TRIP. AND I WANT IT TO ARRIVE ON TIME, IN PLACE, AND WITH A FULL TANK. UNDERSTOOD?
UNDERSTOOD.

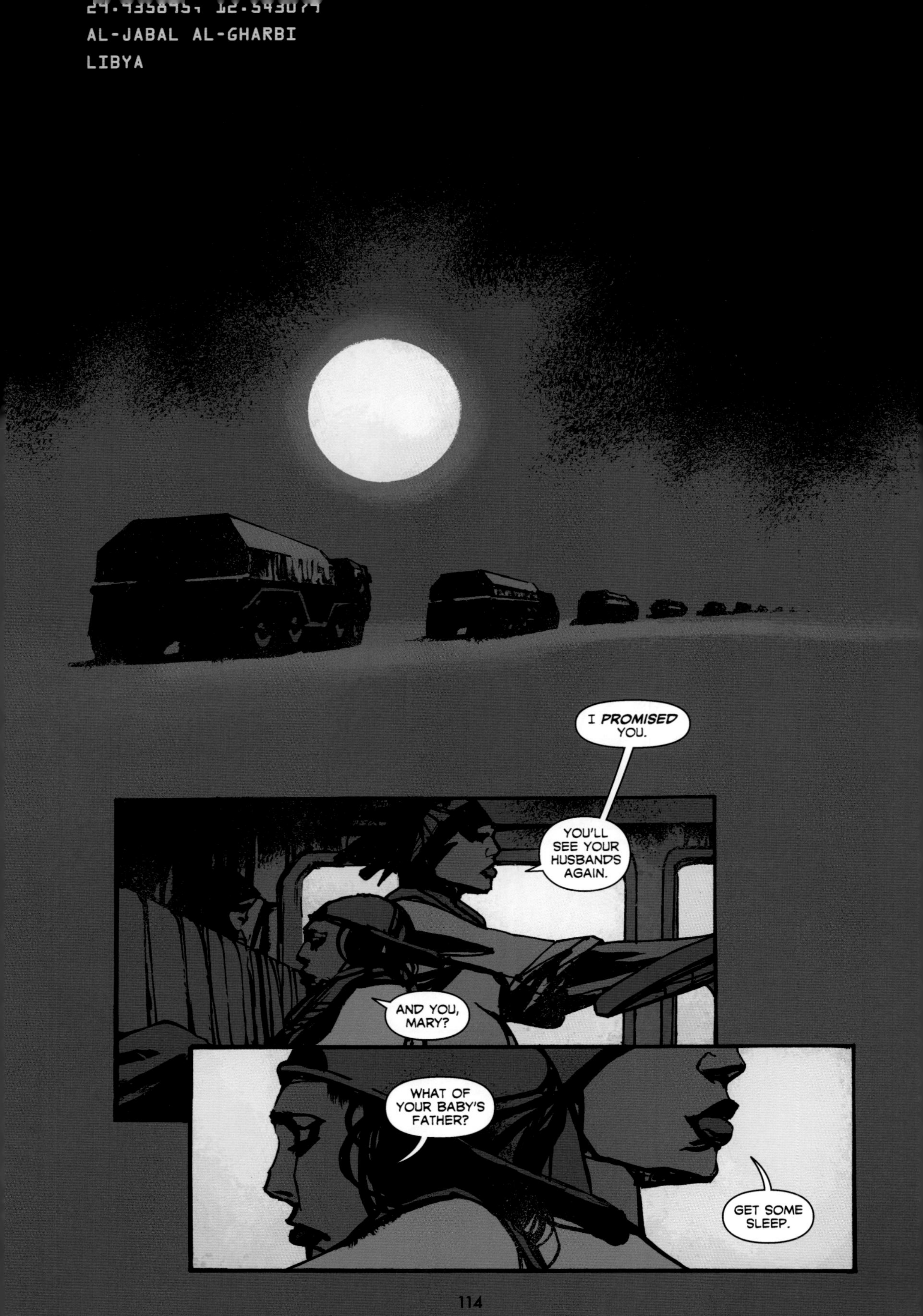
29.935875, 12.543079
AL-JABAL AL-GHARBI
LIBYA
I PROMISED YOU.
YOU'LL SEE YOUR HUSBANDS AGAIN.
AND YOU, MARY?
WHAT OF YOUR BABY'S FATHER?
GET SOME SLEEP.

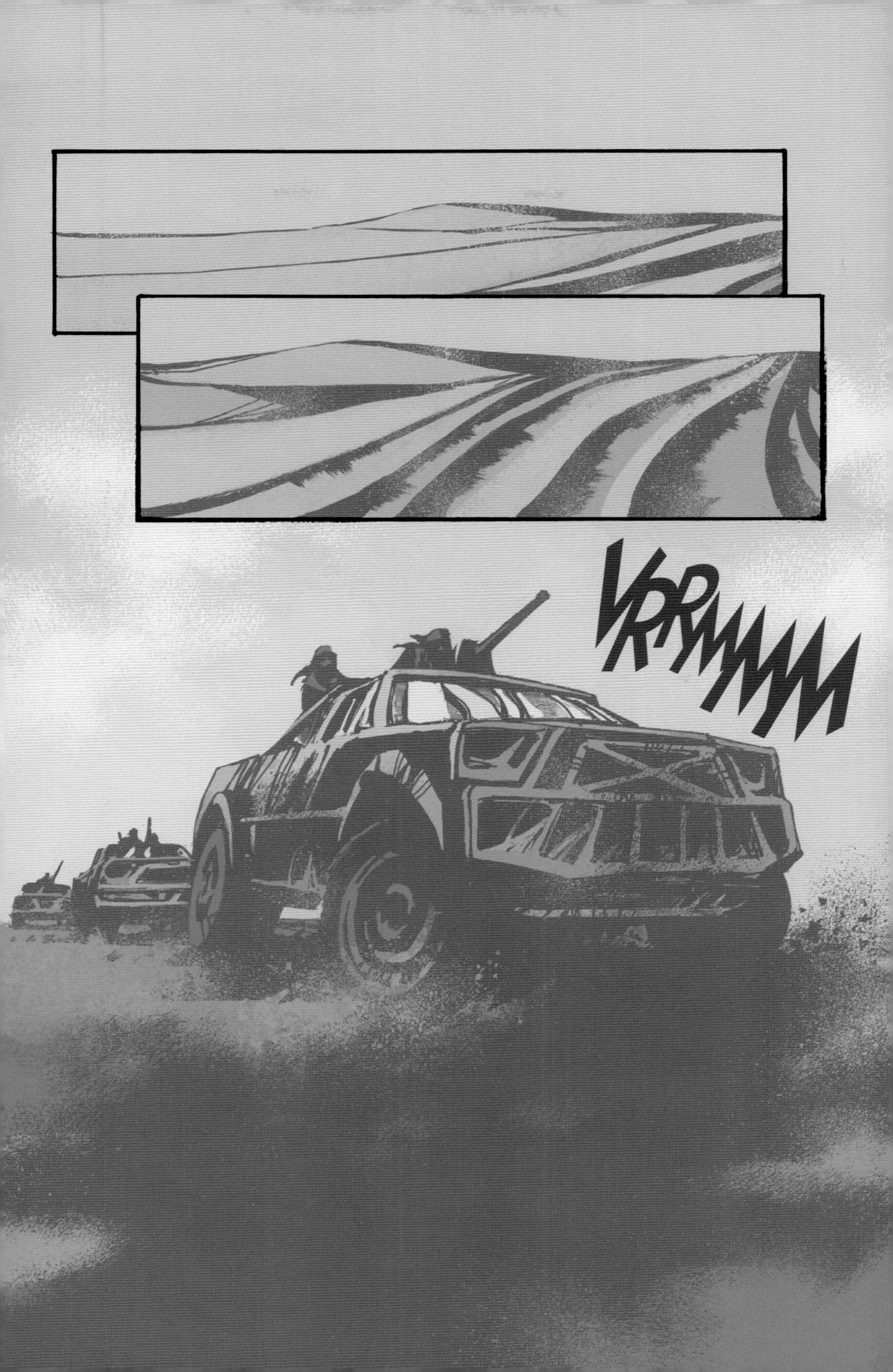
VRRMMMM

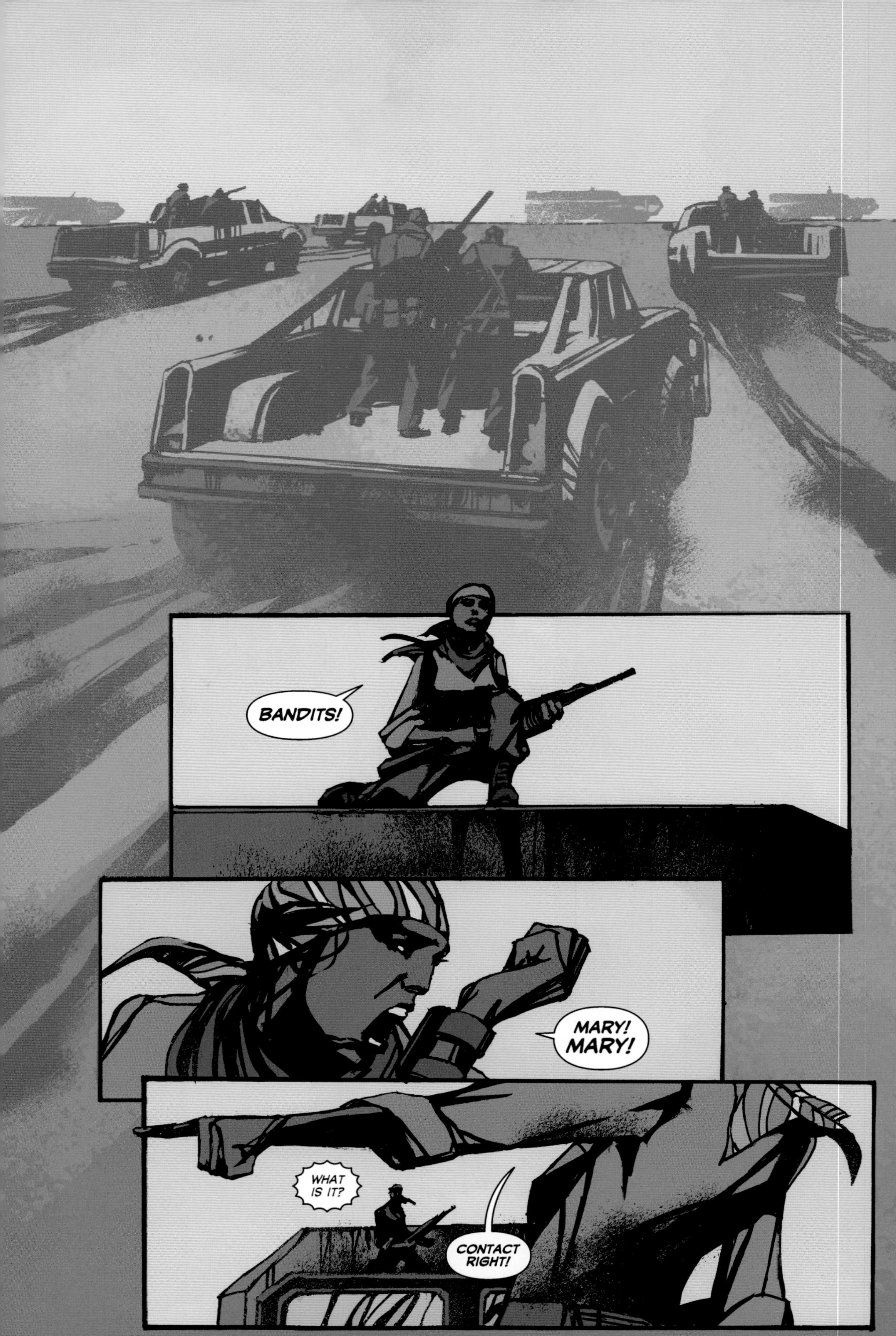
BANDITS!
MARY! MARY!
WHAT IS IT?
CONTACT RIGHT!

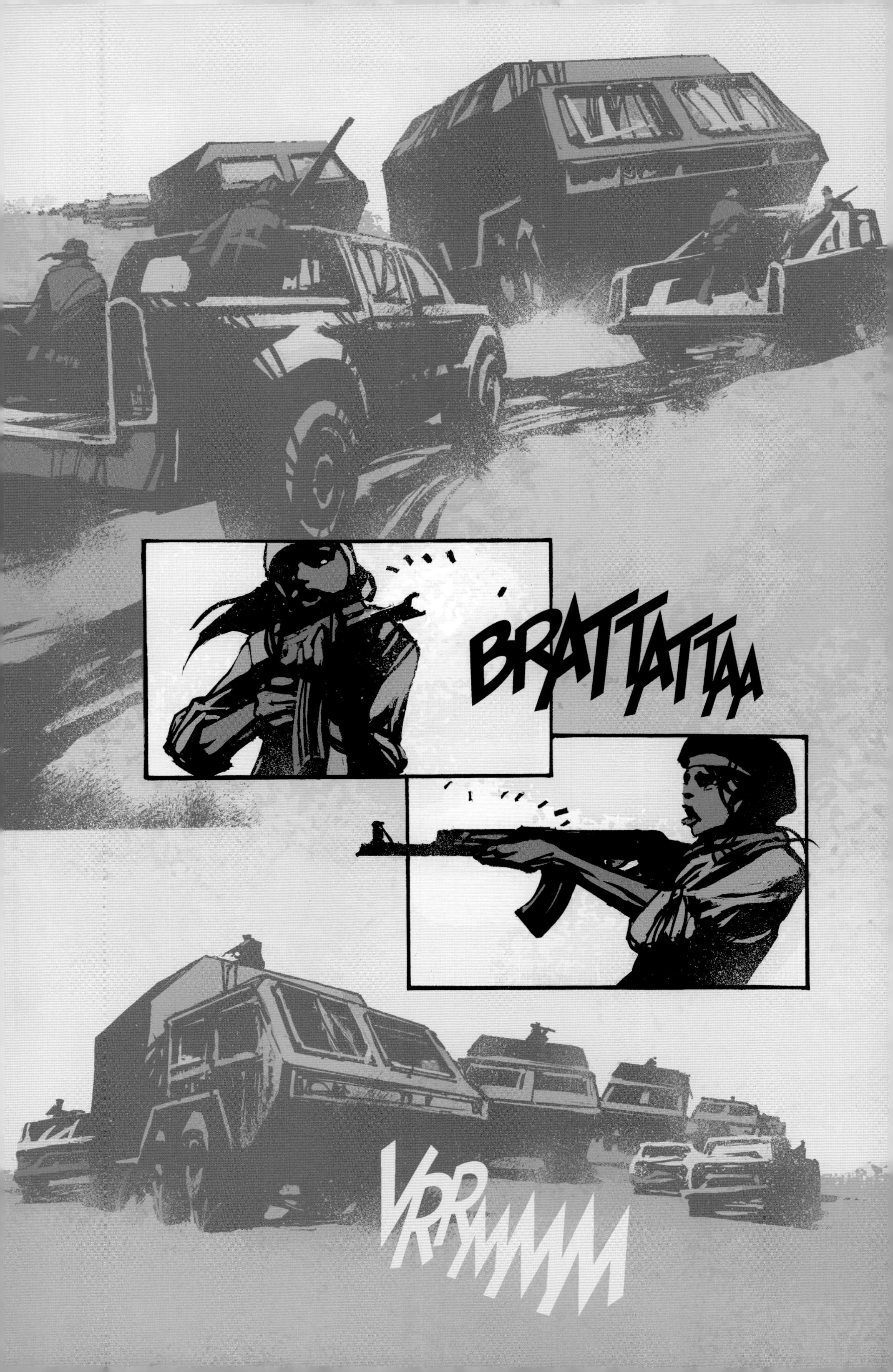
BRATTATTAA
VRRMMMM

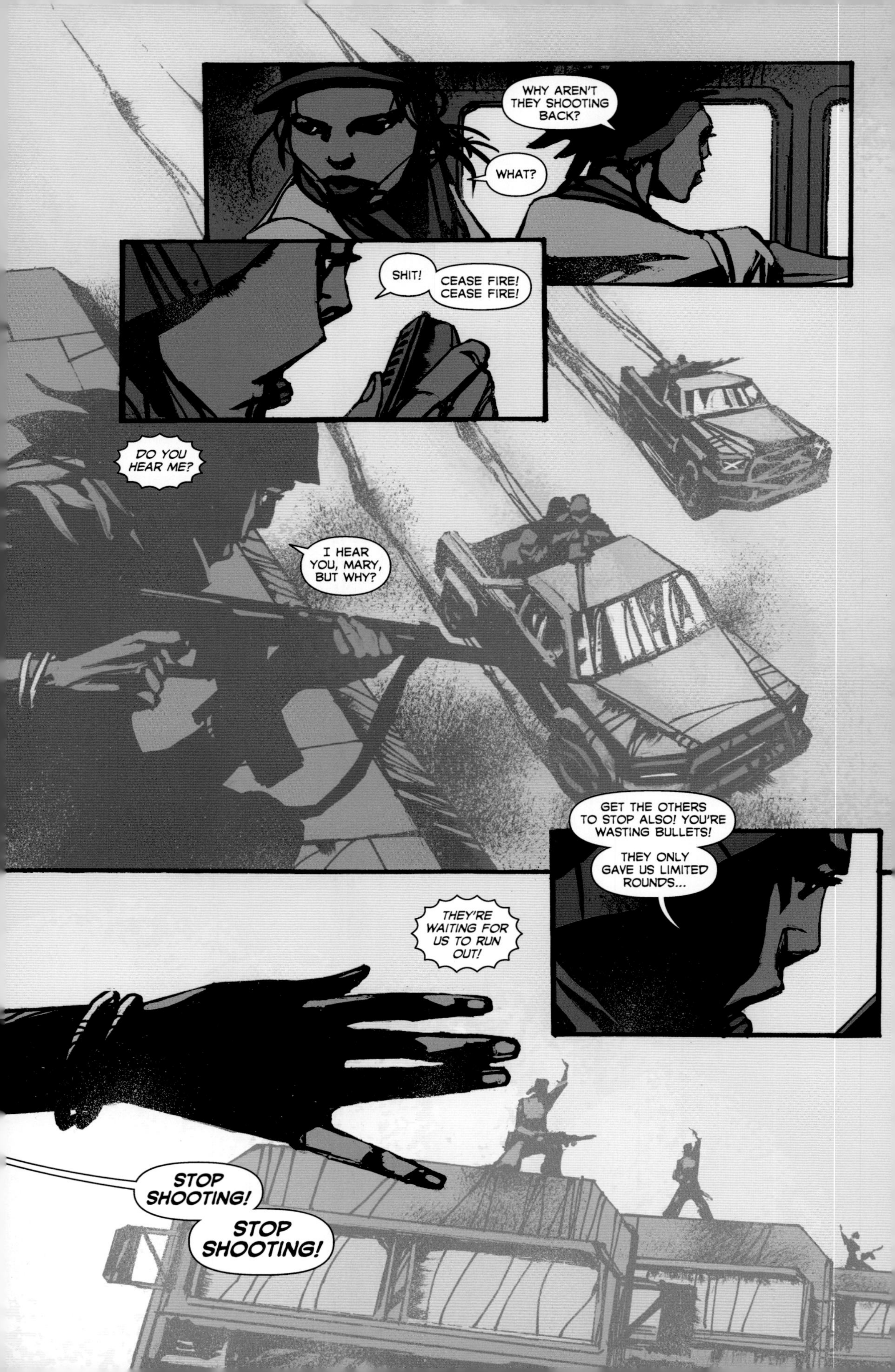
WHY AREN'T THEY SHOOTING BACK?
WHAT?
SHIT!
CEASE FIRE! CEASE FIRE!
DO YOU HEAR ME?
I HEAR YOU, MARY, BUT WHY?
GET THE OTHERS TO STOP ALSO! YOU'RE WASTING BULLETS!
THEY ONLY GAVE US LIMITED ROUNDS...
THEY'RE WAITING FOR US TO RUN OUT!
STOP SHOOTING!
STOP SHOOTING!

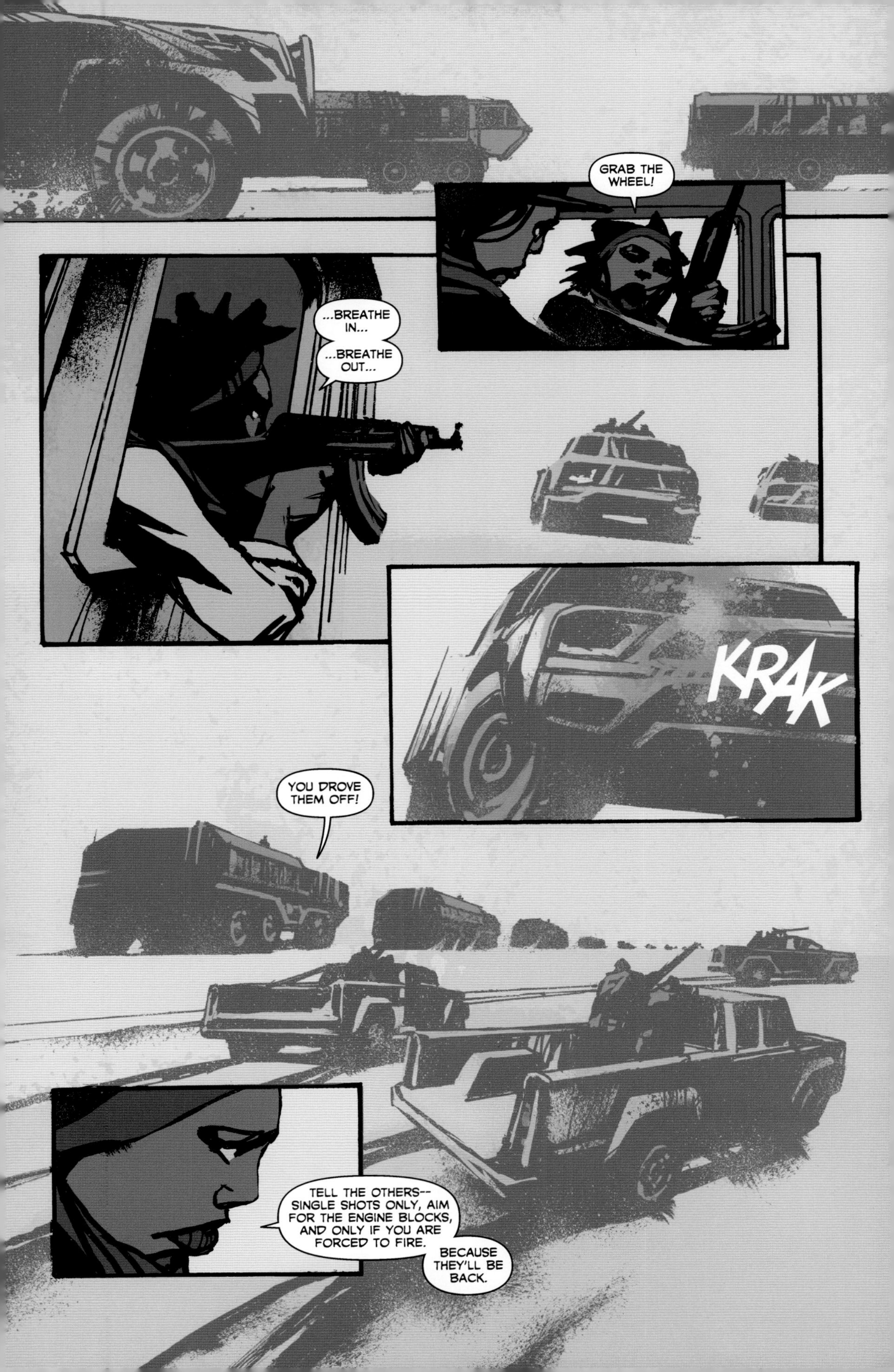
GRAB THE WHEEL!
...BREATHE IN...
...BREATHE OUT...
KRAK
YOU DROVE THEM OFF!
TELL THE OTHERS-- SINGLE SHOTS ONLY, AIM FOR THE ENGINE BLOCKS, AND ONLY IF YOU ARE FORCED TO FIRE.
BECAUSE THEY'LL BE BACK.

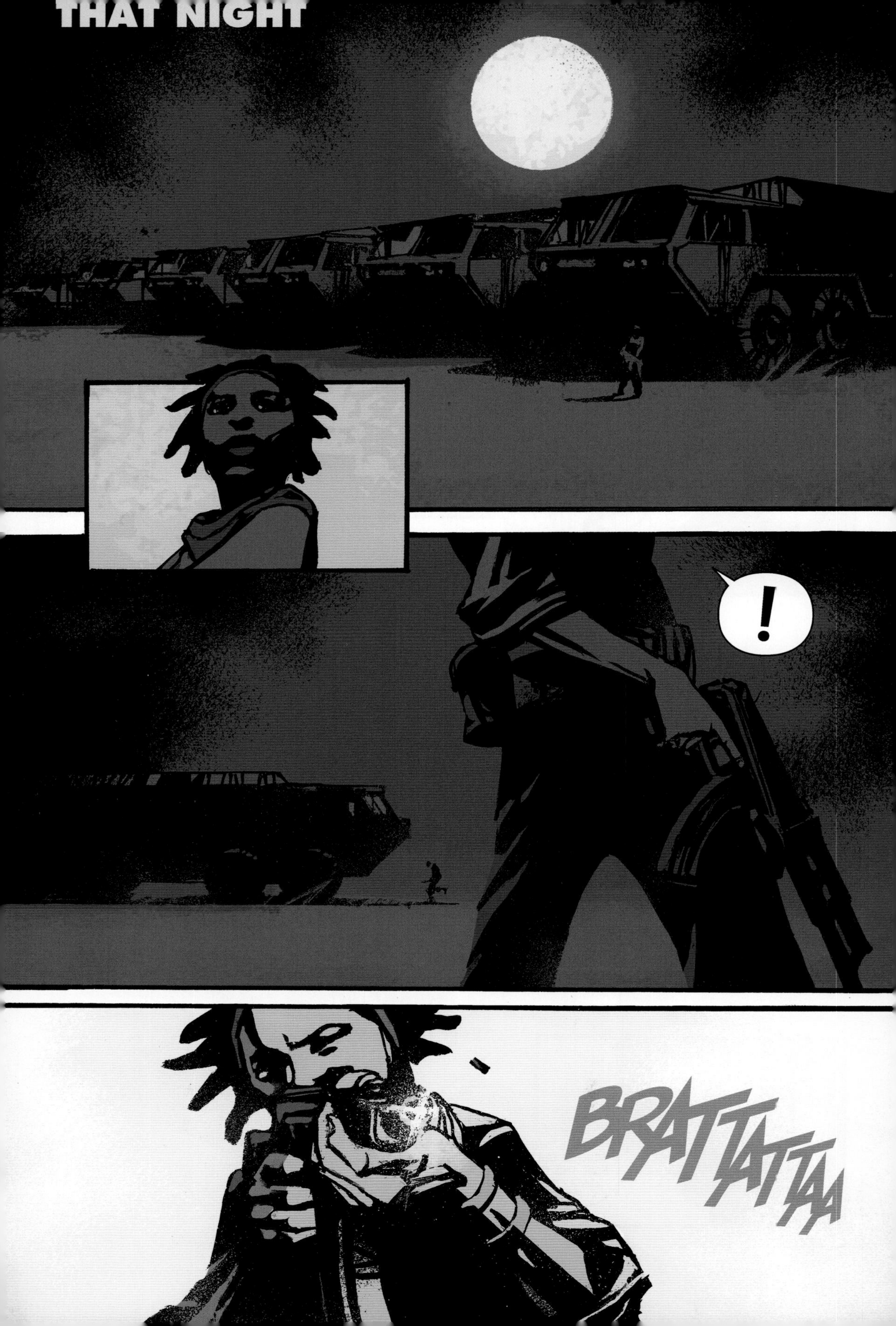
THAT NIGHT
!
BRATTATTAA

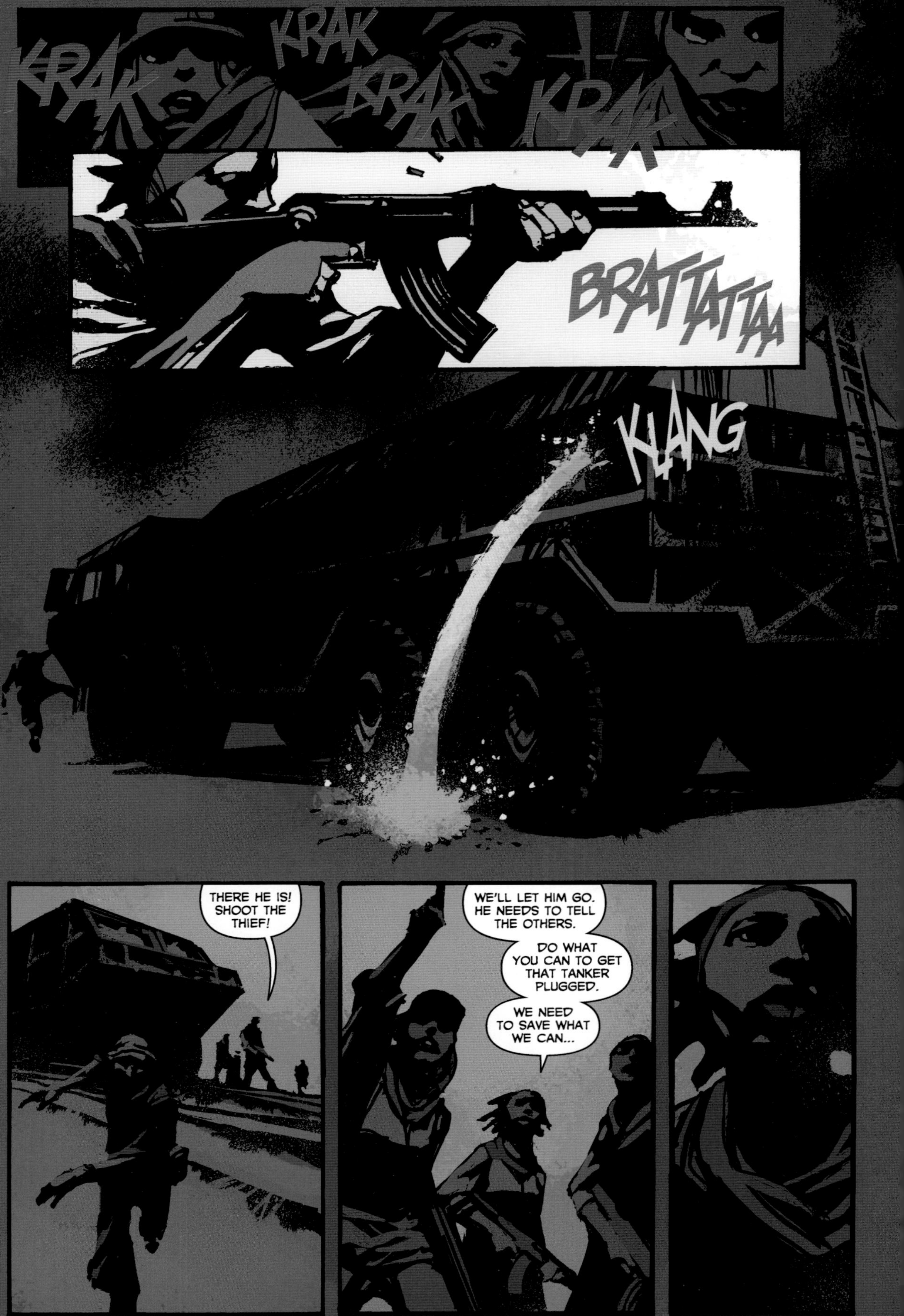
KRAK
KRAK
KRAK
KRAK
BRATTATTAA
KLANG
THERE HE IS! SHOOT THE THIEF!
WE'LL LET HIM GO. HE NEEDS TO TELL THE OTHERS.
DO WHAT YOU CAN TO GET THAT TANKER PLUGGED.
WE NEED TO SAVE WHAT WE CAN...

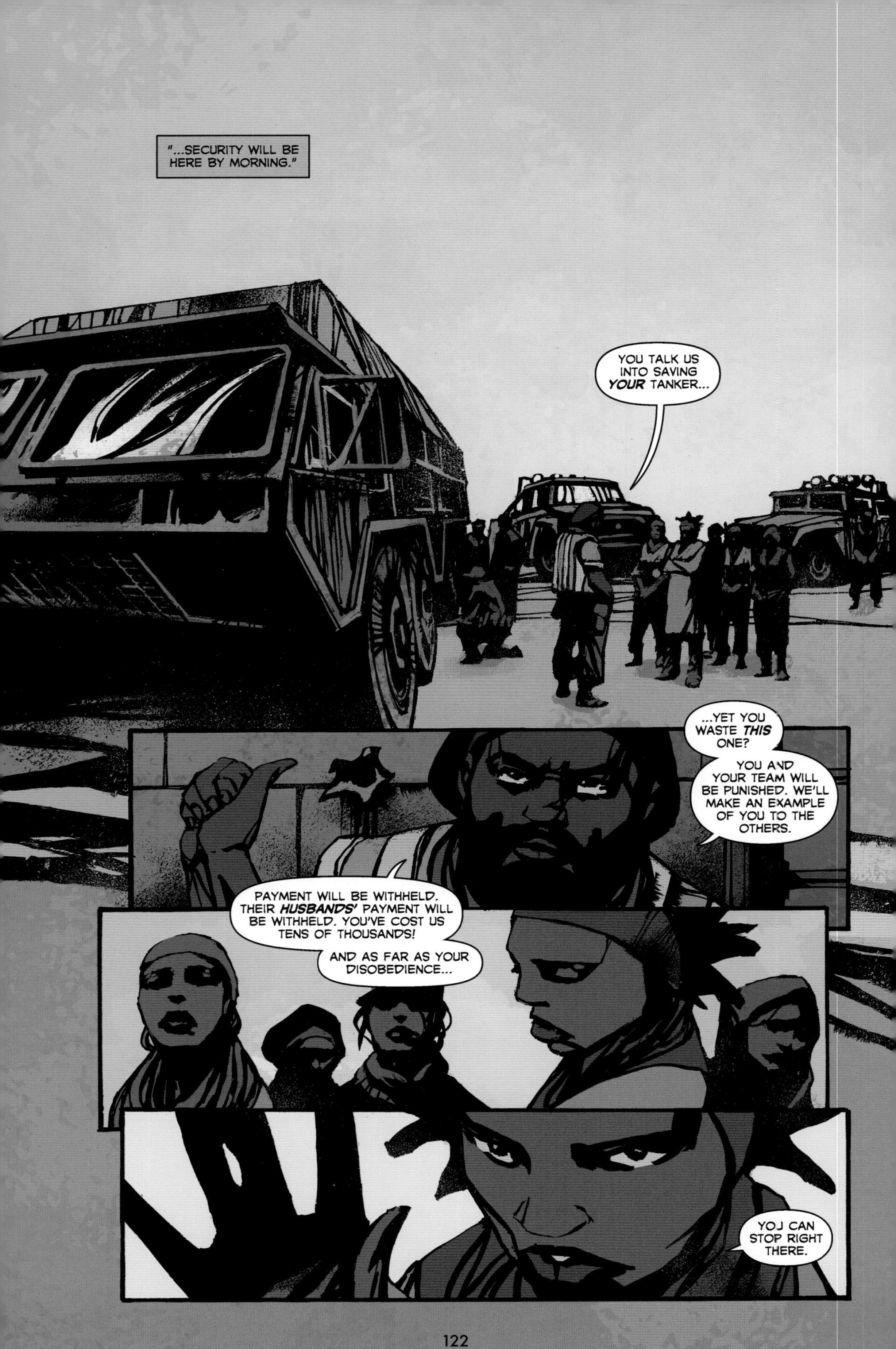
"...SECURITY WILL BE HERE BY MORNING."
YOU TALK US INTO SAVING *YOUR* TANKER...
...YET YOU WASTE *THIS* ONE?
YOU AND YOUR TEAM WILL BE PUNISHED. WE'LL MAKE AN EXAMPLE OF YOU TO THE OTHERS.
PAYMENT WILL BE WITHHELD. THEIR *HUSBANDS'* PAYMENT WILL BE WITHHELD. YOU'VE COST US TENS OF THOUSANDS!
AND AS FAR AS YOUR DISOBEDIENCE...
YOJ CAN STOP RIGHT THERE.

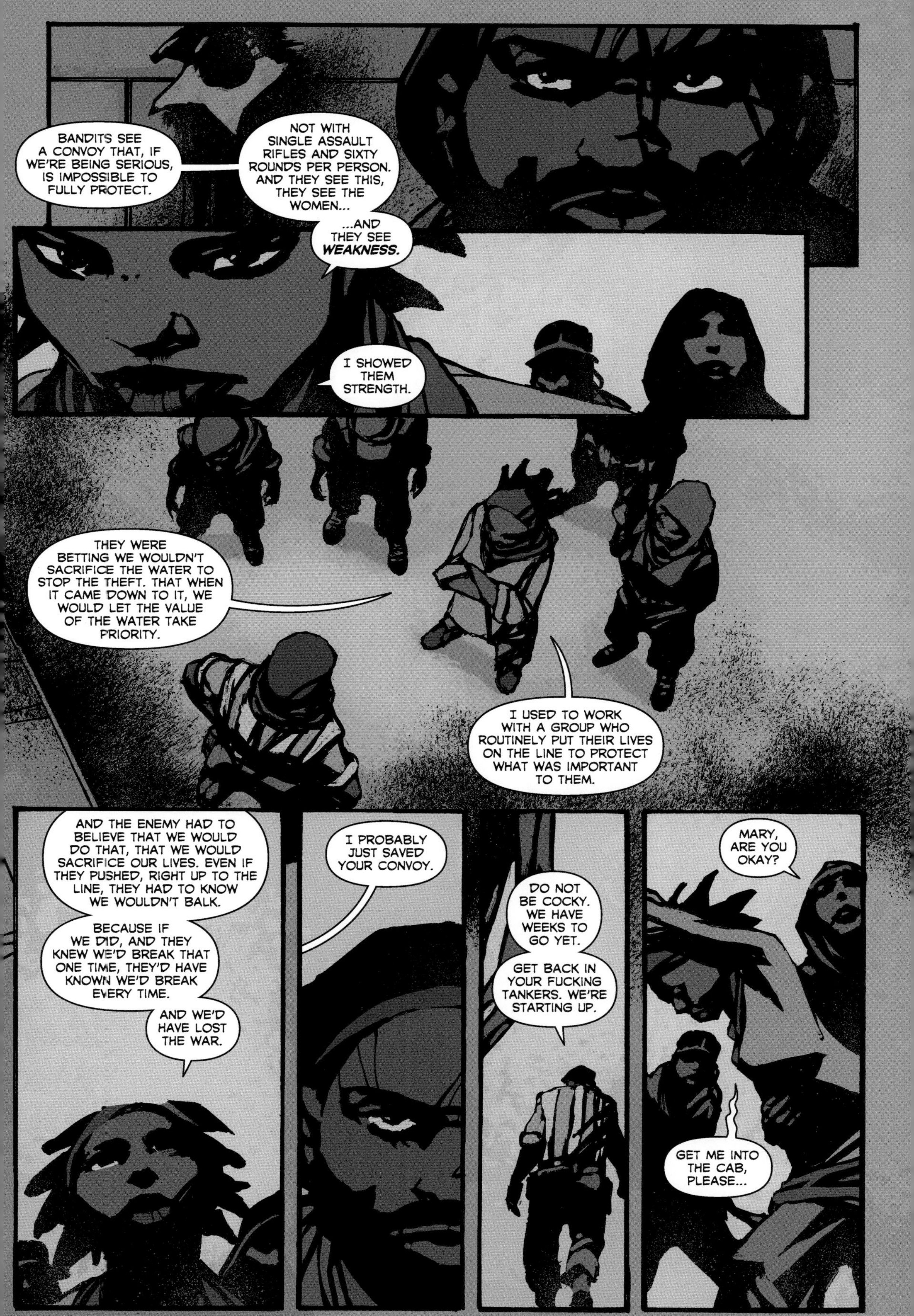
BANDITS SEE A CONVOY THAT, IF WE'RE BEING SERIOUS, IS IMPOSSIBLE TO FULLY PROTECT.
NOT WITH SINGLE ASSAULT RIFLES AND SIXTY ROUNDS PER PERSON. AND THEY SEE THIS, THEY SEE THE WOMEN...
...AND THEY SEE ***WEAKNESS.***
I SHOWED THEM STRENGTH.
THEY WERE BETTING WE WOULDN'T SACRIFICE THE WATER TO STOP THE THEFT. THAT WHEN IT CAME DOWN TO IT, WE WOULD LET THE VALUE OF THE WATER TAKE PRIORITY.
I USED TO WORK WITH A GROUP WHO ROUTINELY PUT THEIR LIVES ON THE LINE TO PROTECT WHAT WAS IMPORTANT TO THEM.
AND THE ENEMY HAD TO BELIEVE THAT WE WOULD DO THAT, THAT WE WOULD SACRIFICE OUR LIVES. EVEN IF THEY PUSHED, RIGHT UP TO THE LINE, THEY HAD TO KNOW WE WOULDN'T BALK.
BECAUSE IF WE DID, AND THEY KNEW WE'D BREAK THAT ONE TIME, THEY'D HAVE KNOWN WE'D BREAK EVERY TIME.
AND WE'D HAVE LOST THE WAR.
I PROBABLY JUST SAVED YOUR CONVOY.
DO NOT BE COCKY. WE HAVE WEEKS TO GO YET.
GET BACK IN YOUR FUCKING TANKERS. WE'RE STARTING UP.
MARY, ARE YOU OKAY?
GET ME INTO THE CAB, PLEASE...

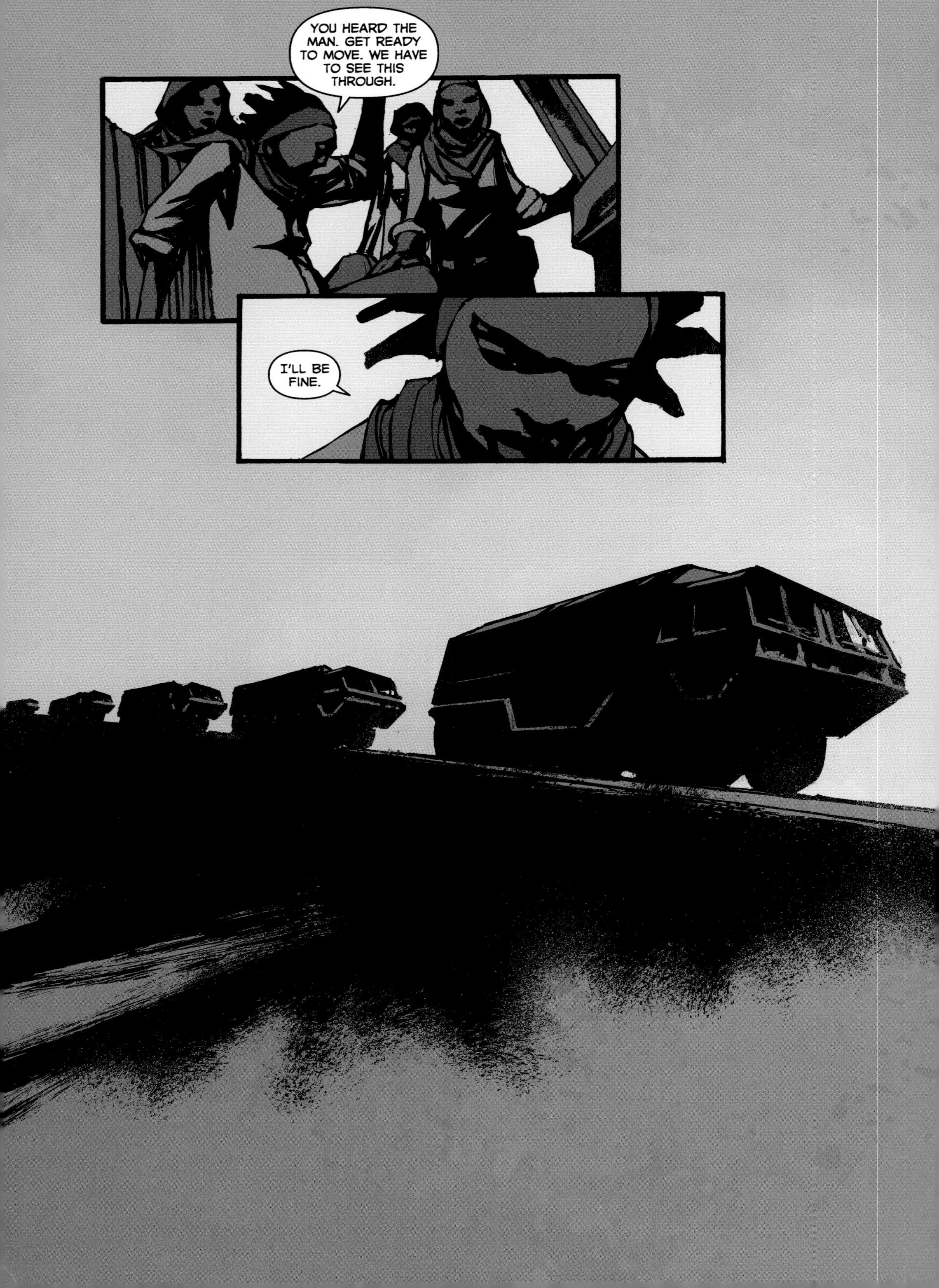
YOU HEARD THE MAN. GET READY TO MOVE. WE HAVE TO SEE THIS THROUGH.
I'LL BE FINE.

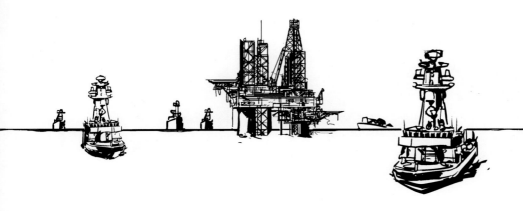

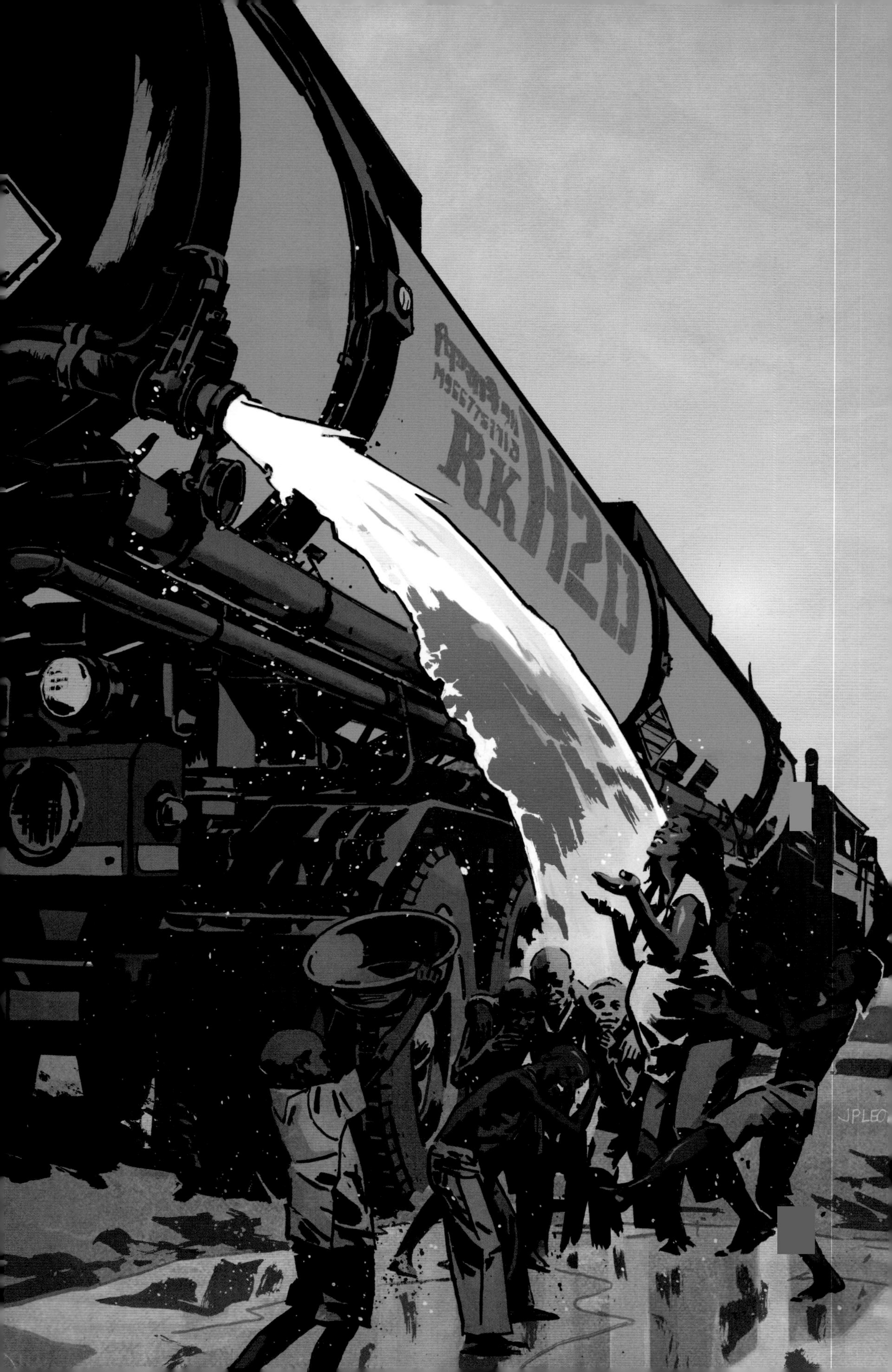
RKH2O
JPLEO

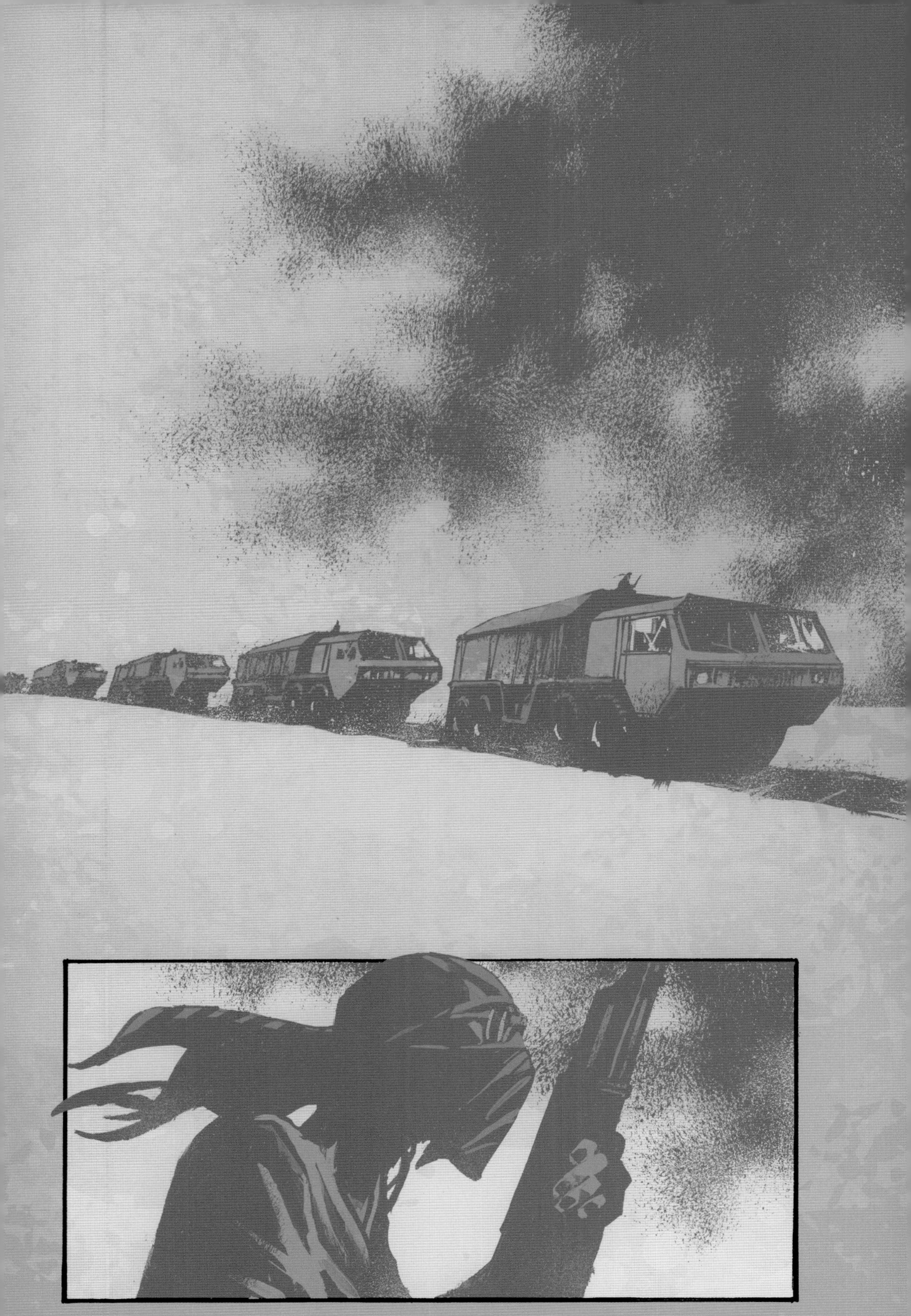

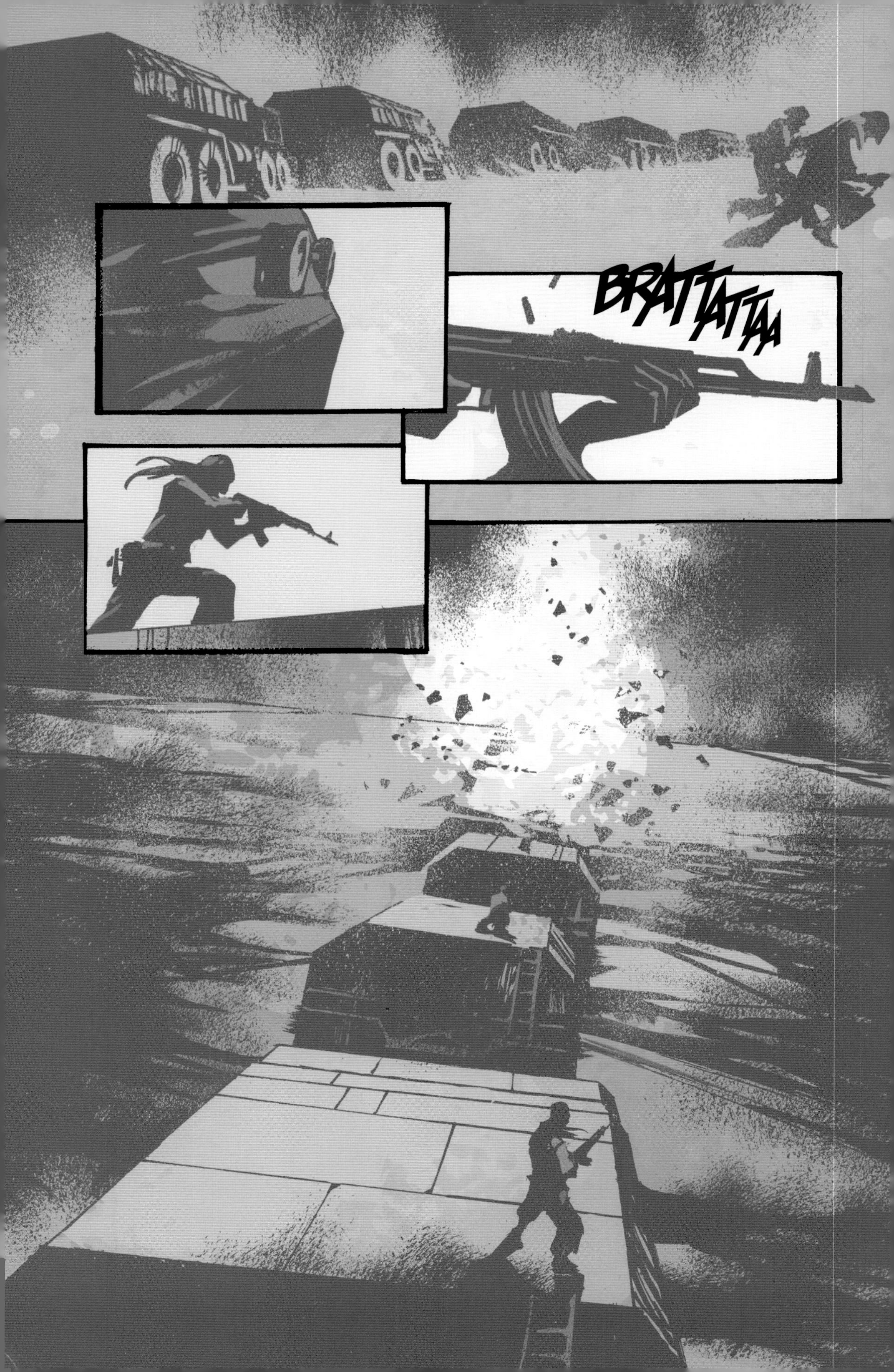
BRATTATTAA

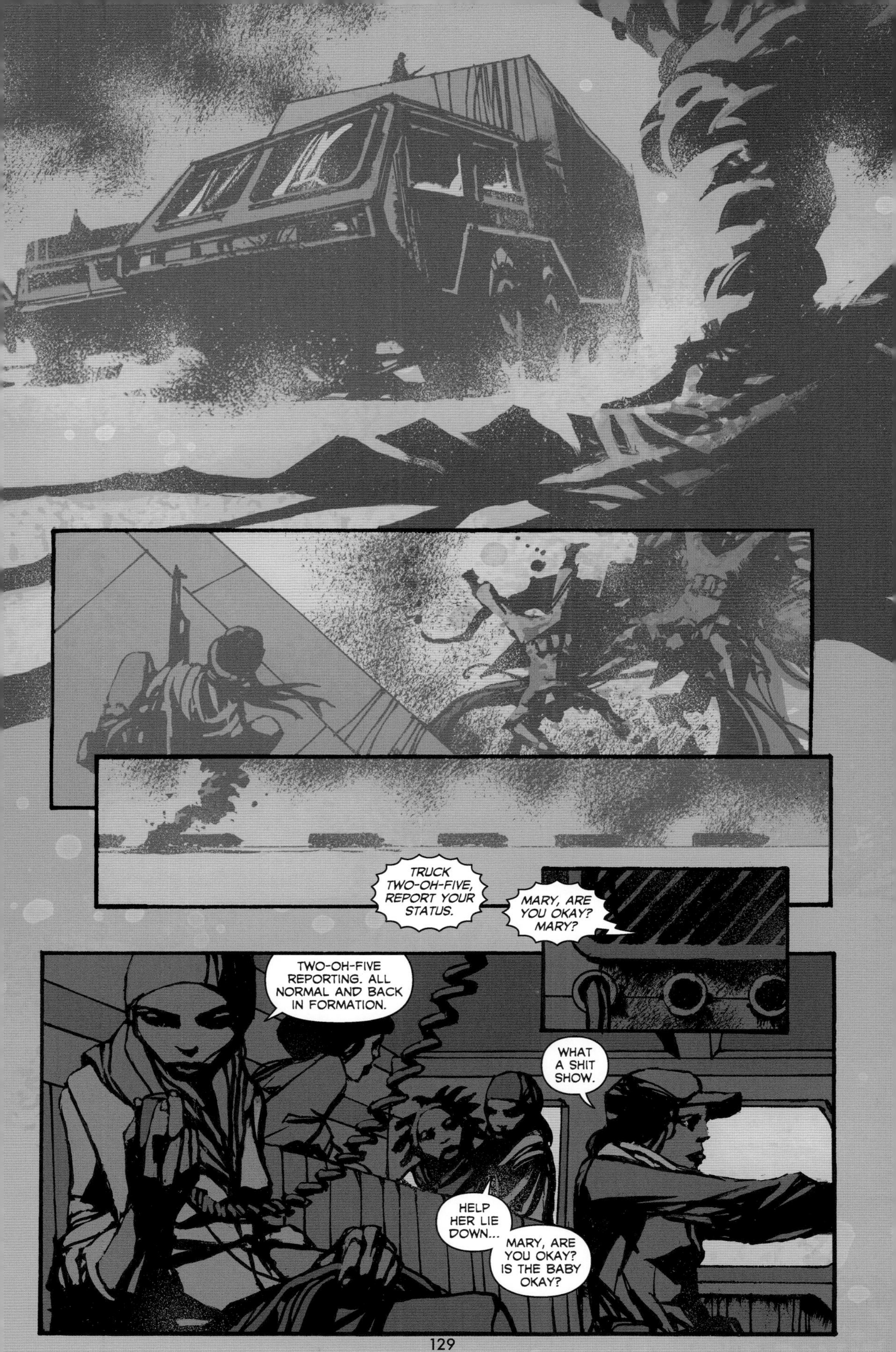

TRUCK TWO-OH-FIVE, REPORT YOUR STATUS.
MARY, ARE YOU OKAY? MARY?
TWO-OH-FIVE REPORTING. ALL NORMAL AND BACK IN FORMATION.
WHAT A SHIT SHOW.
HELP HER LIE DOWN...
MARY, ARE YOU OKAY? IS THE BABY OKAY?

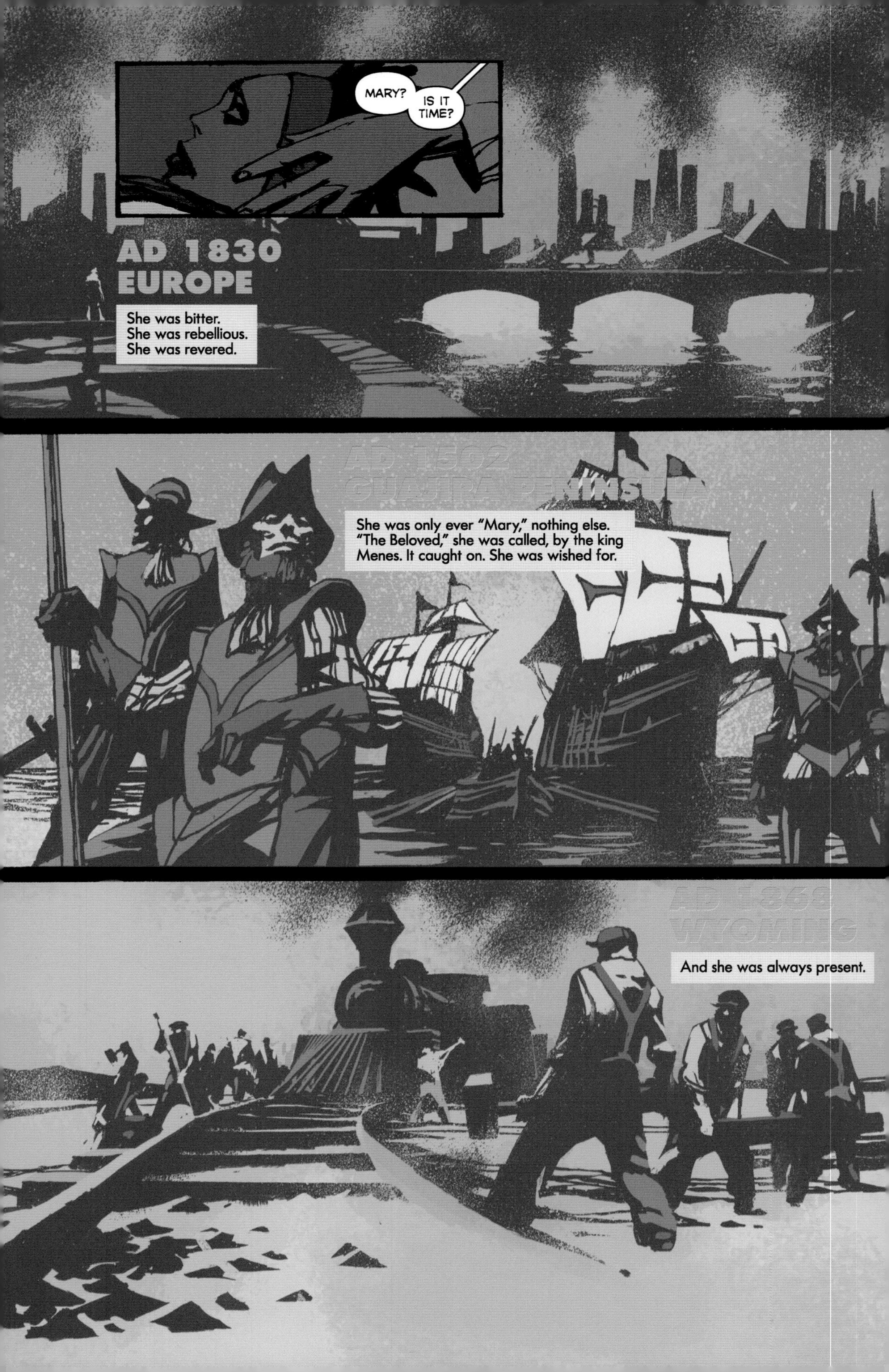
MARY?
IS IT TIME?
AD 1830
EUROPE
She was bitter.
She was rebellious.
She was revered.
AD 1502
GUAJIRA PENINSULA
She was only ever "Mary," nothing else. "The Beloved," she was called, by the king Menes. It caught on. She was wished for.
AD 1868
WYOMING
And she was always present.

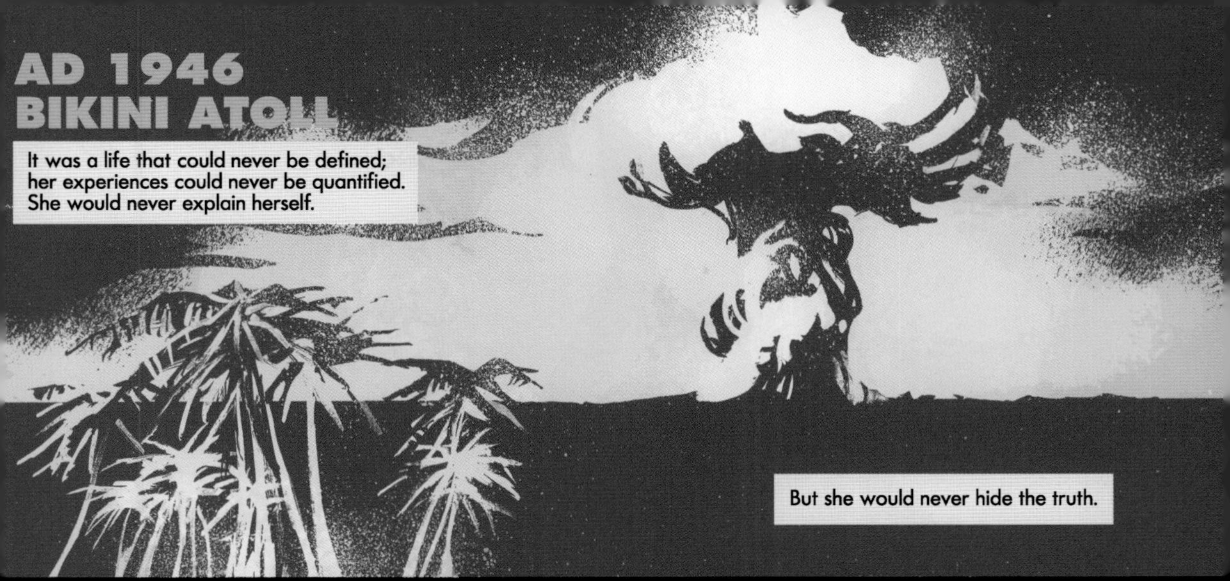
AD 1946
BIKINI ATOLL
It was a life that could never be defined; her experiences could never be quantified. She would never explain herself.
But she would never hide the truth.

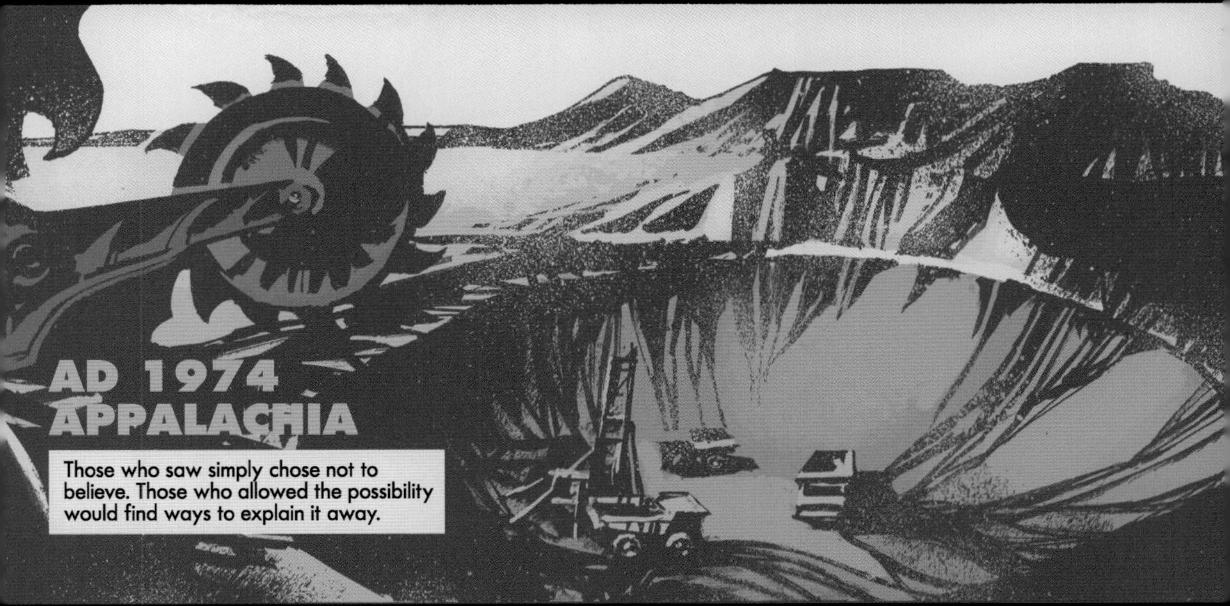
AD 1974
APPALACHIA
Those who saw simply chose not to believe. Those who allowed the possibility would find ways to explain it away.

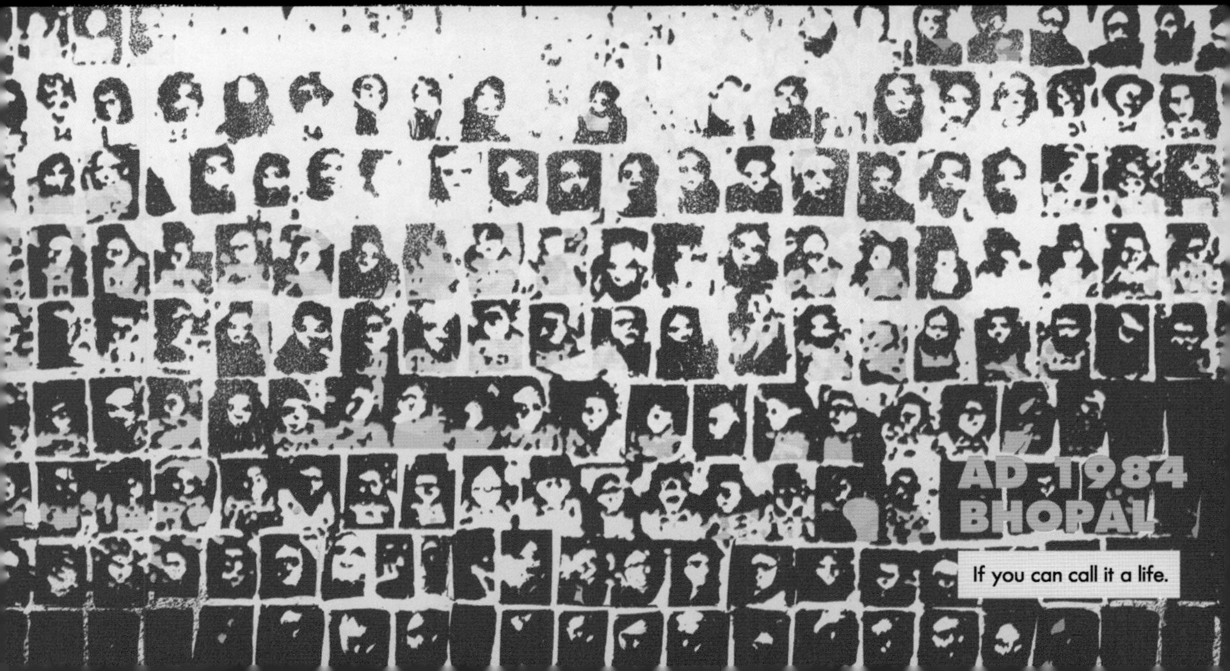
AD 1984
BHOPAL
If you can call it a life.

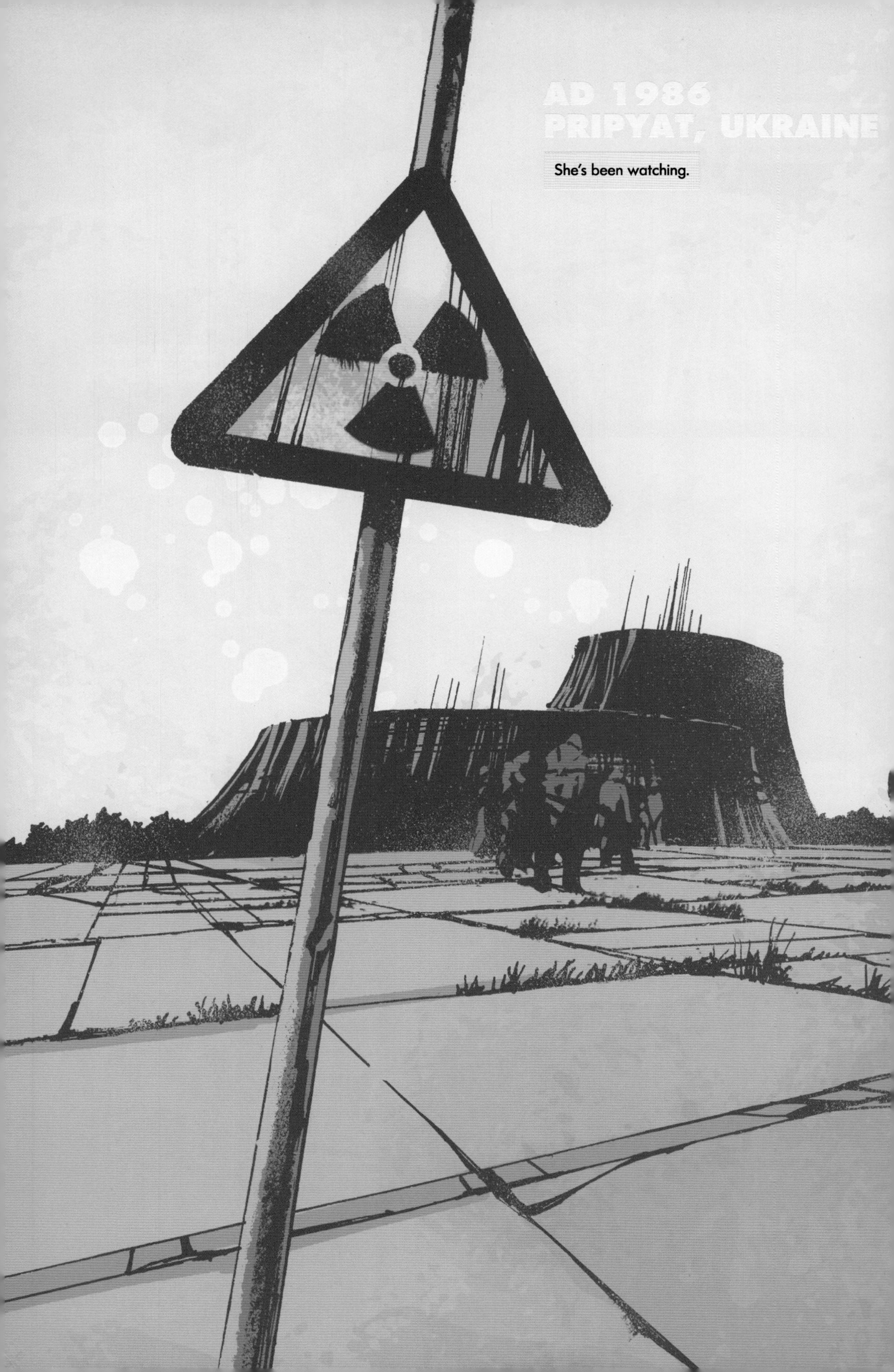
AD 1986
PRIPYAT, UKRAINE
She's been watching.

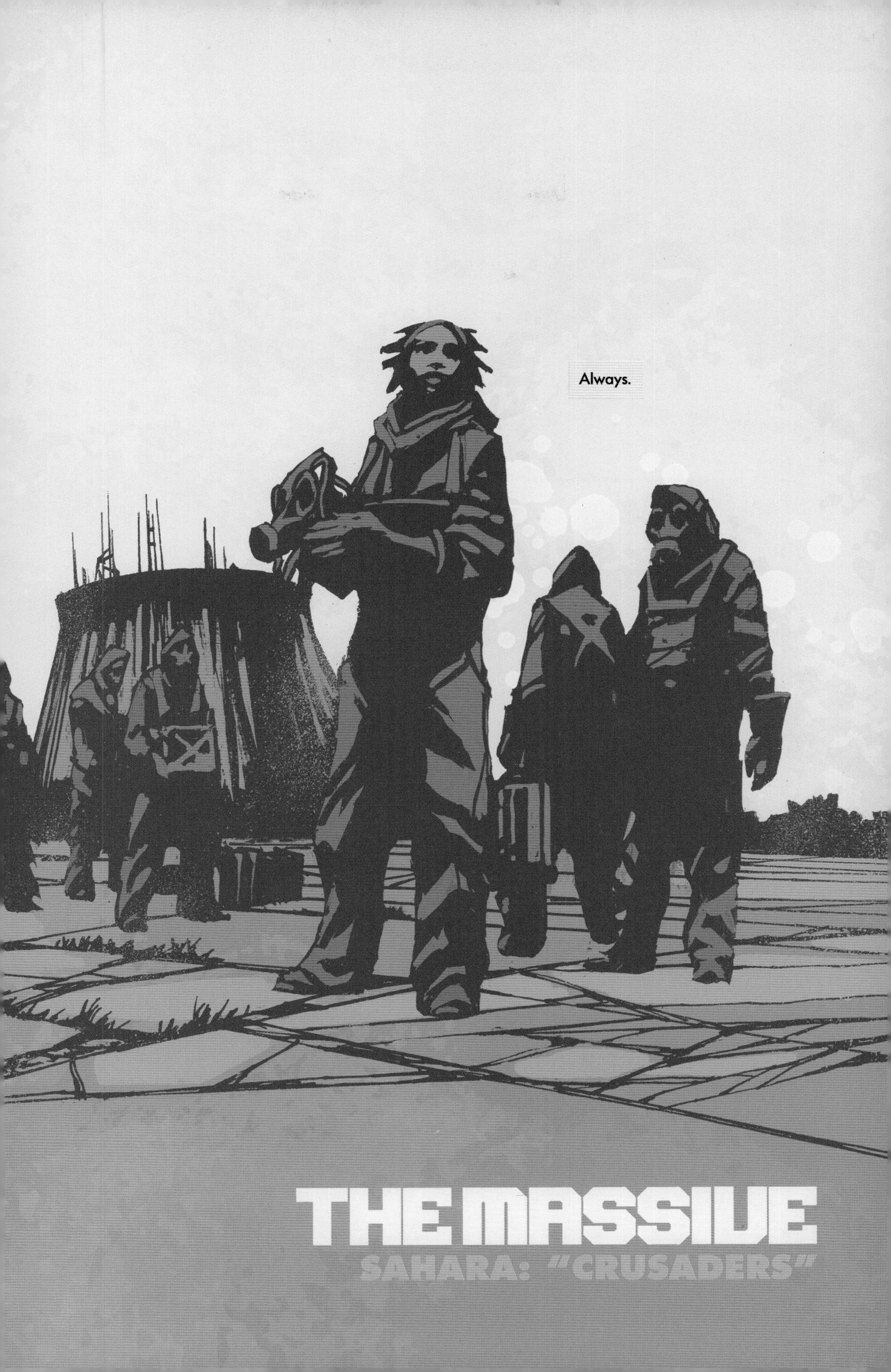
Always.
THE MASSIVE
SAHARA: "CRUSADERS"

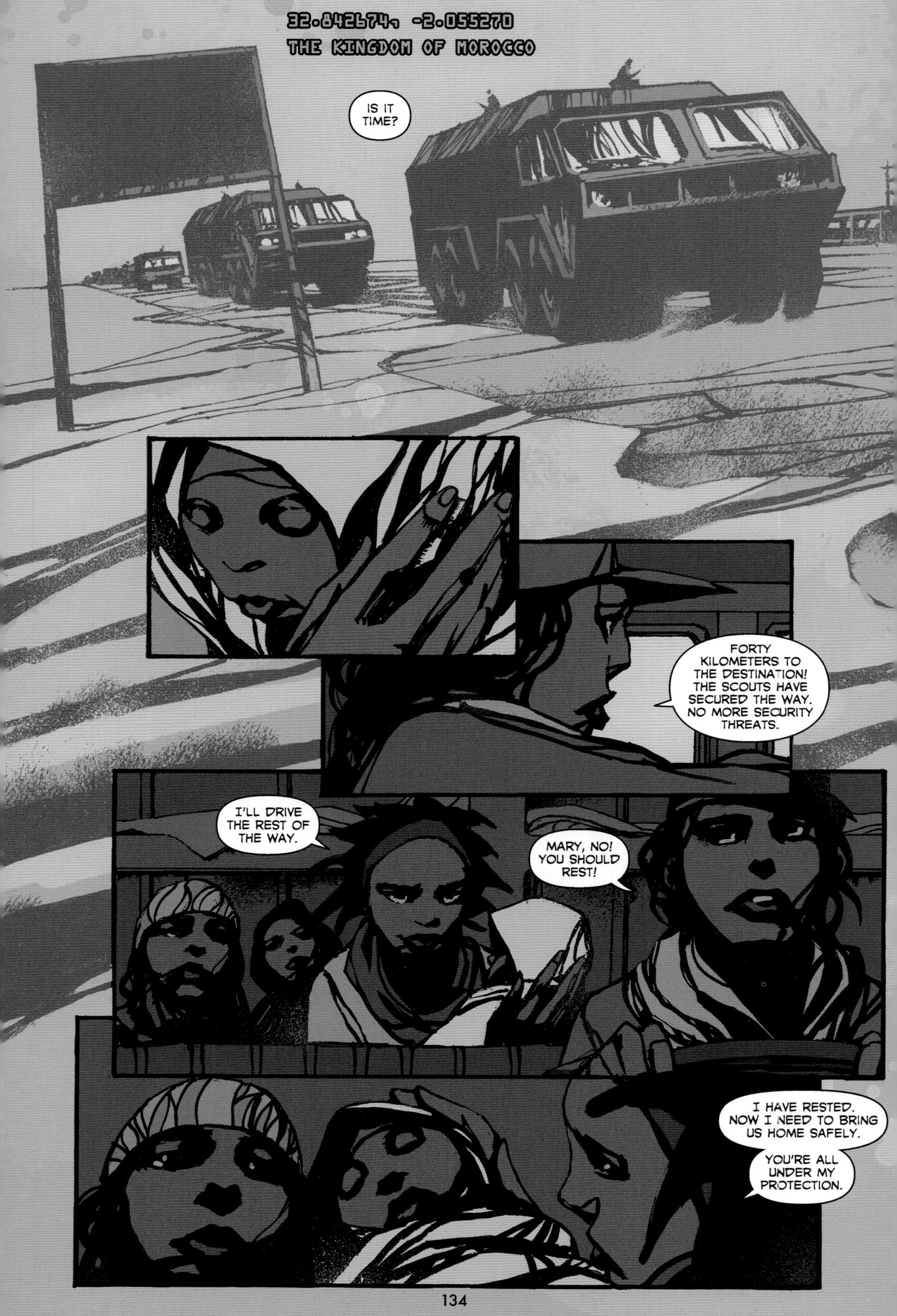
32.842674, -2.055270
THE KINGDOM OF MOROCCO
IS IT TIME?
FORTY KILOMETERS TO THE DESTINATION! THE SCOUTS HAVE SECURED THE WAY. NO MORE SECURITY THREATS.
I'LL DRIVE THE REST OF THE WAY.
MARY, NO! YOU SHOULD REST!
I HAVE RESTED. NOW I NEED TO BRING US HOME SAFELY.
YOU'RE ALL UNDER MY PROTECTION.

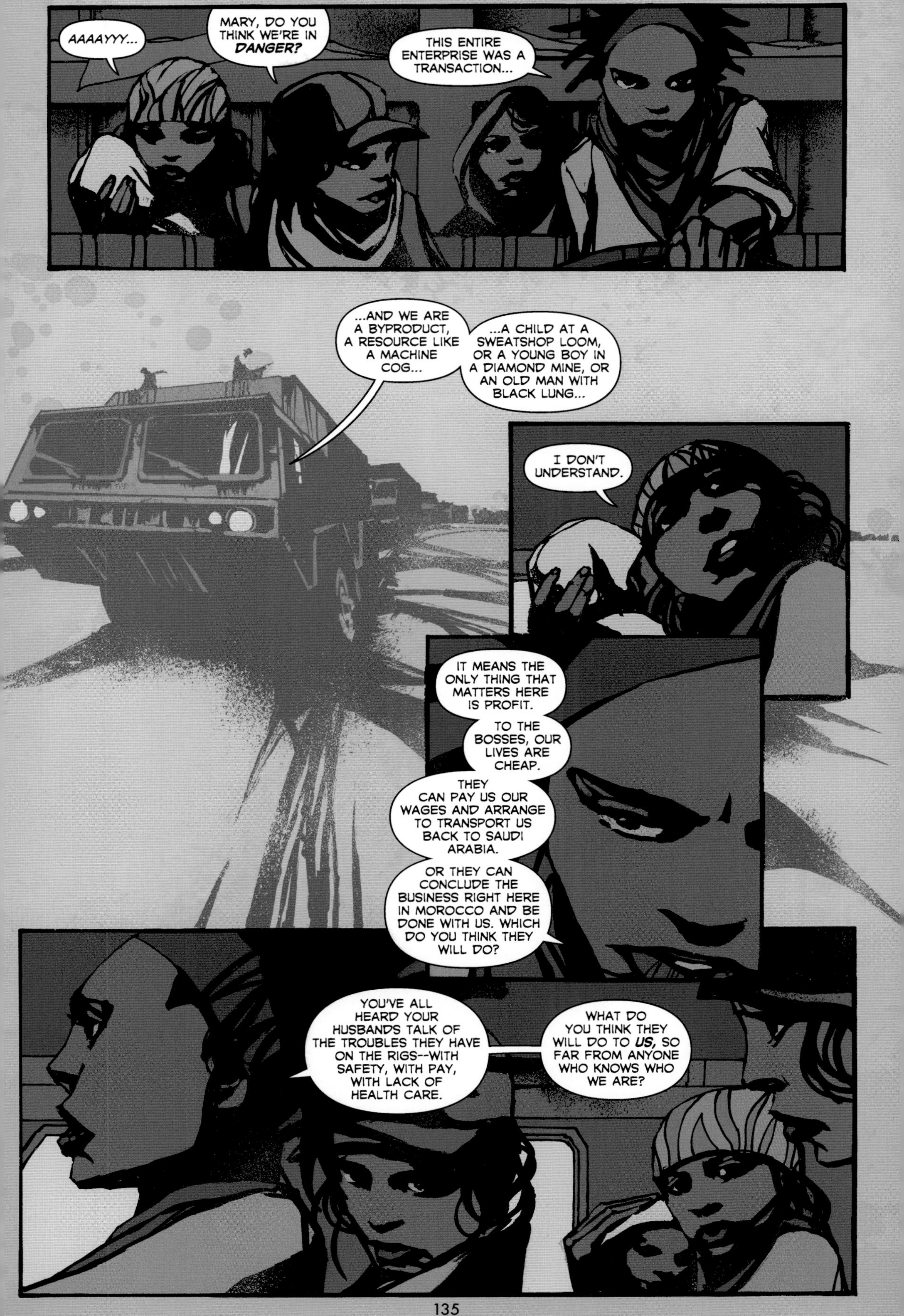
AAAAYYY...
MARY, DO YOU THINK WE'RE IN DANGER?
THIS ENTIRE ENTERPRISE WAS A TRANSACTION...
...AND WE ARE A BYPRODUCT, A RESOURCE LIKE A MACHINE COG...
...A CHILD AT A SWEATSHOP LOOM, OR A YOUNG BOY IN A DIAMOND MINE, OR AN OLD MAN WITH BLACK LUNG...
I DON'T UNDERSTAND.
IT MEANS THE ONLY THING THAT MATTERS HERE IS PROFIT.
TO THE BOSSES, OUR LIVES ARE CHEAP.
THEY CAN PAY US OUR WAGES AND ARRANGE TO TRANSPORT US BACK TO SAUDI ARABIA.
OR THEY CAN CONCLUDE THE BUSINESS RIGHT HERE IN MOROCCO AND BE DONE WITH US. WHICH DO YOU THINK THEY WILL DO?
YOU'VE ALL HEARD YOUR HUSBANDS TALK OF THE TROUBLES THEY HAVE ON THE RIGS--WITH SAFETY, WITH PAY, WITH LACK OF HEALTH CARE.
WHAT DO YOU THINK THEY WILL DO TO US, SO FAR FROM ANYONE WHO KNOWS WHO WE ARE?

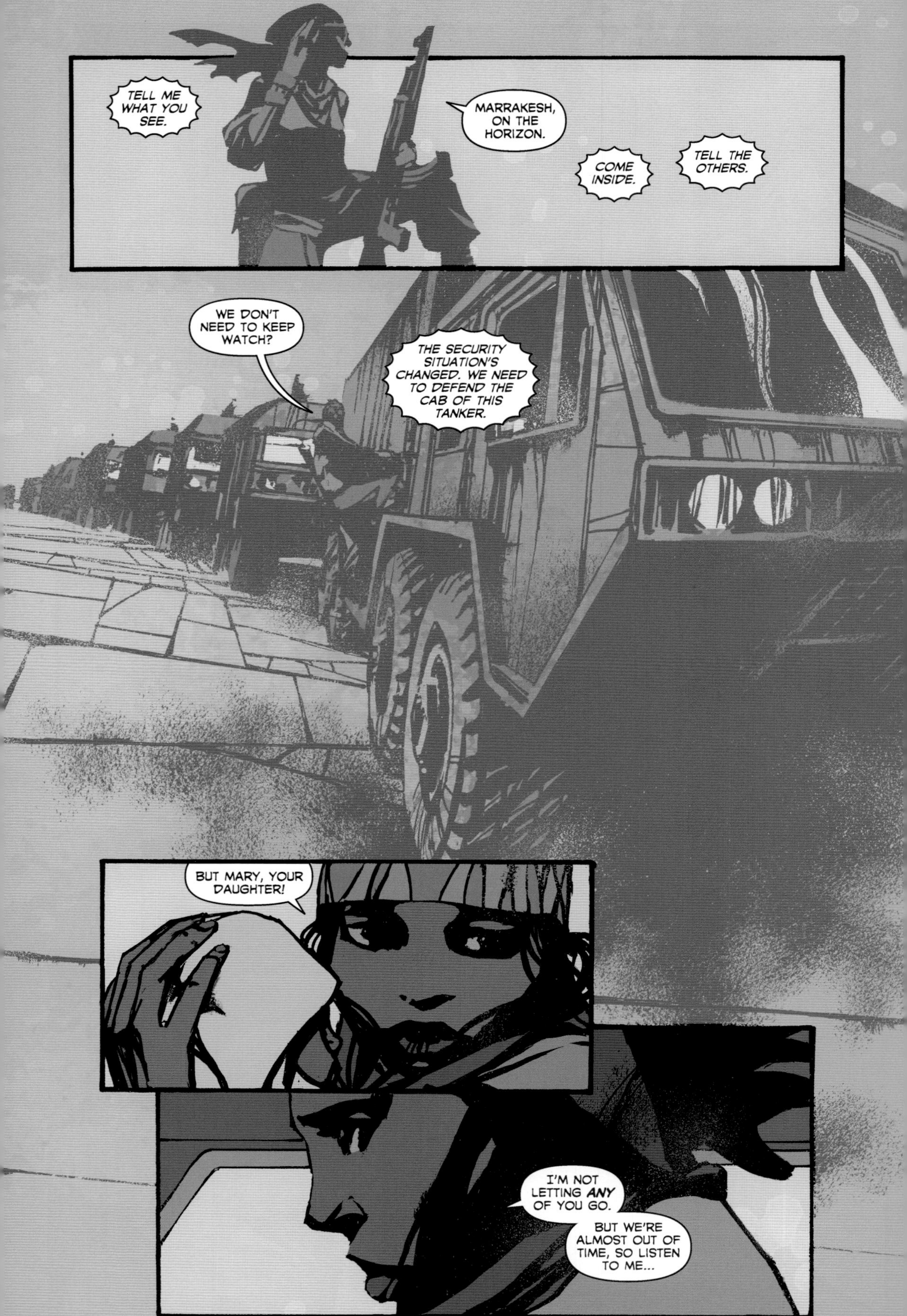
TELL ME WHAT YOU SEE.
MARRAKESH, ON THE HORIZON.
COME INSIDE.
TELL THE OTHERS.
WE DON'T NEED TO KEEP WATCH?
THE SECURITY SITUATION'S CHANGED. WE NEED TO DEFEND THE CAB OF THIS TANKER.
BUT MARY, YOUR DAUGHTER!
I'M NOT LETTING **ANY** OF YOU GO.
BUT WE'RE ALMOST OUT OF TIME, SO LISTEN TO ME...

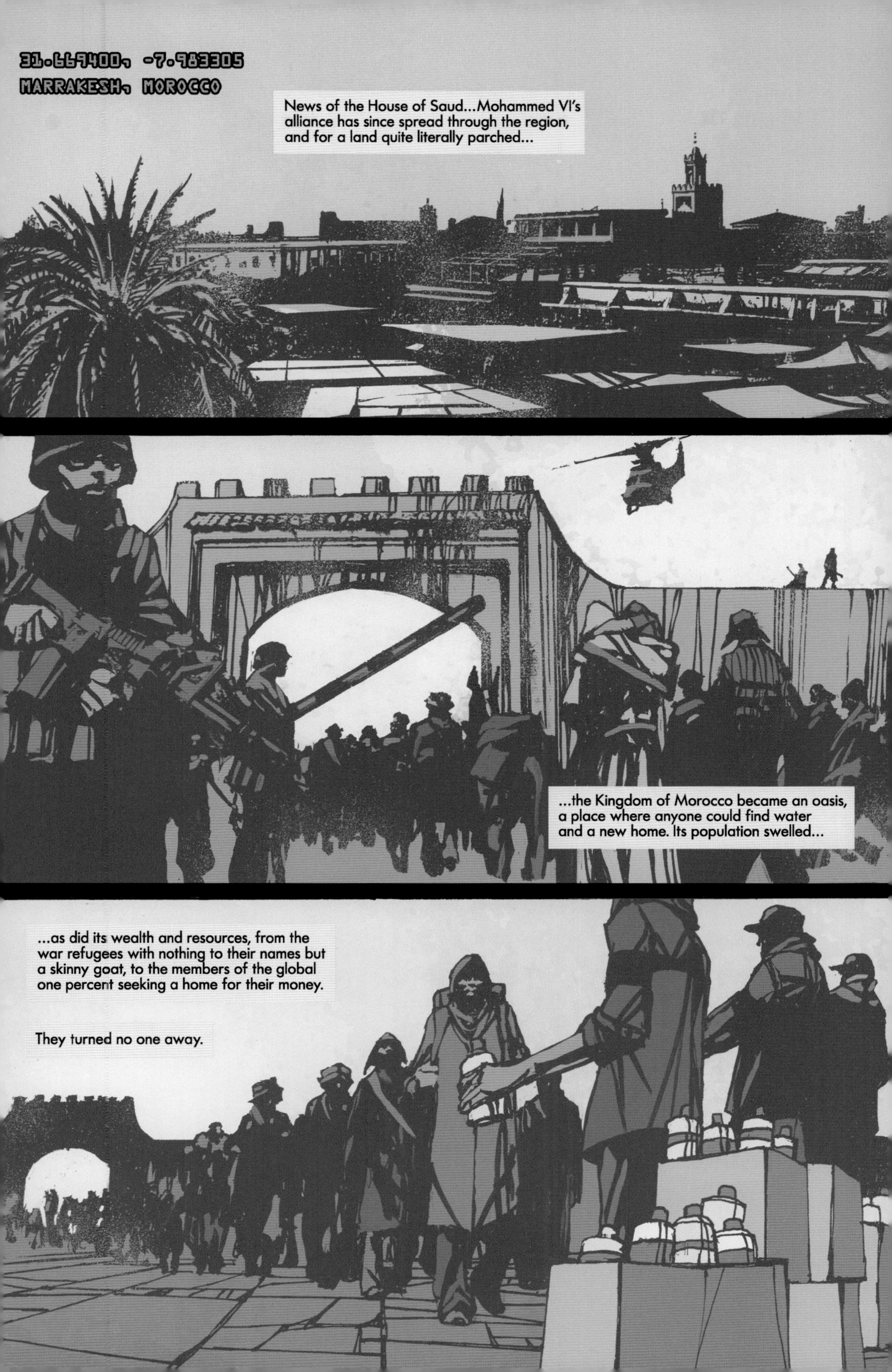
31.669400, -7.983305
MARRAKESH, MOROCCO
News of the House of Saud...Mohammed VI's alliance has since spread through the region, and for a land quite literally parched...
...the Kingdom of Morocco became an oasis, a place where anyone could find water and a new home. Its population swelled...
...as did its wealth and resources, from the war refugees with nothing to their names but a skinny goat, to the members of the global one percent seeking a home for their money.
They turned no one away.

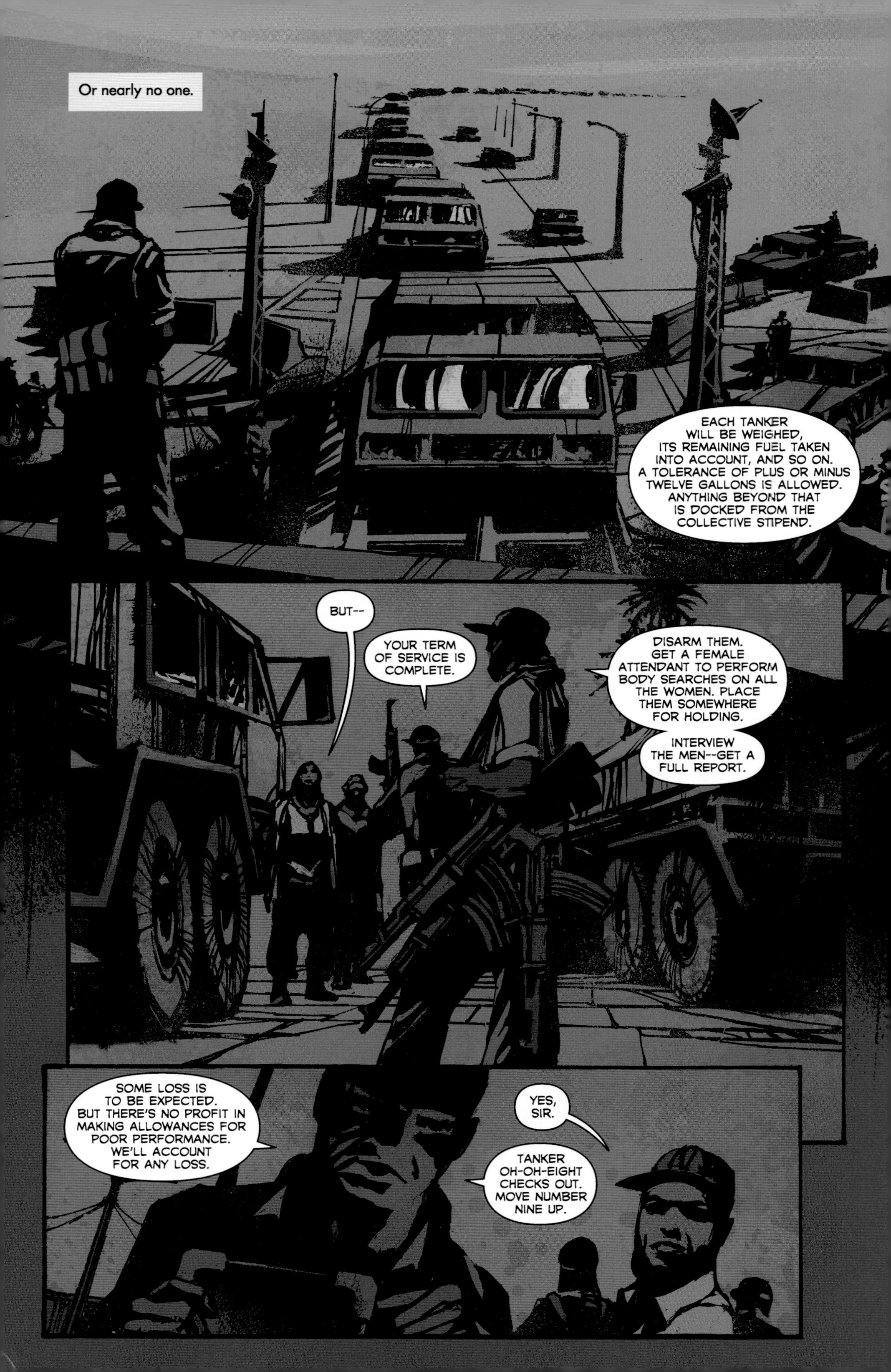
Or nearly no one.
EACH TANKER WILL BE WEIGHED, ITS REMAINING FUEL TAKEN INTO ACCOUNT, AND SO ON. A TOLERANCE OF PLUS OR MINUS TWELVE GALLONS IS ALLOWED. ANYTHING BEYOND THAT IS DOCKED FROM THE COLLECTIVE STIPEND.
BUT--
YOUR TERM OF SERVICE IS COMPLETE.
DISARM THEM. GET A FEMALE ATTENDANT TO PERFORM BODY SEARCHES ON ALL THE WOMEN. PLACE THEM SOMEWHERE FOR HOLDING.
INTERVIEW THE MEN--GET A FULL REPORT.
SOME LOSS IS TO BE EXPECTED. BUT THERE'S NO PROFIT IN MAKING ALLOWANCES FOR POOR PERFORMANCE. WE'LL ACCOUNT FOR ANY LOSS.
YES, SIR.
TANKER OH-OH-EIGHT CHECKS OUT. MOVE NUMBER NINE UP.

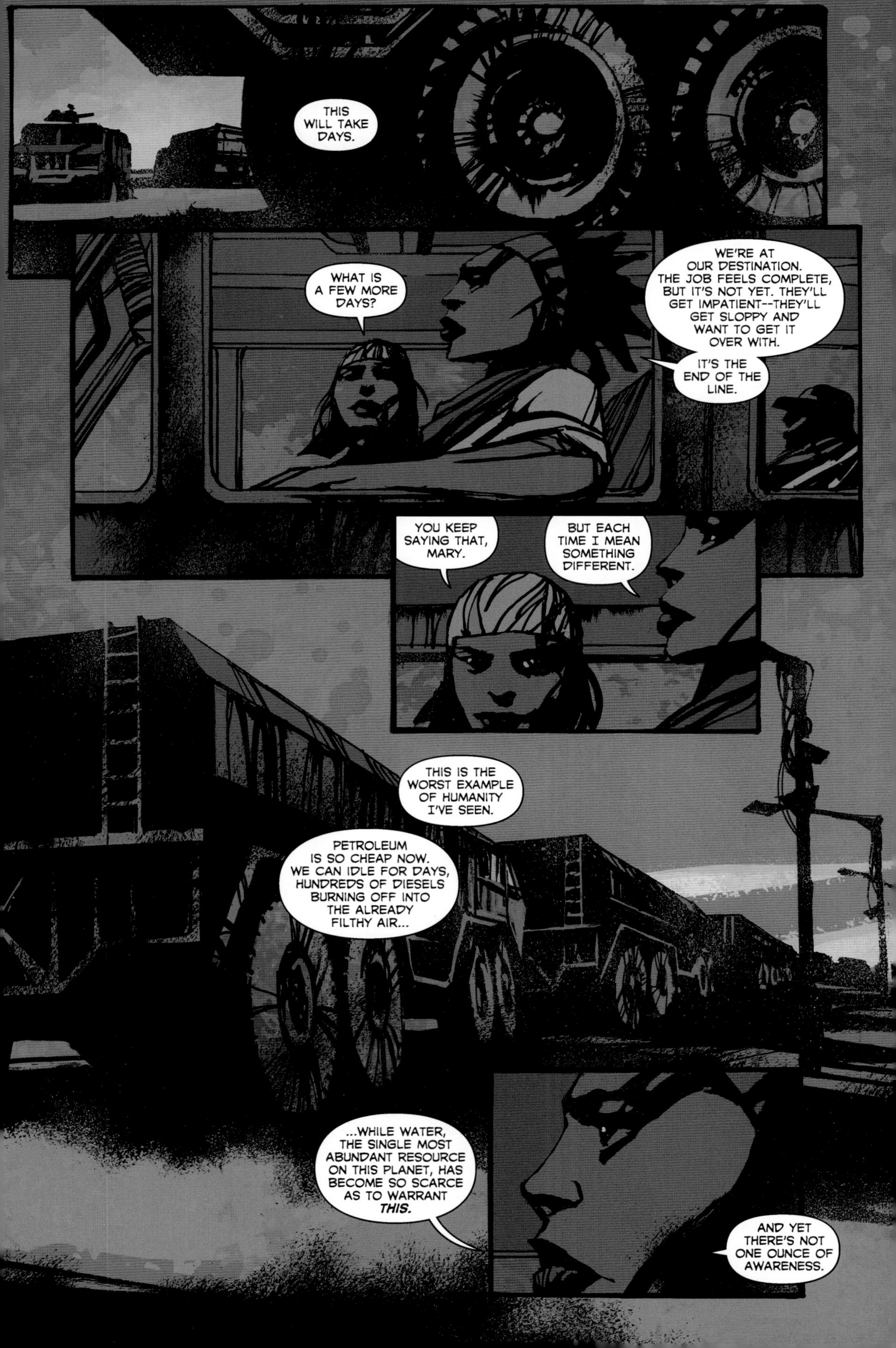
THIS WILL TAKE DAYS.
WHAT IS A FEW MORE DAYS?
WE'RE AT OUR DESTINATION. THE JOB FEELS COMPLETE, BUT IT'S NOT YET. THEY'LL GET IMPATIENT--THEY'LL GET SLOPPY AND WANT TO GET IT OVER WITH.
IT'S THE END OF THE LINE.
YOU KEEP SAYING THAT, MARY.
BUT EACH TIME I MEAN SOMETHING DIFFERENT.
THIS IS THE WORST EXAMPLE OF HUMANITY I'VE SEEN.
PETROLEUM IS SO CHEAP NOW. WE CAN IDLE FOR DAYS, HUNDREDS OF DIESELS BURNING OFF INTO THE ALREADY FILTHY AIR...
...WHILE WATER, THE SINGLE MOST ABUNDANT RESOURCE ON THIS PLANET, HAS BECOME SO SCARCE AS TO WARRANT ***THIS.***
AND YET THERE'S NOT ONE OUNCE OF AWARENESS.

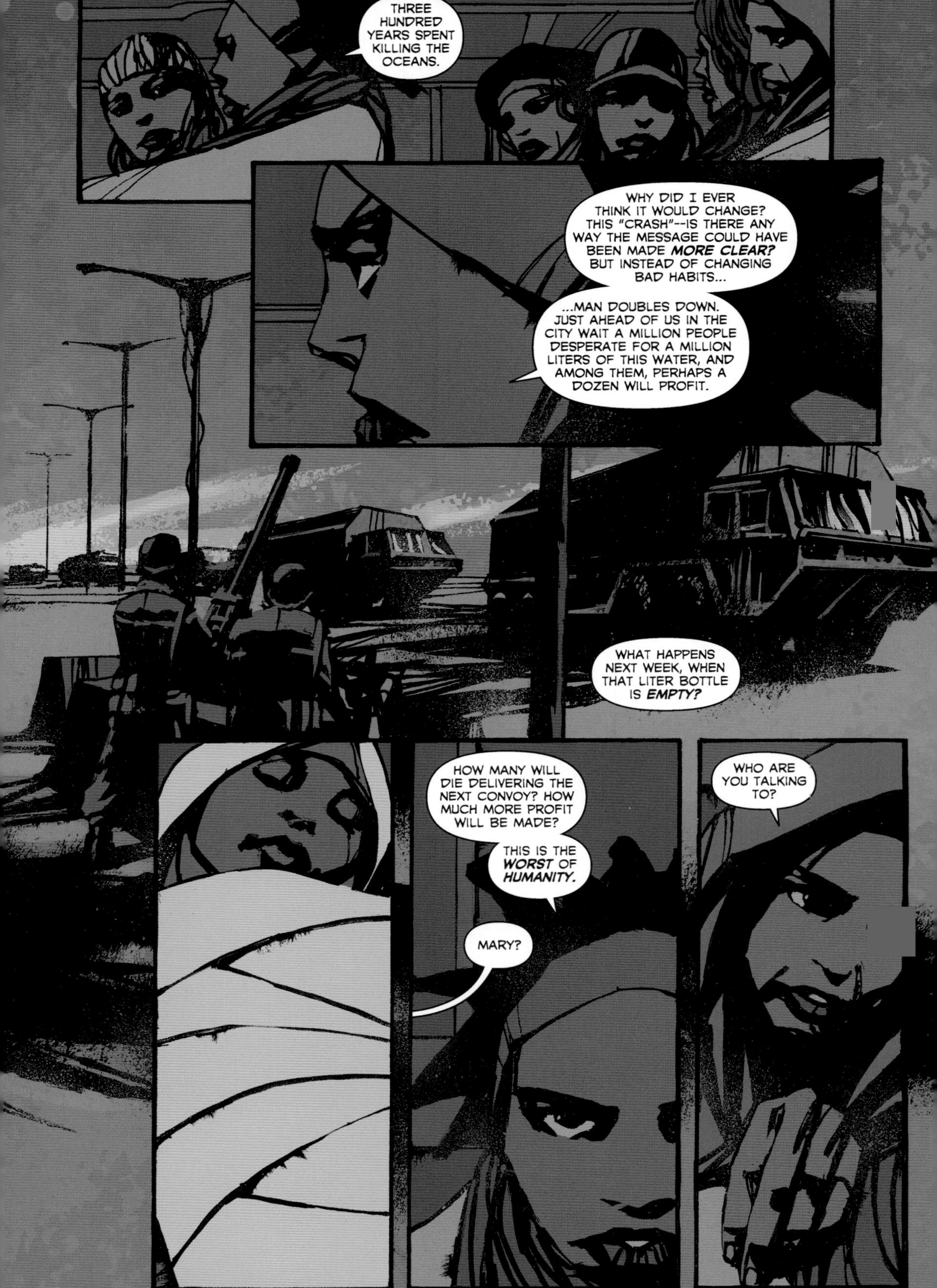
THREE HUNDRED YEARS SPENT KILLING THE OCEANS.
WHY DID I EVER THINK IT WOULD CHANGE? THIS "CRASH"--IS THERE ANY WAY THE MESSAGE COULD HAVE BEEN MADE MORE CLEAR? BUT INSTEAD OF CHANGING BAD HABITS...
...MAN DOUBLES DOWN. JUST AHEAD OF US IN THE CITY WAIT A MILLION PEOPLE DESPERATE FOR A MILLION LITERS OF THIS WATER, AND AMONG THEM, PERHAPS A DOZEN WILL PROFIT.
WHAT HAPPENS NEXT WEEK, WHEN THAT LITER BOTTLE IS EMPTY?
HOW MANY WILL DIE DELIVERING THE NEXT CONVOY? HOW MUCH MORE PROFIT WILL BE MADE?
THIS IS THE WORST OF HUMANITY.
MARY?
WHO ARE YOU TALKING TO?

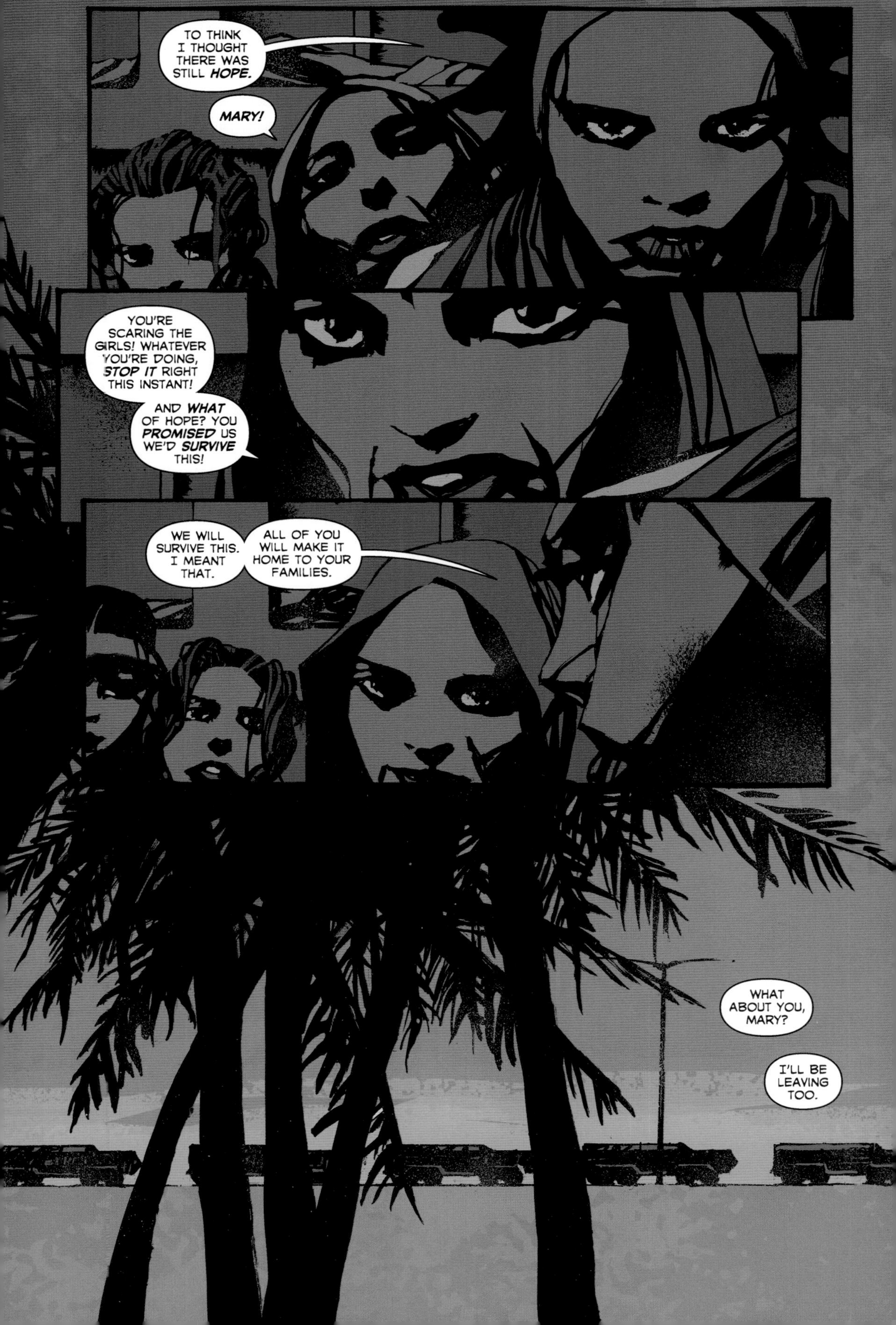
TO THINK I THOUGHT THERE WAS STILL *HOPE.*
MARY!
YOU'RE SCARING THE GIRLS! WHATEVER YOU'RE DOING, *STOP IT* RIGHT THIS INSTANT!
AND *WHAT* OF HOPE? YOU *PROMISED* US WE'D *SURVIVE* THIS!
WE WILL SURVIVE THIS. I MEANT THAT.
ALL OF YOU WILL MAKE IT HOME TO YOUR FAMILIES.
WHAT ABOUT YOU, MARY?
I'LL BE LEAVING TOO.

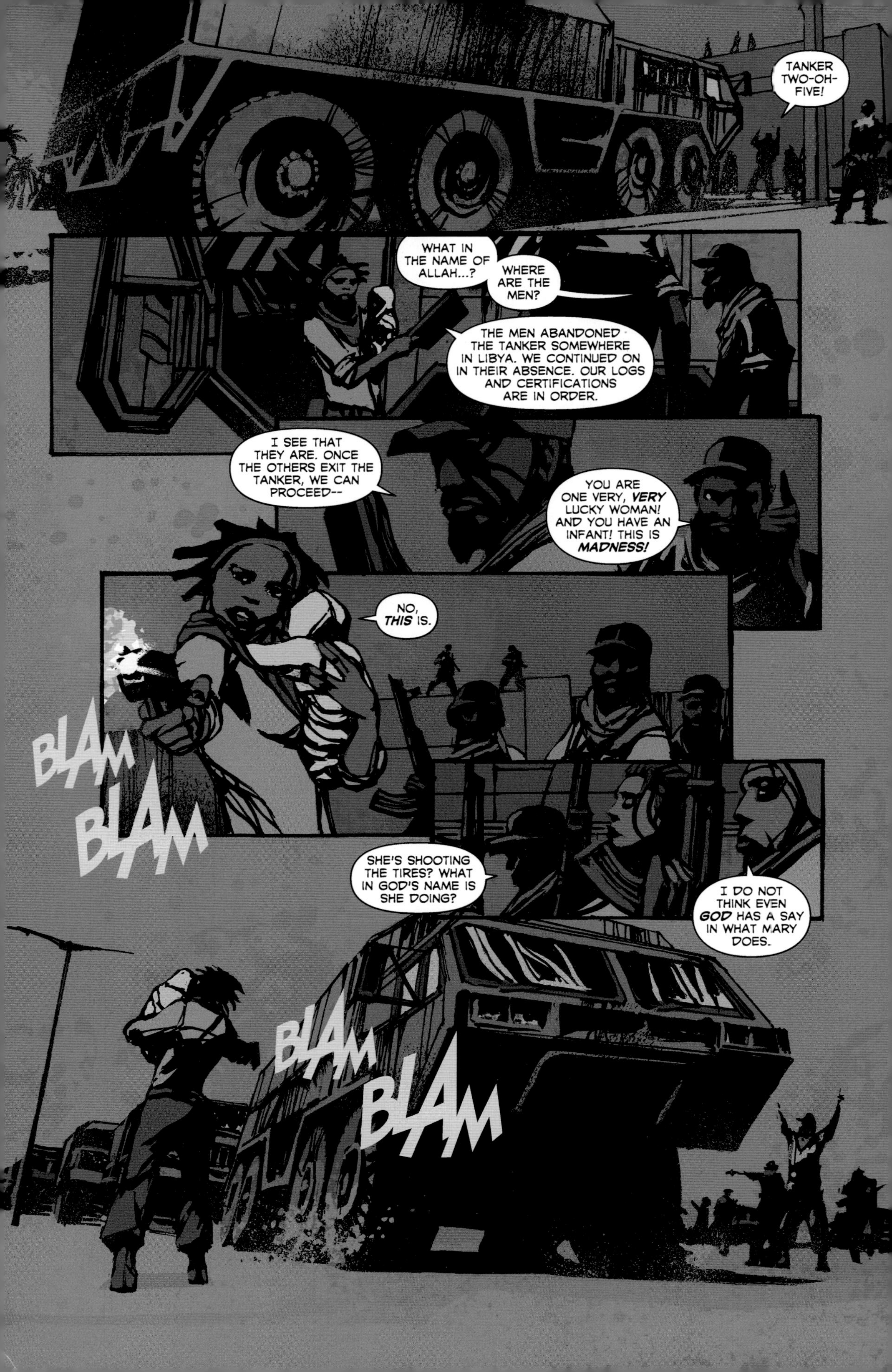

TANKER TWO-OH-FIVE!
WHAT IN THE NAME OF ALLAH...?
WHERE ARE THE MEN?
THE MEN ABANDONED THE TANKER SOMEWHERE IN LIBYA. WE CONTINUED ON IN THEIR ABSENCE. OUR LOGS AND CERTIFICATIONS ARE IN ORDER.
I SEE THAT THEY ARE. ONCE THE OTHERS EXIT THE TANKER, WE CAN PROCEED--
YOU ARE ONE VERY, VERY LUCKY WOMAN! AND YOU HAVE AN INFANT! THIS IS MADNESS!
NO, THIS IS.
BLAM
BLAM
SHE'S SHOOTING THE TIRES? WHAT IN GOD'S NAME IS SHE DOING?
I DO NOT THINK EVEN GOD HAS A SAY IN WHAT MARY DOES.
BLAM
BLAM

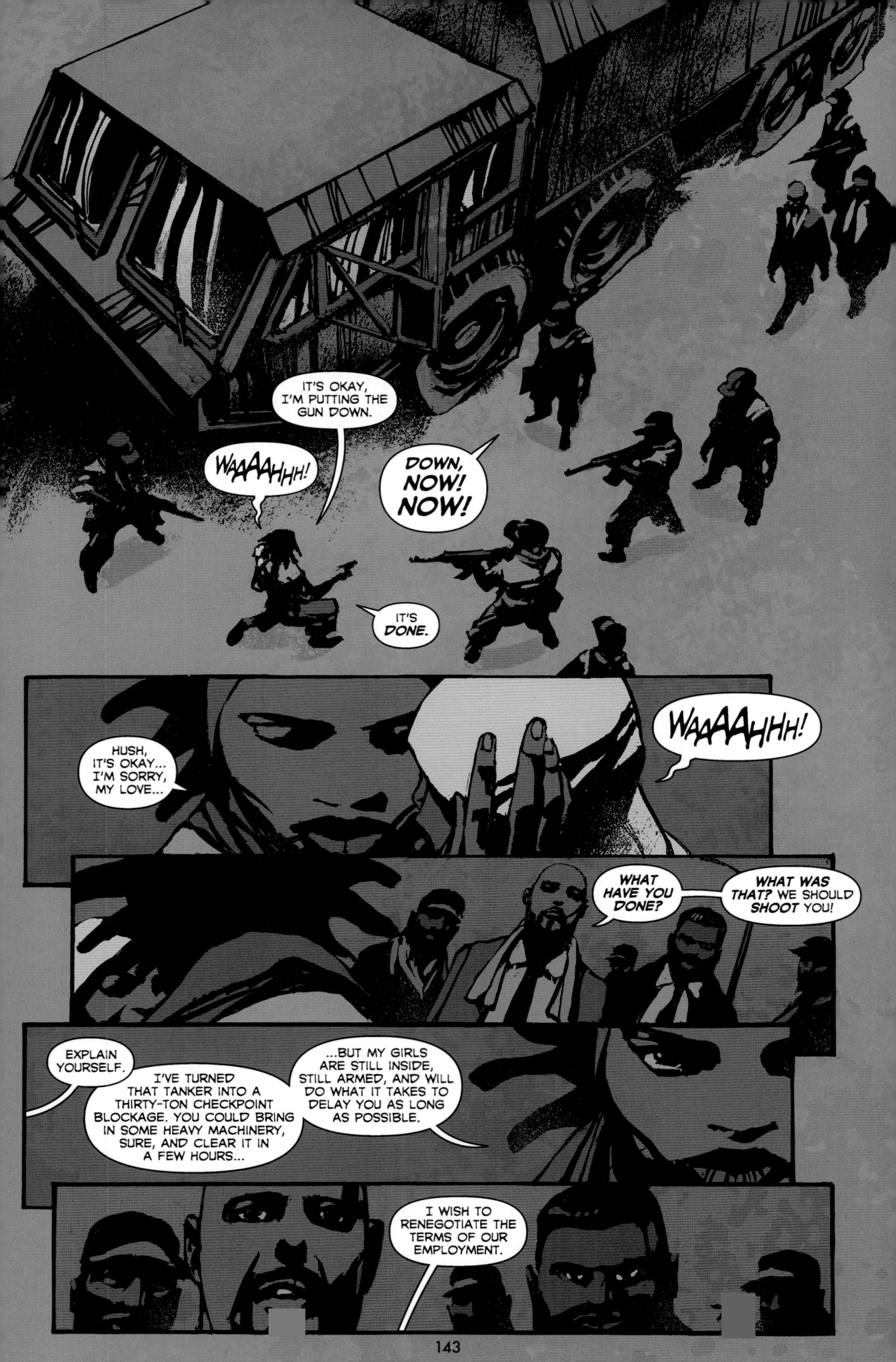
IT'S OKAY, I'M PUTTING THE GUN DOWN.
WAAAAHHH!
DOWN, NOW! NOW!
IT'S DONE.
HUSH, IT'S OKAY... I'M SORRY, MY LOVE...
WAAAAHHH!
WHAT HAVE YOU DONE?
WHAT WAS THAT? WE SHOULD SHOOT YOU!
EXPLAIN YOURSELF.
I'VE TURNED THAT TANKER INTO A THIRTY-TON CHECKPOINT BLOCKAGE. YOU COULD BRING IN SOME HEAVY MACHINERY, SURE, AND CLEAR IT IN A FEW HOURS...
...BUT MY GIRLS ARE STILL INSIDE, STILL ARMED, AND WILL DO WHAT IT TAKES TO DELAY YOU AS LONG AS POSSIBLE.
I WISH TO RENEGOTIATE THE TERMS OF OUR EMPLOYMENT.

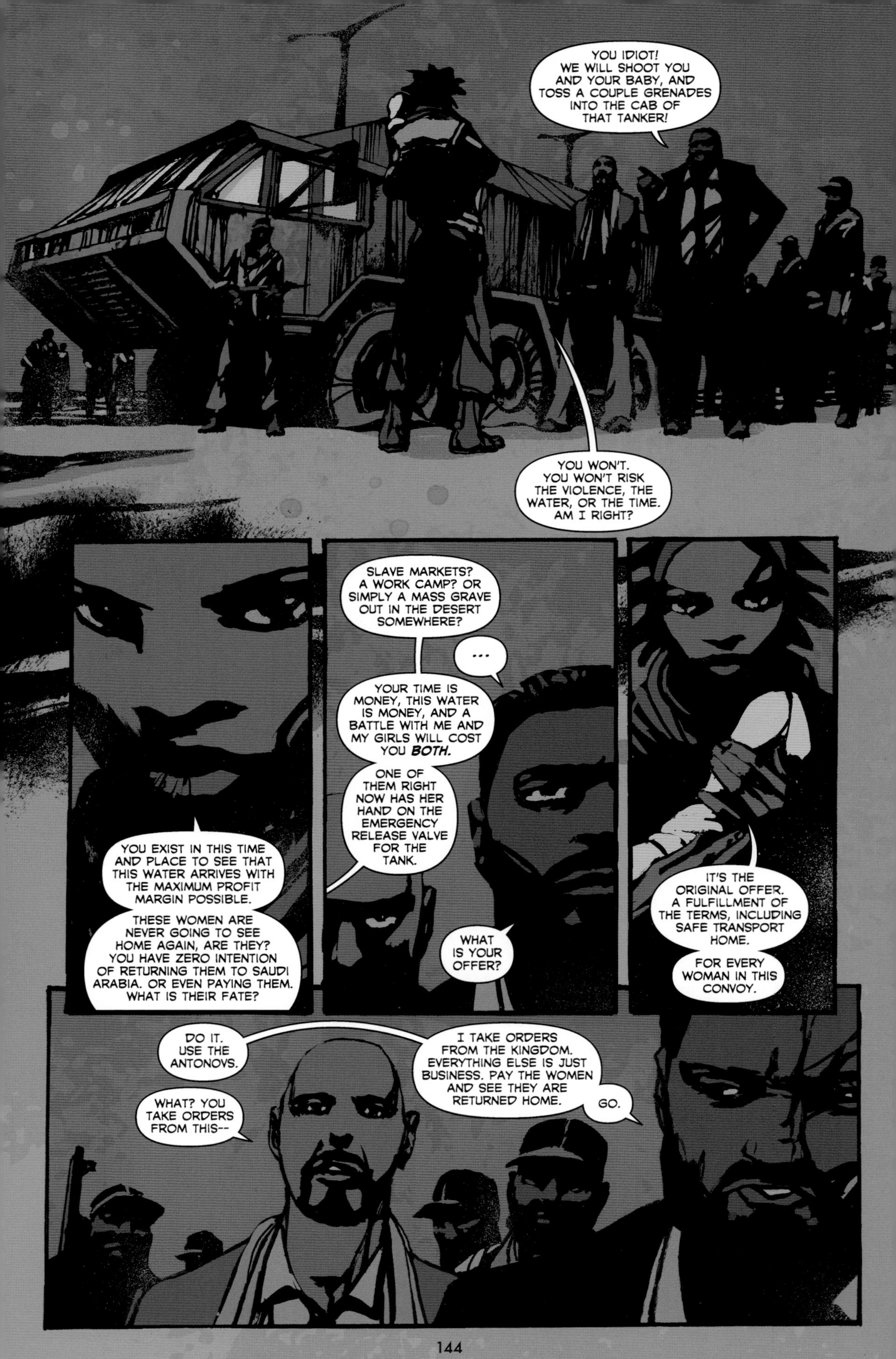
YOU IDIOT! WE WILL SHOOT YOU AND YOUR BABY, AND TOSS A COUPLE GRENADES INTO THE CAB OF THAT TANKER!
YOU WON'T. YOU WON'T RISK THE VIOLENCE, THE WATER, OR THE TIME. AM I RIGHT?
YOU EXIST IN THIS TIME AND PLACE TO SEE THAT THIS WATER ARRIVES WITH THE MAXIMUM PROFIT MARGIN POSSIBLE.
THESE WOMEN ARE NEVER GOING TO SEE HOME AGAIN, ARE THEY? YOU HAVE ZERO INTENTION OF RETURNING THEM TO SAUDI ARABIA. OR EVEN PAYING THEM. WHAT IS THEIR FATE?
SLAVE MARKETS? A WORK CAMP? OR SIMPLY A MASS GRAVE OUT IN THE DESERT SOMEWHERE?
...
YOUR TIME IS MONEY, THIS WATER IS MONEY, AND A BATTLE WITH ME AND MY GIRLS WILL COST YOU ***BOTH.***
ONE OF THEM RIGHT NOW HAS HER HAND ON THE EMERGENCY RELEASE VALVE FOR THE TANK.
WHAT IS YOUR OFFER?
IT'S THE ORIGINAL OFFER. A FULFILLMENT OF THE TERMS, INCLUDING SAFE TRANSPORT HOME.
FOR EVERY WOMAN IN THIS CONVOY.
DO IT. USE THE ANTONOVS.
WHAT? YOU TAKE ORDERS FROM THIS--
I TAKE ORDERS FROM THE KINGDOM. EVERYTHING ELSE IS JUST BUSINESS. PAY THE WOMEN AND SEE THEY ARE RETURNED HOME.
GO.

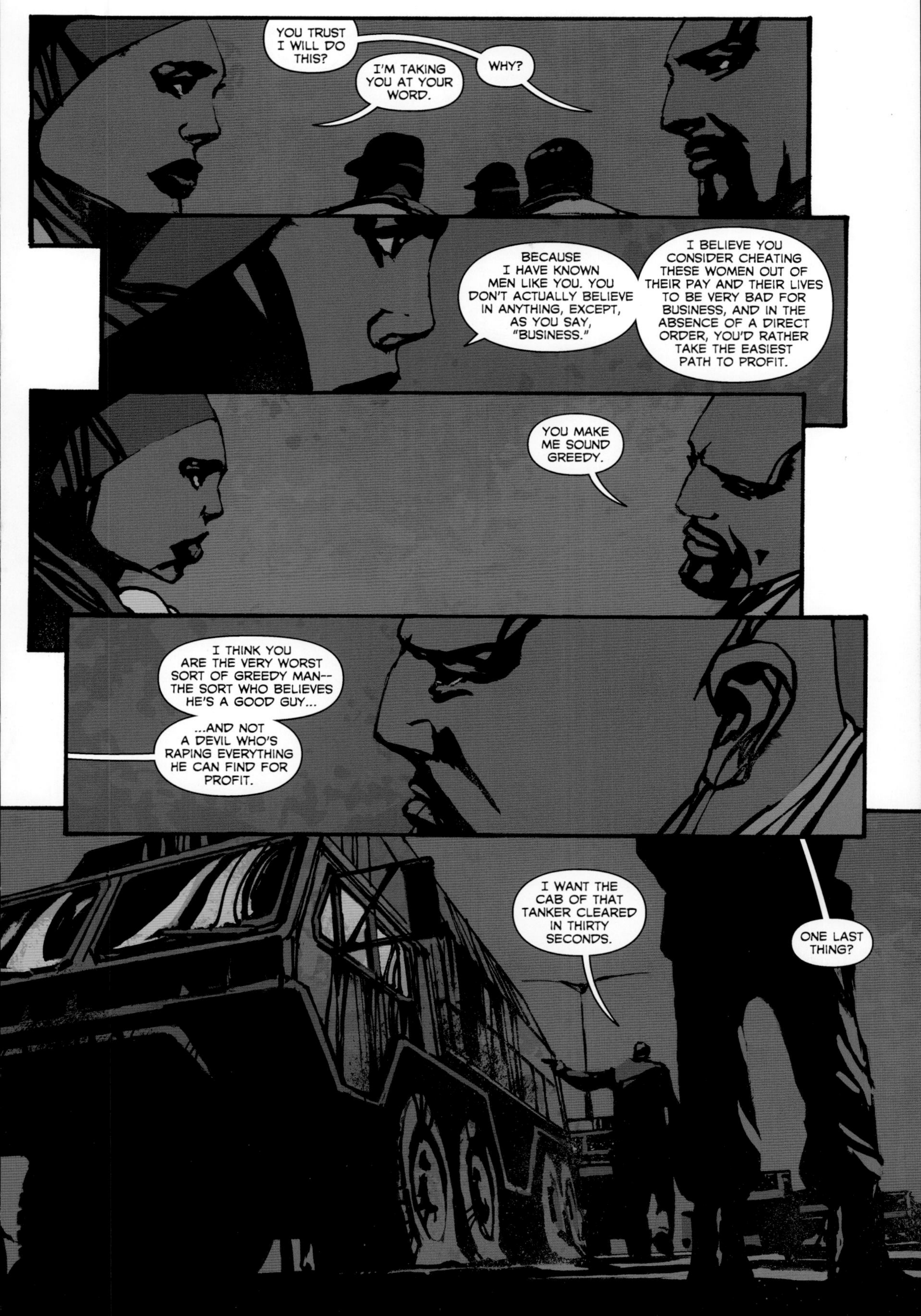
YOU TRUST I WILL DO THIS?
I'M TAKING YOU AT YOUR WORD.
WHY?
BECAUSE I HAVE KNOWN MEN LIKE YOU. YOU DON'T ACTUALLY BELIEVE IN ANYTHING, EXCEPT, AS YOU SAY, "BUSINESS."
I BELIEVE YOU CONSIDER CHEATING THESE WOMEN OUT OF THEIR PAY AND THEIR LIVES TO BE VERY BAD FOR BUSINESS, AND IN THE ABSENCE OF A DIRECT ORDER, YOU'D RATHER TAKE THE EASIEST PATH TO PROFIT.
YOU MAKE ME SOUND GREEDY.
I THINK YOU ARE THE VERY WORST SORT OF GREEDY MAN-- THE SORT WHO BELIEVES HE'S A GOOD GUY...
...AND NOT A DEVIL WHO'S RAPING EVERYTHING HE CAN FIND FOR PROFIT.
I WANT THE CAB OF THAT TANKER CLEARED IN THIRTY SECONDS.
ONE LAST THING?

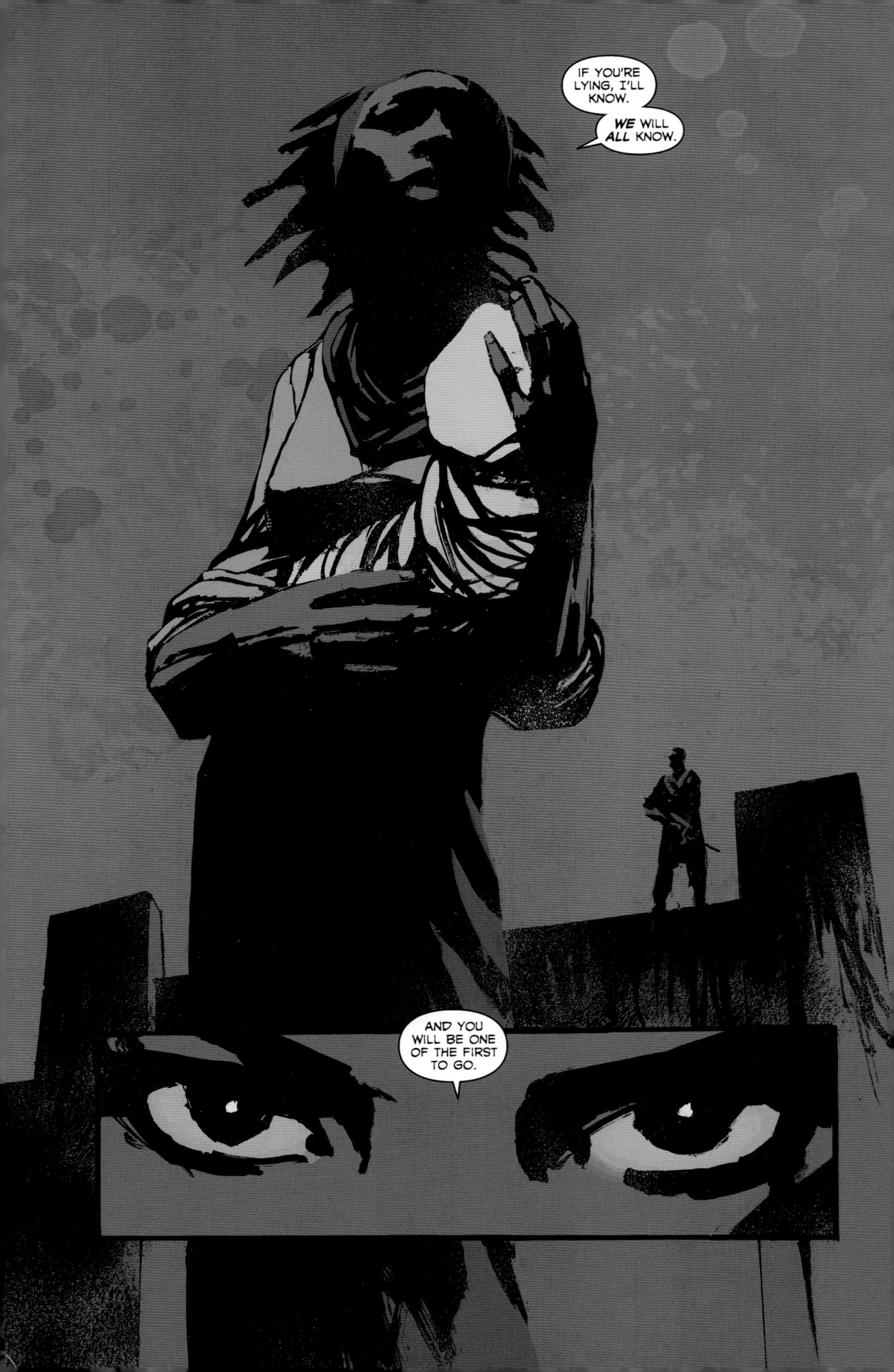
IF YOU'RE LYING, I'LL KNOW.
WE WILL ALL KNOW.
AND YOU WILL BE ONE OF THE FIRST TO GO.

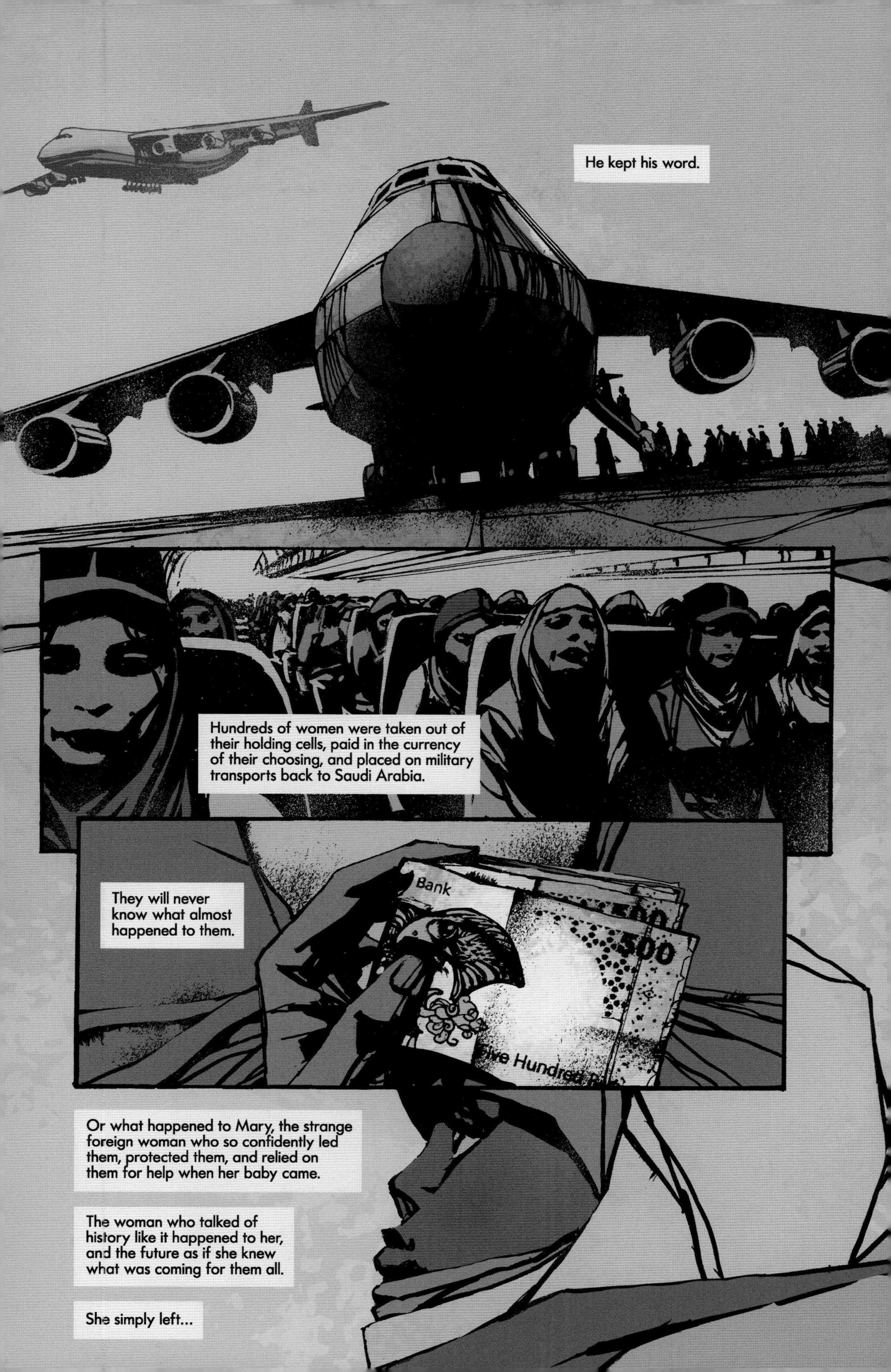
He kept his word.
Hundreds of women were taken out of their holding cells, paid in the currency of their choosing, and placed on military transports back to Saudi Arabia.
They will never know what almost happened to them.
Bank
500
Five Hundred
Or what happened to Mary, the strange foreign woman who so confidently led them, protected them, and relied on them for help when her baby came.
The woman who talked of history like it happened to her, and the future as if she knew what was coming for them all.
She simply left...

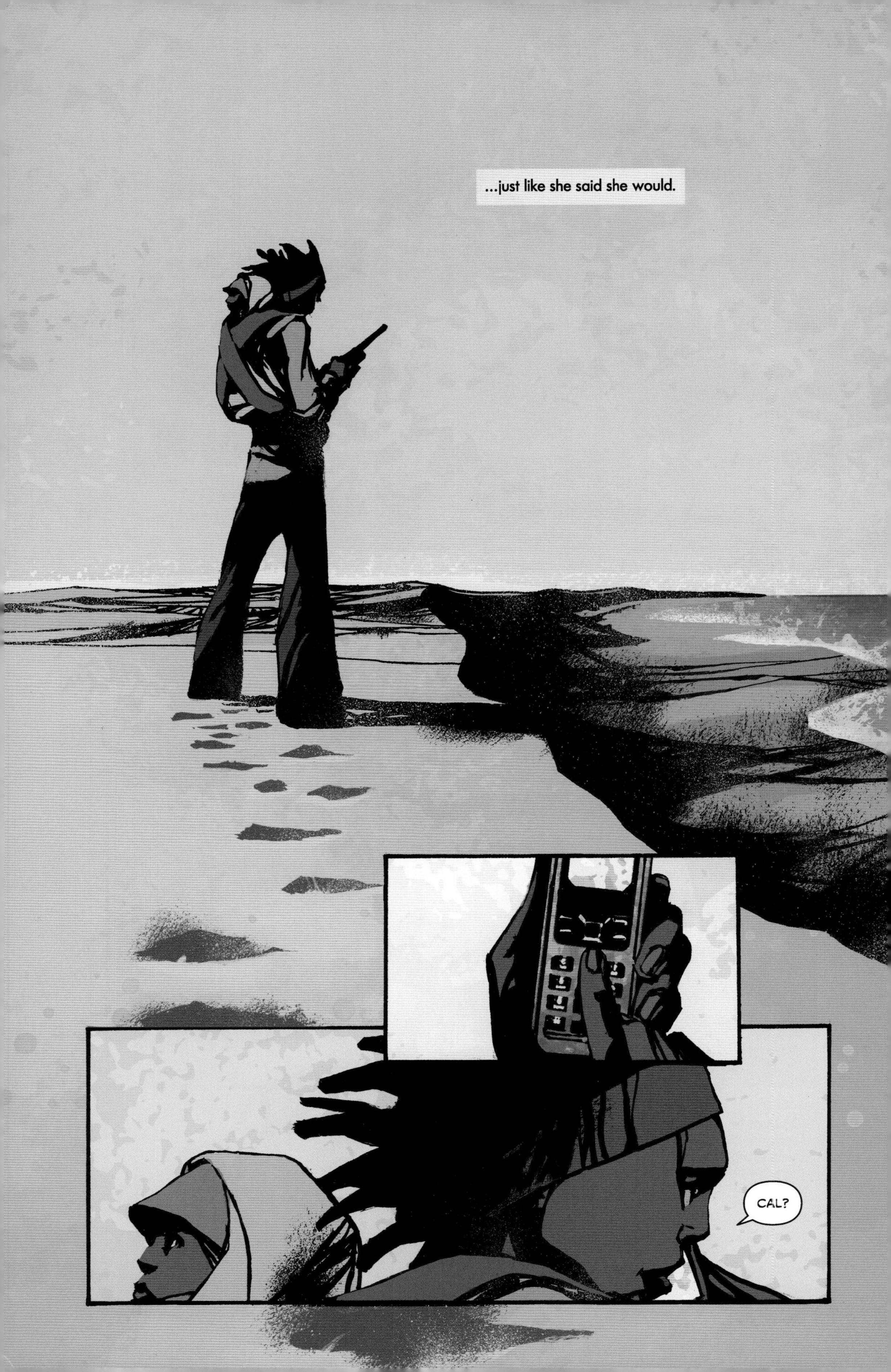
...just like she said she would.
CAL?

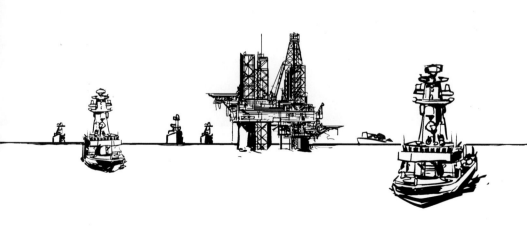

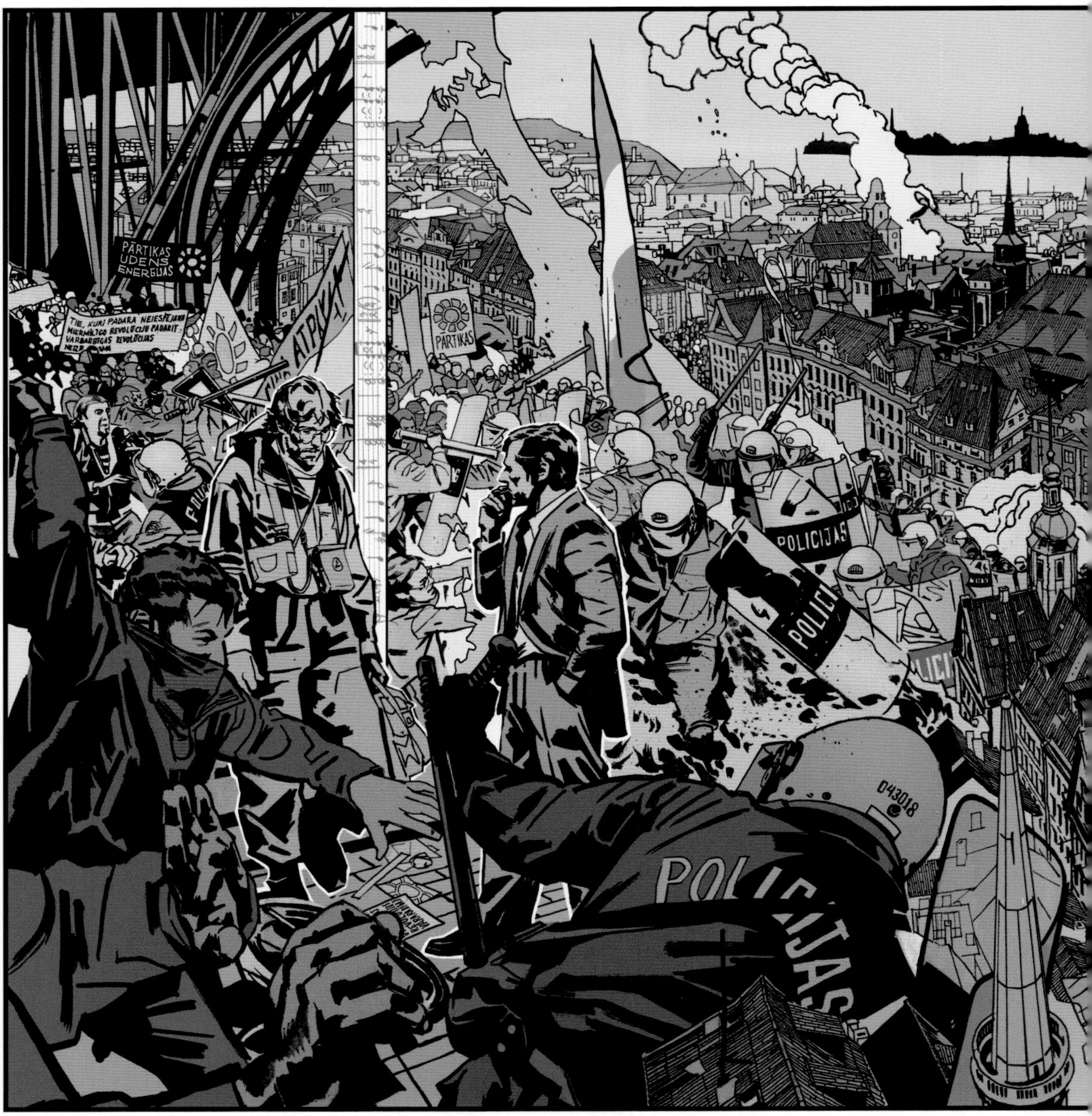
PARTIKAS
UDENS
ENERGIJAS
PARTIKAS
POLICIJAS
D43018
POLICIJAS

J. P. Leon's cover art for *The Massive* #19–#21.

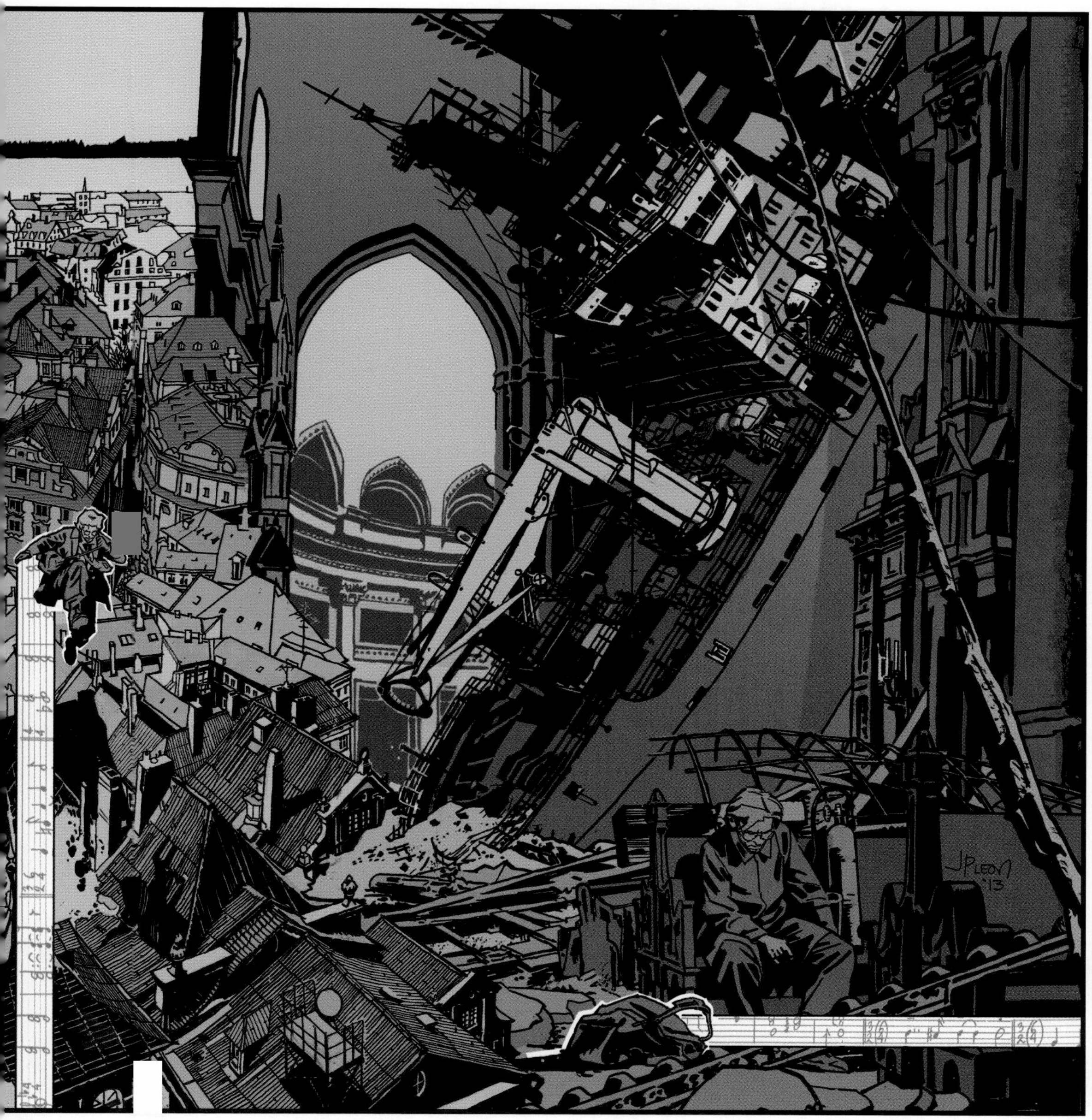
JP LEON
'13

MORE FROM *NEW YORK TIMES* BEST-SELLING AUTHOR

BRIAN WOOD

"Someone remembered what comics are for. Meet Brian Wood."
—Warren Ellis

BRIAN WOOD • KRISTIAN DONALDSON • GARRY BROWN • DAVE STEWART
THE MASSIVE
BLACK PACIFIC

THE MASSIVE

Written by Brian Wood, Art by Kristian Donaldson and Garry Brown

In this first volume of Brian Wood's new, sprawling postapocalyptic epic, follow the crew of the *Kapital* from the flooded remnants of Hong Kong to Unalaska, with stops in Antarctica and Mogadishu, as post-Crash ethics and economics are explored across a broken world.

Volume 1: Black Pacific
ISBN 978-1-61655-132-2 | $19.99

Volume 2: Subcontinental
ISBN 978-1-61655-316-6 | $19.99

Volume 3: Longship
ISBN 978-1-61655-446-0 | $19.99

Volume 4: Sahara
ISBN 978-1-61655-508-5 | $19.99

STAR WARS
IN THE SHADOW OF YAVIN
BRIAN WOOD · CARLOS D'ANDA

STAR WARS VOLUME 1: IN THE SHADOW OF YAVIN

Written by Brian Wood, Art by Carlos D'Anda, Ryan Odagawa, and Gabe Eltaeb, Cover by Alex Ross

After the destruction of the Death Star, the Rebels are hounded by the Empire. Suspecting a spy in their ranks, Princess Leia forms a secret X-wing squadron—which includes Luke Skywalker—to expose the spy and find a safe home. Meanwhile, Han Solo and Chewbacca are sent on a covert mission!

ISBN 978-1-61655-170-4 | $19.99

THE NEW YORK FOUR

Written by Brian Wood, Art by Ryan Kelly

Worlds collide when four young women begin college at the prestigious New York University. But that freedom comes at a price: roommate drama, mysterious love interests, school troubles, and family conflicts. Welcome to adulthood!

ISBN 978-1-61655-605-1 | $19.99

BRIAN WOOD
CHANNEL ZERO
THE COMPLETE COLLECTION
WITH BECKY CLOONAN

CHANNEL ZERO

Written by Brian Wood, Art by Becky Cloonan

A blistering take on media control in a repressive future America! *DMZ* and *The Massive* creator Brian Wood launched an all-out assault on the comics medium in 1997 with *Channel Zero*, an influential, forward-thinking series that combined art, politics, and graphic design in a unique way.

ISBN 978-1-59582-936-8 | $19.99

CONAN
QUEEN OF THE BLACK COAST

CONAN VOLUME 13: QUEEN OF THE BLACK COAST

Written by Brian Wood, Art by Becky Cloonan and James Harren

Conan turns his back on the civilized world and takes to the Western Ocean. Finding first danger and then passion in the arms of the pirate queen Bêlit, the Cimmerian begins a new life of pleasure and pillage along the Black Coast, in this epic of romance and terror!

TPB: ISBN 978-1-61655-043-1 | $19.99
HC: ISBN 978-1-61655-042-4 | $24.99

CONAN VOLUME 14: THE DEATH

Written by Brian Wood, Art by Becky Cloonan, Vasilis Lolos, and Declan Shalvey

Conan returns to Cimmeria to track down an impostor destroying villages in his name, only to discover a tragic connection to his own past!

TPB: ISBN 978-1-61655-123-0 | $19.99

AVAILABLE AT YOUR LOCAL COMICS SHOP OR BOOKSTORE! • To find a comics shop in your area, call 1-888-266-4226.
For more information or to order direct visit DarkHorse.com or call 1-800-862-0052 Mon.–Fri. 9 AM. to 5 PM. Pacific Time. Prices and availability subject to change without notice.

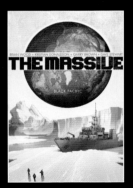

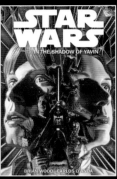

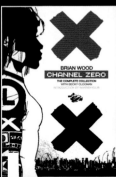

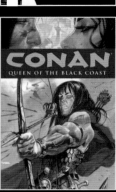